Well, it is odd and sad that our minds should be such seed-beds, and we without power to choose the seed. But man is an odd, sad creature as yet, intent on pilfering the earth, and heedless of the growths within himself. He cannot be bored about psychology. He leaves it to the specialist, which is as if he should leave his dinner to be eaten by a steam-engine.
— *E. M. Forster*, Howards End

THE SHAME
EXPERIENCE

*To My Mother Judith, My Father Albert,
and My Sisters Lisa and Laura*

THE SHAME EXPERIENCE

Susan Miller

 THE ANALYTIC PRESS
1985

Distributed by
LAWRENCE ERLBAUM ASSOCIATES, PUBLISHERS
Hillsdale, New Jersey   London

Distributed solely by

Lawrence Erlbaum Associates, Inc., Publishers
365 Broadway
Hillsdale, New Jersey 07642

Library of Congress Cataloging in Publication Data

Miller, Susan (Susan Beth)
    The shame experience.

    Originally presented at the author's thesis (doctoral—
University of Michigan)
    Bibliography: p.
    Includes index.
    1. Shame. I. Title.
BF575.S45M55   1985   152.4   85-3984
ISBN 0-88163-017-9

Printed in the United States of America
10 9 8 7 6 5 4 3 2 1

Contents

Foreword

This monograph deals with a familiar, clinically important and, among clinicians, an only recently rediscovered feeling state, that of shame. The study method is phenomenological, that is to say it sets about trying to identify and understand the many nuances of the shame state from subjective reports of remembered shame experiences. Most phenomenological studies of feeling states have been carried out in the existentialist tradition, by investigators who are often inclined to represent their work as antithetical to psychoanalysis. It is noteworthy that this study is both phenomenological and psychoanalytic. The monograph demonstrates the rich yield that awaits a marriage between phenomenological research and psychoanalysis. What existential phenomenologists have failed to realize, something that anyone familiar with Freud's clinical papers knows well, is that all of Freud's discoveries emerge from and rest solidly upon a bedrock of empathy with his patients. The psychoanalytic process at its best, and as originally formulated by Freud, is a study in phenomenological existentialism. What has given psychoanalysis a bad name among existentialists has been Freud's wish to build a more complex theory by drawing from his phenomenological data ever more complex and more abstract generalizations. Phenomenologists are averse to extending their findings in this fashion, unlike Freud, who aligned himself with the scientific tradition. Phenomenologists have a marked aversion to Freud's "metapsychology," which sought to establish natural laws that govern the full range of behaviors of human beings.

In an out-of-the-way paper[1], now largely inaccessible, I suggested that psychoanalysis speaks three different languages. One is the language one uses with one's patients. At its best, this is the language that captures in vivo the elusive but very meaningful nuances of a person's life. It is the language best suited to talk with a patient about his own experiences. This is a language rich in metaphors, a language that is often closer to poetry than to science. The second language of psychoanalysis is that which the analyst uses *after* the consultation, when he tries to formulate for himself the themes of a patient's hour; the flow of feelings, the twists and turns of a patient's (and analyst's) ideation as he gives himself over to the play of forces mobilized in a treatment session. This is a language that comprises the clinical theories of psychoanalysis. The third language is the language in which one formulates what Rapaport called the general theory of psychoanalysis. This is the language of Freud's metapsychology, which the psychoanalyst uses when he backs off from the intensely personal material of the clinical hours and examines his findings in broadest perspective. It is in its dependence on this third language of psychoanalysis that the psychoanalyst departs from his phenomenologist cousins. At its best, psychoanalysis is a rich interweaving of formulations at all three levels of discourse. Unfortunately, it does not always live up to this ideal. Sometimes it becomes overly absorbed in its third voice, its metapsychology. And it is then that it lays itself open to attack by existentialists. Psychoanalytic researchers have, for example, had much to say about "affect" as a "discharge phenomenon," but precious little to say about affects as distinctive and very human feeling states. What is especially puzzling about this state of affairs in its theory building is that psychoanalysis is nothing if not an attempt to uncover and unravel the affects of its patients. That was the essence of psychoanalysis from its earliest beginnings, and the attunement to a patient's affect has remained the indispensable divining rod of every skillful psychoanalyst to this day. As Brierley put it, affects are "the Ariadne thread" for finding one's way correctly to the understanding of a person's neurotic transferences. The metapsychologizing of feelings was a later development in psychoanalysis. It was not evident in psychoanalysis at first.[2] Freud told us early on that people suffer from "strangulated affects." I have yet to find a more apt metaphor with which to replace this early formulation. When, in his *Studies on Hysteria*, Freud

---

[1]Mayman, M. (1960). Early memories and abandoned ego states. *Proceedings of the Academic Assembly on Clinical Psychology*, Montreal, McGill University Press, 1963, pp. 97–117.

[2]Except for the posthumously published *Project for a Scientific Psychology*..

proposed that the hysteric has cut himself off from undischarged feelings because those feelings have for one reason or another become intolerable, or because the person lacks the courage to face them. Psychoanalysis, whatever else we may wish to define it as, is the systematic attempt to help people discover and get back in touch with what they feel. For this reason, if for no other, a monograph of the kind Sue Miller has written is to be welcomed. It provides a masterful attempt to put words to a particular feeling state that pains all human beings to some extent, and that plagues some to an overpowering extent.

People are enlarged when they can capture their thoughts in words. Surely this is even more true of feelings. The Wild Boy of Aveyron was more creature than human being until he learned human speech. Nor is this much different with those chimps who learn to "speak," whether this be with the aid of a computer console or only through the finger-speech of the deaf. Chimps who developed a repertoire of several hundred words with which to communicate with their human trainers, seemed to the trainers to become more human and less chimplike than their less articulate brothers. Perhaps it was anthropomorphism, but it seemed to some trainers that the chimps regarded *themselves* as more human than animal, tied more closely to human relationships than to chimpanzee relationships. The writings of Wharf and Langer and Chomsky provide rich embellishment for Freud's skeletal writings about the importance of language for human consciousness.

There has been a recent resurgence of interest in the relationship of words to feeling states, most recently in the writings of Krystal. He and others find a severe crippling of the personality in those people who show a virtual absence in their vocabulary of words with which to correctly designate feelings. Such people seem not only to be lacking in the words for feelings, but in the feelings themselves. Their feeling life is impoverished, and affect seems to play little overt role in their lives. A rapidly growing literature on "alexythymia" explores the relationship of such affect alexia to psychopathology.

This deficit is not confined only to severely narcissistic or borderline personalities. I remember one patient with a quite high IQ and a capacity to be very articulate, except where feelings were concerned. In response to some provocation, he told me he had gotten "angry." When asked how he knew he was angry, what anger felt like to him, he described a band of tension across his forehead from a point roughly above one eye to a point roughly above the other. Whenever he felt that band of tension he knew he was "angry." No other feelings were associated by him with that word. Another person comes to mind, a brilliant, vivacious graduate student of philosophy who quite sincerely claimed that she didn't know what the word "feeling" meant, that she was quite convinced that she had no experiences to which the word "feeling" might appropriately apply, and moreover, she really doubted that any such thing as a feeling existed for anyone else. This conviction disappeared dramatically in the course of her three years of therapy, and it became possible to understand how this total disowning of feelings had come about. The therapy in this case could obviously be characterized as a search for her lost affects. The psychoanalyst is engaged in the same kind of search with all patients, though not in so blatantly apparent a way.

Another oddity one finds in the way a person communicates with himself and with others about his feelings is the highly idiosyncratic meaning he often attaches to affect words, a kind of affect *dys*lexia. In conjunction with a dissertation study on shame,[3] subjects were asked to describe in words a striking shame experience they had had, and then to do the same with a striking guilt experience. Independently of this task, the subjects were judged as to whether they were primarily shame-prone people or primarily guilt-prone people. We found that shame-prone people were very adept at presenting a vivid account of some shameful event, but seemed not quite to comprehend what was meant by the word "guilty"; their account of a guilt experience was indistinguishable from a shame experience. The reverse was equally true. Guilt-prone people understand the word "guilt" very well, but do not seem to understand the word "shame" and easily confuse it with guilt. Their account of a shame experience sounded like their own and others' accounts of guilt experiences. If such individual differences characterize the use of all affect words, then surely this is an area that deserves far more study than it has received, and is something that psychotherapists in particular should be especially attentive to.

A comprehensive study of the nature of feeling states articulated with the help of a language that accurately represents the nature of those states is an almost virgin territory for psychoanalytic research. I am especially appreciative, therefore, of the subtlety and sensitivity with which the research described in this monograph was undertaken and carried out. I feel certain that this is one of what will become in the course of the next ten years a rich literature on the nature and meaning of feeling states.

Martin Mayman
University of Michigan

---

[3]Binder, J. (1970). *Relative Proneness to Shame or Guilt as a Dimension of Character.* Unpublished doctoral dissertation, University of Michigan.

Acknowledgments

This monograph was based on my doctoral dissertation completed at the University of Michigan in 1981. For their steady support for a nontraditional research approach, I especially wish to thank my dissertation committee: Howard Wolowitz, Chairman; Eric Bermann; Bill Gerler; and Bob Weisbuch. I also wish to thank the other colleagues, instructors, and friends at the University of Michigan who provided many forms of help and encouragement during the dissertation phase or as I developed the dissertation into a monograph. These include Howard Shevrin, Estela Rivero, Roberta Caplan, Michael Jackson, Irv Leon, Dick Hertel, Matt Dochoda, Helga Ashley, George Rosenwald, and Suraleah Michaels. A special thanks is due Beverly Knickerbocker who typed and retyped this manuscript with enormous patience and skill. Invaluable financial support was given by the University of Michigan, first with a generous Rackham dissertation grant, later with a psychology research internship in the Adult Psychiatry Department and a postdoctoral fellowship in clinical psychology in the Department of Psychiatry. I am grateful to Marty Mayman for writing the Foreword to this volume and for his creative and insightful teaching over the years. The staff of *The Analytic Press* made my work easier through their patient and professional approach. My family and friends gave their encouragement throughout this long project. The thoughtful self-explorations of my research interviewees and psychotherapy patients were the indispensable stimulus and informant for the conceptualizing efforts undertaken.

THE SHAME
EXPERIENCE

1

Semantic Issues in the Study of Feeling States

> *We ought to say a feeling of* and *and a feeling of* if, *a feeling of* but, *and a feeling of* by. . . . *Yet we do not: so inveterate has our habit become of recognizing the existence of the substantive parts alone, that language almost refuses to lend itself to any other use. The Empiricists have always dwelt on its influence in making us suppose that where we have a separate name, a separate thing must needs be there to correspond with it; and they have rightfully denied the existence of the mob of abstract entities, principles, and forces, in whose favor no other evidence than this could be brought up. But they have said nothing of that obverse error . . . of supposing that where there is* no *name,* no *entity can exist. All* dumb, *or anonymous psychic states have, owing to this error, been cruelly suppressed; or, if recognized at all, have been named after the substantive perception they led to, as thoughts "about" this object or "about" that, the stolid word* about *engulfing all their delicate idiosyncrasies in its monotonous sound. Thus, the greater and greater accentuation and isolation of the substantive parts have continually gone on.*
>
> —William James (1890)

William James' words doubly chasten our thinking about feeling. We ought to speak to the nameless feelings—the *and's, but's,* and *if's* that invite no substantial name like shame or guilt. And periodically we

1

should suspect "shame," "guilt," and "disgust," our solid citizens, of fraud: They may promise more meaning than they can deliver. The relationship between states and words that propose to label states is complex. Some writers and researchers invest great faith in the common labels of states. They begin their inquiries into emotion with these labels, which they take to be highly significant categorizations of experience. They see the entire domain of emotional experience as fully describable by a list of "the emotions." Entries on the list vary from writer to writer, but all are familiar emotion words of the language. A typical list of the emotions includes shame, guilt, surprise, joy, disgust, fear, anger, contempt, and interest (Izard, 1971). Other writers reject the orientation toward emotions as discrete events, moments of recognizable contempt or surprise or anger. Emotion is omnipresent as the qualitative or tonal aspect of consciousness. It is "the colorfulness of human life" (Goldstein, 1951, p. 33), or the comprehension that one's "well-being is implicated in a transaction, for better or worse" (Lazarus, 1984, p. 124). Shevrin (1978) refers to affects as "a form of awareness or cognition. . . . [I]n higher organisms they play an ever-widening role because they provide important information about the state of vital internal processes" (p. 269). The concept of emotion or feeling as defined by these writers recognizes an essential similarity between the moment of joy, the second of hesitation before crossing a busy street, and the feeling of pleasantly cool water on the hand. Each has a feeling component, a component of the self experiencing the inner and outer worlds and their significance for one's state of being. The moment of joy is experienced intensely. It is strong and clear, and it is remembered as a moment centrally defined by its feeling aspect. In the moment before the street-crossing, the sense of caution and analytic attention may occur alongside thoughts about the evening's plans. The person is half-immersed in one activity, half in the other. Minutes later he or she may not remember the feeling of cautious scanning associated with crossing the busy street. Nevertheless, the feeling aspect of that moment differs in no *essential* way from the feeling in the moment of joy. Both forms of feeling represent the basic human capacity for sensing the personally meaningful activity of the mind and body.

Those concerned with listing the emotions often proceed to schematize them. Particular emotions are designated as signal-scanning emotions (Engel, 1962, 1963), emotions of partial or fused drives (Engel, 1963), expectancy emotions (Panksepp, 1982), or recognition emotions (De Rivera, 1977). Scores of such taxonomies have been suggested. Certain problems attend these efforts, and here we return to James. The emotion categories themselves command more respect than they deserve. We are asked to believe that all emotional experiences fit nicely into 9, or 12, or 20 categories. But this assumption contradicts experience. Most people do not easily state the difference between shame and guilt for example. Nor do they easily place their experiences within one or the other category. The second problem attending taxonomies of emotions as types A, B, or C is that no particular significance is identified for the typologies established. Writers proceed as if their goal is to arrive at a single, correct classification of the emotions. They imply that some such correct classification eventually will be discovered or established. An alternative approach endorsed by Novey (1963) recognizes that all classifications are artificial in that each represents a point of view imposed on the data, not an identification of the fundamental order of emotional events. Feelings may be grouped together because their neurological components are similarly activated. Or a classification schema may reflect felt similarities or psychodynamic relatedness. For example, one emotion might function as a reaction-formation against the other. Or evolutionary relatedness may be introduced as an organizer as in the case of Knapp's (1967) conceptualization of shame and disgust as nature's appetite-curbing mechanisms. Just as psychoanalytic writers recognize that psychological events can be analyzed from multiple viewpoints—dynamic, economic, genetic, structural, and adaptive—emotion theorists must recognize that typologies of emotion represent particular points of view. The value of adopting any one point of view should be specified. For example, a typology might be useful in relation to a specific line of research. When each writer presents his or her classification schema as the ultimate classification of the emotions, endless unproductive controversy follows.

If we disdain emotion names and typologies altogether and refuse to grant them any meaning, we encounter other difficulties. From an evolutionary standpoint, such lists of basic feelings may have significance. Data exist to support the notion that certain clusters of behaviors, especially facial expressions and body postures, appear across cultures and sometimes across species. Some of these behavior clusters emerge at predictable points in the individual's development (Darwin, 1872). These data of universal facial and postural expression must be integrated into concepts of emotion. Our aim though should be to give the data their due significance, and no more. We can recognize that certain emotional expressions, probably indicative of felt experience, are inherited as potentials, some of which express themselves in early infancy and some later in childhood. Whatever experience attends these expressions might then contribute to the development of an individual's store of remembered feeling experiences. The inherited expressions and feeling capacities would also contribute powerfully to the individual and cultural process of categorizing emotion. Thus we find that the obvious emotion-expressions generally have associated names (e.g., disgust) that designate reasonably clear categories of experience. The fact that some well defined expressions are passed on through the genes ought not, however, to compel us to believe that the whole enterprise of categorizing feeling has been established hereditarily. Guilt appears to have no inherited expressions but it is a meaningful, uniquely human category that is related to but (for most people) not interchangeable with shame. We may inherit the blueprint for an expression of disgust and for a rudimentary feeling that is largely a bodily affair, but with time and experience the category, disgust, rooted undoubtedly in the universal esophageal peristalsis, becomes greatly enriched, beyond such a basic format, for each individual. Each person's disgust category will share certain elements with each other person's, but the individual variation in category formation will remain as interesting as the common ground. Also, we find some people fussy about naming their feelings. They decline to find a place for all that they experience in one of the basic groupings named with single words. Others care little for the precise matching of label to experience, and they settle for approximate convergences.

Another confusing practice involving emotion names is that of using a label like shame or anxiety without reference to actual felt experience. Piers and Singer's (1953) discussion of shame exemplifies this practice. They explicitly state that they do not intend "shame" to refer to feeling, but to "a distinctly differentiated form of inner tension (p. 17). . . . Shame arises out of a tension between the ego and the ego ideal" (p. 23). Thus their reference is structural, psychoanalytically speaking. What relationship have these structures to experience? Translated into experiential language, Piers and Singer's use of "tension" implies either conscious, experienced tension or tension existing at a non-conscious level between neurological structures that (a) represent structural products of conscious or unconscious mental processes and (b) continue to give rise to and undergo modification by conscious mental processes. Such tension is said to exist between the ego and the ego ideal. "Ego ideal" can be paraphrased as a constellation of images of how one wishes the self to be. I am not certain how to paraphrase "ego" in this context, but I believe Piers and Singer mean to refer to tension between that which one wishes to be and that which one is. However one understands their use of ego, the claim of no experiential referent allows them to group a vast number of rather different experiences under one term. Piers and Singer believe that these diverse experiences all relate to conscious or non-conscious confrontations that a person makes with some real or imaged personal inferiority. In response to such a confrontation, a person may feel ashamed, or angry, or lethargic, or depressed. But whatever the feeling experience, Piers and Singer label the situation shame based on their definition of shame as a tension between the ego and the ego ideal. This nonspecific use of "shame" discourages attention to the great variety of felt experiences (e.g., anger, depression, withdrawal, anxiety, or humiliation) with which a person may respond to a perception of failing. It also leads to confusion over whether conscious or unconscious mental activity is intended when a reference to shame is made. And it allows us to assume unconscious activity without confronting how and in what form such activity is psychologically meaningful.

Piers and Singer explicitly claim no experiential referent. Their clarity on this point helps to keep their intended meaning apparent. But the use of feeling labels without intention to designate felt experience at times can cause greater confusion. Typically, these problems occur when a feeling label is used to denote some state or situation that is assumed to motivate the actually experienced state. "Anxiety" is often designated as the cause for behavioral symptoms, ideas, or other experienced feelings, when no experienced anxiety is intended. Such uses of "anxiety" are difficult to avoid. They have great explanatory power; nevertheless, they should be avoided. They circumvent the important theoretical question of what actually is happening, consciously or unconsciously, that produces an outcome we naively might expect to result from *experienced* anxiety. If one restricts the use of affect labels to the domain of felt experience, one challenges oneself to specify (to whatever extent possible) the form of those events that do not *feel like* anxiety, but have an anxiety-like impact on some aspect of functioning.

When words such as anxiety are used without reference to felt experience, often it is implied that the relevant events take place outside of consciousness. Most writers reject phrases like "unconscious anxiety" or "unconscious experience" because they involve such an apparent contradiction in terms, but psychoanalytic clinical theory and metapsychology assume events outside of consciousness that are in some ways equivalent to felt emotion. For example, an unconscious event might equate with experienced anxiety in its impact on defenses. Postulation of unconscious events that profoundly influence consciousness at times appears to be well justified. Clinical observation constantly calls for such a concept. However, once the concept has been integrated into clinical explanation, it opens the door to a number of abuses. One such abuse relevant to the study of emotion is the practice of too quickly labeling as unconscious all formulations of a patient's experience that the clinician can articulate but the patient apparently cannot. The designation "dynamic unconscious" should be reserved for that which is completely and totally unavailable to introspection yet clearly of consequence in determining an individual's actions, feelings, or thoughts. Many states of consciousness are difficult to verbalize. Often the individual who experiences them barely attends to them and may forget them quickly. Yet such inarticulate states are conscious states, and they may contain rich data about the self and its motives. The central position in psychoanalytic theory of a concept of unconscious events that influence consciousness may draw attention away from many states of inarticulate consciousness too quickly labeled unconscious. For example, a male patient's free associations might abound with castration imagery and with themes of shame. From these data the clinician might conclude that the patient is ashamed of his sense of himself as castrated. But when confronted with the question of whether he feels ashamed, the patient denies any such feelings because he has not conceptualized his shifting, weakly attended feeling states in terms of the category, shame. Persuaded by the themes within the clinical material, the clinician concludes that the feeling, or some physiological equivalent of it, is fully unconscious. And the assumption is made that at some earlier point in the person's life the designated feeling probably was experienced in a clear and specific form that initiated defensive consequences. Novey (1963) states the clinician's position well:

> Clinically, one occasionally observes behavioral patterns which one has reason to believe are related to certain emotional states. It is a tantalizing problem, indeed, when the actual feeling state as experienced and reported by the patient seems incongruous with the accompanying behavioral pattern. I should suppose that based upon the observational data, this is about all one would be entitled to say. In practice, however, we are in the habit of making logical, perhaps dangerous, assumptions about linkages, presumed to be present and as yet unrevealed, between the behavioral pattern, for instance, and some emotional experience not within the realm of specific awareness—and we do this despite the paradox of talking of the feeling which is not felt! As indefensible as this position may be on many grounds, it has the virtue of clinical usefulness and a classificatory system of affects must, at least if it is to be useful to the clinician, take cognizance of such observations. (p. 298)

Although Novey gives it no further attention in his brief article, the word "specific" modifying "awareness" deserves consideration. It is possible that the shame-denying person has absolutely no conscious data that could help to identify a shame potential in the self, but it is equally probable that the person does have some non-specific, conscious experience that when carefully introspected and articulated would add up to what we generally call shame. One may have no specific awareness of shame, that is, no fully articulated, readily recognized feeling, but yet have some experience, not yet put into words or concepts, that when scrutinized appears to be a shame-like experience. The therapeutic process of making the unconscious conscious in certain cases might be better described as making the inarticulate articulate. The reasons for emotional experience taking inarticulate form also deserve consideration. For example, some feeling states may have been vague and undefined, yet disturbing, even when first experienced in childhood. Others may have been strong and clear and they were rendered vague as part of a defensive quest for unconsciousness; or the vagueness may represent the influence of time and of the complex interplay of many frames of experience.

Gendlin (1962) calls this type of inarticulate experience *preconceptual*. Early infantile experience must be entirely preconceptual. At that early stage of life, ideas (i.e., relationships between states or perceptions) are felt; they are not articulated with words and formal concepts. Later in life, verbal expressions of ideas supplement and alter the felt experience. What is preconceptual is not unconscious but may appear to be because the subject may deny the experience when asked about it, and then, after further therapy, he or she may recognize the experience. The importance in psychoanalytic theory of the concept of the unconscious makes it easy for us to ignore distinctions between what may be strictly and entirely unconscious and what is conscious but remains in an inarticulate or transient form that makes conceptualization and study difficult. Individuals who are attentive to and comfortable with the inarticulate stream of consciousness make good reporters of such intermediate states. Those who distrust the inchoate inner world will quickly deny this unformed, inarticulate experience, and thus they will prevent it from reaching articulate form.

Inquiry into nuances of actually experienced emotion is not the sole legitimate domain of the study of emotion. But it does constitute an important area of study that has been undervalued—not in the practice of psychotherapy but in formal studies of emotion. A close look at the experienced content of a category such as shame ought to be of value in several respects. Such inquiry elucidates the meaningfulness—or lack of meaningfulness—of the linguistic category itself. It tells us how seriously we can regard the category designation. And the inquiry shows us how various individuals struggle with relationships between language and actual experiences. What else should such inquiry reveal? Psychoanalysis is interested in depth psychology, that is, in core conflicts variously expressed, disguised, or avoided at the experiential surface of personality. Shame experience is implicated in some of these conflicts, for example, conflict over sexual exhibitionism.

Psychoanalysis tells us that shame means more than or other than what it feels like it means. Shame means the opposite of what it feels like. It means reaction-formation. The experience is taken to be a deception that hides the true motivation enlivening the personality. How does psychoanalysis know these things? There are various routes to psychological knowing. One can discover empirically, for example by noting that a feeling suddenly disappears and is replaced by another feeling that is intelligible if regarded as a transformation of the original. Thus, self-hate in melancholia has been hypothesized to be a transformation of object hate. Extrapolation from theory is another route to knowing. Thus, De Rivera's (1977) theory of emotions predicts that certain feelings have opposites on key dimensions. When the opposites cannot be found they are assumed to be undiscovered but still existent, just as the presence of the planet Pluto could be predicted, according to certain natural laws, long before it was discovered. Another route to psychological knowing is the direct recognition of the significance of feeling through the experiencing of it. The psychology of the mind surrenders certain of its secrets to the individual who listens to the emotional tones of communication. Though this route to knowledge contains many pitfalls, there exists no smoothly paved route. We accept the theory of reaction-formation in part because we are able to *hear directly* the pretense in the sweetness sufficiently often to make a reaction-formation concept plausible. Thus the surface of feeling that we experience—in the case of our own feeling—or hear in another's verbalizations, always remains richly communicative and worthy of study. It points the way to classifications, dynamics, and tests of theories. And it informs us of patterns within the surface or experienced layer of personality. It tells us how the individual's tendencies in the shame domain (e.g., his or her intensity, or articulateness, or blandness) might relate to broader patterns of emotional experience characterizing that individual.

The direct experience of feeling also can be a great deceiver. The palpable intensity of a feeling may succeed in totally obscuring its defensive aspect unless one has a psychological theory to point the way to those hidden realms. Thus a person who is profoundly fearful of delivering a speech may find it inconceivable that such dread derives from conflict over a pleasurable wish.

In this monograph then, considerable respect, but not blind allegiance, belongs to felt experience and what it can tell us. The work is in the spirit of James' (1890) interest in the stream of consciousness, of Gendlin's (1962) fascination with preconceptual experience, and of all psychotherapists' and bewildered dreamers' admiration for the mind's eye.

2 Literature Review

Psychoanalytic writing on shame concerns itself with the question, what is the ashamed person actually distressed about? Some writers view the shame experience as itself the articulate expression of a concern. These writers identify the ashamed person's problem by attending closely to what the shame experience feels like to the individual. Shame then is just what it says it is. All we need do is attend to the complainant's words and physiognomy. Other writers regard the shame experience as a disguise rather than a direct expression. In their view, the structure of shame is like the structure of a symptom. Shame masks an exhibitionistic impulse while giving it partial expression in the form of physiological arousal. For these writers, the concern of the ashamed person reveals itself during analysis of the shame-precipitating situation or from analysis of shame as a defense. The approaches taken by the two groups are not mutually exclusive, as a closer look at each will show.

Two subgroups emerge from a larger grouping of writers who understand shame by examining the psychological situation it interrupts. Freud, Anna Freud, Nunberg, and Jacobson all regard shame as a servant of morality. Comments by Knapp, Kohut, and Lewis place them in a second subgroup. They identify an arousal-blocking function of shame. Unlike the first group, they do not view arousal as necessarily *morally* dangerous; rather, arousal may be threatening to the *ego*.

According to the group to which Freud belongs, shame functions principally as a reaction-formation against exhibitionistic impulses. Prohibitions against exhibitionism drive the ego to create a shame feeling that obliterates awareness of the forbidden wishes. Thus shame is a deputy of sexual morality. Shame's significance lies in its psychological function, not in its experienced content. The negative statements about the self that often form the core of experienced shame are not taken to be true statements of self-evaluation, but are taken instead to be psychic decoys that divert a person away from exhibitionism. A few passages from Freud demonstrate his consistent interpretation of shame as a sexual reaction-formation in the service of morality:

> [On hearing smut] instead of this excitement [intended by the speaker] the other person may be led to feel shame or embarrassment, which is only a reaction against the excitement and, in a roundabout way, is an admission of it. (Freud, 1905/53, p. 97)

> During the period of life which may be called the period of "sexual latency"—i.e., from the completion of the fifth year to the first manifestations of puberty (round about the eleventh year)—reaction-formations, or counter-forces, such as shame, disgust, and morality, are created in the mind. They are actually formed at the expense of the excitations proceeding from the erotogenic zones, and they rise like dams to oppose the later activity of the sexual instincts. (Freud, 1908/53, p. 171)

> Even before puberty, extremely energetic repressions of certain instincts have been effected under the influence of education, and mental forces such as shame, disgust and morality have been set up, which, like watchmen, maintain these repressions. So that when at puberty, the high tide of sexual demands is reached, it is met by these mental reactions or resistant structures like dams, which direct its flow into what are called normal channels and make it impossible for it to reactivate the instincts that have undergone repression. (Freud, 1909/53, p. 45)

> But thereafter this early efflorescence of sexuality passes off; the sexual impulses which have shown such liveliness are overcome by repression and a *period of latency* follows, which lasts until puberty and during which the *reaction-formations* of morality, shame and disgust are built up. (Freud, 1925/53, p. 37)

> During that period of life, after the early efflorescence of sexuality has withered, such attitudes of the ego as shame, disgust and morality arise which are destined to stand up against the later tempest of puberty and to lay down the path of the freshly awakened sexual desires. (Freud, 1926/53, pp. 210–211)

In Freud's view, the self-diminishing, self-hiding quality of the shame experience represents its function as a dam against *morally forbidden* exhibitionistic excitement. Many others share Freud's emphasis on reaction-formation. Anna Freud (1965) states, "The qualities of shame, disgust, pity, are known not to be acquired by any child except as results of internal struggles with exhibitionism, messing, cruelty" (p. 16). Jacobson (1964) makes a similar point:

> Feelings of disgust and shame, a reaction-formation to exhibitionistic wishes, from now on assist the child in his struggle with his forbidden pregenital and, later on, genital wishes. (p. 100)

Nunberg's (1955) formulation differs only slightly from those above:

> It follows from all of this that shame is a reaction-formation of the ego to the wish to exhibit. Castration is the motive power of this reaction-formation. (p. 157)

Freud proposes morality as the motive behind shame, and superego as the relevant agency; Nunberg designates castration anxiety and ego. Because psychoanalytic theory regards castration anxiety as a motive for morality, the difference between the two views may not be highly significant. Nunberg's view may imply a slightly earlier (phallic phase) point of origin for shame experience than Freud's view, which implies an oedipal origin. But Freud, Anna Freud, Jacobson, and Nunberg all see shame as a reaction-formation against exhibitionism, motivated by the belief that exhibitionism is forbidden. Thus, to indulge in it will bring negative consequences. These may be guilt (attack from within) or castration (attack from without).

As comprehensive shame theories, the reaction-formation theories focus too narrowly on a single dynamic. Although they identify the commonplace situation in which shame experience interrupts morally forbidden exhibitionism, they mistake that function for the defining core of the shame experience. One can prop open a window with a book, but that does not mean that a book is essentially a window prop. It means only that the book's structure is such that it lends itself to that purpose, among others. The reaction-formation theorists have studied a particular function of shame—that of superego deputy—and have neglected to study the shame experience itself. They present shame as an experience of personal inferiority that does not in fact represent a real negative conviction about the self. Instead, shame signifies an attempt to deflect attention away from impulses to exhibit an erotically viewed self or body. The public display of the body or sexual self would bring guilt or, in Nunberg's view, castration anxiety. Freud and others of the reaction-formation persuasion sometimes use "shame" *in context* in a way that appears to reflect a view of shame as a straightforward expression of true negative self-evaluation, but their formal theory regards shame as a defense only and gives it no real expressive function. While there are problems with theories such as Freud's that analyze one state solely as a means to deliver a person from a second, more threatening state and not at all as an expressive event, nevertheless these theories have made a crucial contribution to the psychology of feeling. They reach beyond naive conceptions of feeling that neglect the dynamic interplay between states.

A second group of writers shares with the first group an orientation toward shame as a functional event. These writers see shame as a brake applied against various forms of exhibitionistic excitement, but they do not posit morality as the exclusive motive behind the braking operation. They point to the ego-disruptive impact of overstimulation and to the need for a mechanism to reverse highly stimulated states. Knapp (1967) proposes that shame, like disgust, evolved in order to curb appetites that may be dangerous to the organism. Disgust curbs hunger; shame counters the sexual instinct. Under certain circumstances, one emotion may substitute for the other. Lewis (1971) states, "In a case of 'watching' in a child patient (1963), I suggest that shame functions as a protection against the loss of self-boundaries which is implicit in absorbed sexual fantasy" (p. 24). At times Kohut (1971) appears to understand shame as a feeling state that functions (in combination with states of self-consciousness and hypochondriacal worry) to ground a person who is so overstimulated by feelings of omnipotence that these feelings threaten his or her capacities to resist wholehearted and active commitment to psychotically grandiose beliefs about the self. Some of the "curbing" interpretations of shame rely too exclusively on a physiological principle, homeostasis, that has been imported as an explanation for shifts from highly stimulated to less stimulated feeling states. It is possible to obtain experiential evidence of a homeostatic principle operating in feeling life, but I have not seen this in the shame literature. Patients often report that, while painful in its own way, depression can be experienced as a great relief from the exhausting demands of anxiety, thus the depression has a homeostatic effect. I have not seen any parallel reports that describe shame experience in such a way that it becomes comprehensible as a felt reduction of exhibitionistic excitement or grandiosity. Since shame generally is itself a painfully stimulated state, it is somewhat difficult to accept that shame comes as a relief from excitement. It *is* understandable that overexcitement (for example, in response to wishes to show one's assets to a potential lover) can be experienced as such a disorganized state, with the self not firmly in control, that shame is a meaningful reponse to the state. The person feels diminished by the failure to present the self in a calm and organized way.[1] I have had patients talk of their need to import a familiar negative feeling, such as discouragement or irritation, because they feel ungrounded when they experience unfamiliar forms of pleasure. Shame might serve this same purpose. One woman spoke of feeling lightheaded, dizzy, and fearful of passing out when she felt certain pleasures. She explained her anxiety by the novelty of the pleasure, though I suspected that specific conflicts—as yet unarticulated—accompanied the pleasure and contributed to her response to it. Substitution of shame for pleasure under such circumstances might be seen as a homeostasis-promoting net reduction in stimulation, but it might also be viewed as a switch to a less conflictual *type* of stimulated state. The latter explanation gives weight to the significance of the particular variety of stimulation, not just to its intensity. Intense feeling existing in the absence of familiarity with it or understanding of it will produce fears of unlimited, overwhelming further intensification of stimulation, and such fears, which depend on the meaning of the feeling to the individual and the possibilities for active management of it, certainly might give rise to efforts to reduce stimulation.

A homeostatic physiological tendency might exert some control over conscious experience without giving rise to conscious feelings of relief, such as those reported by the lightheaded patient who welcomes back her annoyance or by anxious patients who find a respite in depression. But without strong evidence for this order of impact on the composition of consciousness, it seems more reasonable first to approach shame as a *psychological* event, the meaning of which is revealed through psychological analysis, whether directed toward the shame experience itself or toward the surrounding psychological events. The analysis of nonpsychological contributions to felt experience poses complex questions not to be considered here in detail. These questions are of current interest due to the widespread belief that affective deviation is directly caused by biochemical abnormality. Such a theory often is taken to mean that the forms of consciousness that accompany affective illness—for example, the self-hate in melancholia—have little to do with an object relational history. The forms of consciousness are epiphenomena of biochemical abnormality. Even if we grant that biochemistry influences decisively the forms of consciousness, no felt experience can be totally apsychological or psychologically irrelevant since the self is always operating to give personal meaning to experi-

---

[1]Lewis presents a similar argument in showing that giddy, excited triumph feelings are experienced as childish; thus they bring shame because of their childishness. This is a dynamic rather than an economic explanation for a shame experience.

ence. Personal integration of biologically induced affect states may occur in a great variety of ways, but it will occur. One recovered depressive may regard his or her delusions as a fevered delirium. Another may regard them as manifestations of previously repressed feelings about the self. Of these views, one may be correct and the other erroneous, but each represents an integration of the experience by the self and a further delineation of the self. While my own current bias is to think about shame as psychologically meaningful and not as a meaningless visitation, the least one can do is to recognize that individuals will give meaning to their experience as part of the ongoing process of maintaining a coherent self. This will be true even when experiences are in some real way visited upon the person by evolution or by biochemistry.

Of the writers considered here, Kohut most closely approaches a convincing presentation of shame as an experience induced in order to curb arousal. He describes states of growing belief in personal omnipotence. Though partially pleasurable, these states create an uncomfortable tension from which a person might seek relief. I am not clear about the specific nature of the discomfort Kohut seeks to identify. Is the discomfort the result of impulses to behave omnipotently, urges that must be energetically resisted because one senses that they could bring personal disaster if enacted? Within such a scenario, it is understandable that a person might feel some relief when omnipotence, which presses for action, is relieved by a state of shame and worry that seeks limitation of contacts with the outer world. The self has found a new organization, painful in its own right, but able to free a person from certain previously experienced stresses. The possible relationships between shame feeling and various types of ego-disruptive excitement remain minimally explored. Any researcher working in this area would need to consider thoughtfully the distinctions between shame as an *experience* of relief and shame determined to be arousal-reducing according to a nonexperiential criterion.

A number of writers—some who conceptualize shame as a reaction-formation and others who do not—see the shame experience as an indicator of conflict around a specific developmental stage or issue. Nunberg is an example of this group. According to Nunberg, shame functions to curtail exhibitionism in order to protect against perceived dangers to the penis. Taken literally, his definition encourages an enormously constricted understanding of shame and of human values in general. No body part or aspect of self other than the male genital is seen as relevant to the shame experience. In his understanding of women's shame, he not only restricts shame to genital concerns; he also sees shame in women as due invariably to feelings of castration.

He neglects the shame felt in response to a woman's assessment that she is inadequately *feminine,* as compared with her mother or another woman. In its linking of shame with a particular developmental phase and body part, Nunberg's definition is among the most restrictive, but others do share his conviction that shame always pertains to a particular psychosexual phase, or at least to feelings about the body rather than to broader, perhaps nonsexual or nonphysical aspects of the self. Mayman (1974) regularly relates shame to the experience of genital inferiority, but he does not share Nunberg's belief that sexual inferiority feelings in women focus exclusively on the absence of a penis. Others, such as Engel (1963), suggest a more variable focus for the shame experience by noting that shame may refer to anal experiences of loss of control or loss of good feeling about body products, or to phallic concern with genital size or function. Still, shame remains invariably linked to a bodily concern. These theories imply that self-investments that lead to the experience of pride are essentially matters of body investment, and that self-disappointments that generate shame are disappointments in body function or appearance. They encourage the view that adult values that bring shame when they are not honored are always to be regarded as later echoes or transformations of the child's body narcissism. Perhaps the best way to integrate these writers' insights about infantile experience and shame would be to state that all adult experiences have a history; therefore, shame in an adult is a reminder of childhood shame experiences, many (but not all) of which focus on the body. But the presence of a shame history associated with all adult shame experiences ought not to be taken to mean that the adult's shame is never anything other than a simple reactivation of infantile shame over bodily shortcomings.

Mayman was mentioned above without attention to a significant distinction between his theory and Nunberg's. Though both writers focus on genital concerns, Nunberg describes shame as a defense against those exhibitionistic feelings that might invite castration, while Mayman describes shame as an expression of sexual inferiority feelings in a person whose early exhibitionistic efforts have left him or her feeling diminished. In other words, Nunberg sees shame as protecting against the castration that potentially could take place and Mayman sees shame as stating that the figurative castration has already occurred. In Mayman's view, the shame-prone adult learned as a child that what he or she wished to display with pride and excitement was regarded by others as laughably small, cute, or underdeveloped. Mayman's analysis of shame is consistent with the results of introspecting certain shame states. He treats the felt meaning of shame as its reality and essence, not as an irrelevant epiphenomenon. He understands the exhibitionistic impulse as the background against which the inferiority feeling develops, not necessarily as the motive for the inferiority feeling.

Horney (1932) argued that all boys suffer a profound loss of self-esteem (presumably generating shame) due to a perception or intuition that their genital is small and inconsequential compared with the mother's vagina, which can swallow it up. She believed that feelings of genital inadequacy in comparison with the mother are more significant to the boy's development and to the adult male's dread of women than are the boy's feelings of inferiority and vulnerability in relation to the father. She argued that the little girl experiences no equivalent loss of self-esteem; her feelings about the father's larger genital revolve around the fear of being damaged by it. Horney sees the phallic phase in boys as a phase of denial of the already intuited, narcissistically threatening female genital. Her theory has obvious implications for shame experience in men, but to my knowledge it has received little attention in the shame literature.

If one takes the position that Mayman's understanding of shame as a straightforward expressive state is essentially more correct than Nunberg's or Freud's interpretation of shame as fundamentally a reaction-formation—the self-critical content of which is only a smoke screen meant to obscure exhibitionistic excitement—then what place does one assign to the reaction-formation theory of shame? The basic psychological significance of shame relates to the experience of the self as inferior. Shame is felt when an injurious situation breeds inferiority feelings. But shame also may grow strong because normal defenses against inferiority feelings cannot be used, or because guilty or self-abusive trends actually encourage such feeling. Shame as reaction-formation would appear to belong to the last category; the reaction-formations are instances of shame that appear because guilt (or other sources of anxiety) over exhibitionism encourages the person to view his or her body or behavior as shameful. This argument will be elaborated later but the point to be made here is that shame in the context of reaction-formation is not without direct expressive significance. The experience of the self as inferior is present and real, as in all shame experiences. But the shame is nourished in part by guilt or other anxieties that restrict the individual to perceiving only the negative narcissistic potential in a situation, not the positive (prideful) potential.

Not all who write about shame feeling immediately associate the feeling with exclusively bodily conflict. A last group of writers define shame as an acute experience of inferiority feeling that may refer to any aspect of self or to the self experienced as a unity. Shame is an experience—often referring to the self as a whole—whose meaning is revealed by the experienced nature of the feeling. Many could be included in this group; I will refer briefly to Kohut, Lewis, Lynd, Grinker, Piers and Singer, and Alexander.

Kohut (1971) repeatedly mentions shame in the context of discussions of the narcissistic personality. He thinks of shame as a collapse of self-esteem that is developmentally linked to parental failures to respond attentively and appreciatively to the child as a whole human being rather than as a collection of body parts and functions. Kohut generally does not place any special emphasis on shame about the genitals. He predicts shame (in combination with hypochondriacal worry and self-consciousness) when regression causes the narcissistically vulnerable individual to experience himself or herself as an unintegrated assemblage of weak parts and functions:

> In a number of instances the regression which follows the disappointment in the idealized object does not stop at the level of archaic narcissism but moves further toward the hypercathexis of the autoerotic, fragmented body-mind-self with painful experiences of hypochondriacal worry and archaic shame. (p. 136)

In the next passage, Kohut describes shame that attends the awareness that one's behavior is infantile:

> True, at times, even the content of the fantasy permits an empathic understanding of the shame and hypochondria, and of the anxiety which the patient experiences: *shame, because revelation is at times still accompanied by the discharge of crude, unneutralized exhibitionistic libido;* and anxiety because the grandiosity isolates the analysand and threatens him with permanent object loss. (p. 149, italics added)

In clear contrast with the theory of shame as a reaction-formation meant to obscure forbidden exhibitionism, here we have a description of shame as a response to undisguised exhibitionism that is judged to be infantile. The shame to which Kohut alludes would appear to be shame over the wish to exhibit one's whole self, not shame over a particular body part or process. Kohut associates shame with problems in self-structure and self-esteem, but his writing often leaves unspecified the precise nature of the shame experience and the role of shame in relation to the self-defects he postulates.

Alexander (1938) also discusses shame without specific reference to feelings about the genitals. He sees shame as resulting from failures to move forward developmentally. The ashamed person often has acquiesced to regressive wishes. In emphasizing developmental failure,

Alexander is partially in accord with Kohut, who talks about shame over infantile forms of exhibitionism, and with Mayman. The experience of having small, cute, or inadequate genitalia—Mayman's emphasis—would represent a perceived developmental failure. But Alexander does not restrict his concept of developmental progress to progress with respect to genitally focused identity. Furthermore, he thinks that shame follows not just from unavoidable weakness, but from normal wishes to be small, protected, and sexually undifferentiated. As with others who look first at the straightforward statement of inferiority that shame carries, and look secondarily at the defensive potential of such statements, Alexander's discussion of shame and guilt highlights the differences between the two experiences. He demonstrates the role of guilt in inhibiting self-development and the role of shame in promoting such development. His dichotomy oversimplifies in that it ignores the demoralizing, paralyzing, self-abusive aspects of profound shame, but it represents a useful counterpoint to the insupportable Freudian notion that shame invariably restricts expressiveness and personal development due to its deputy position vis-à-vis guilt.

Grinker (1955) sees shame as the response to failure to master a developmental task at the normally expected time. He does not reduce shame over relatively late developmental failure to a mere reverberation of some early failure, e.g., of genital self-esteem. The 18-year-old's setbacks in leaving his or her parents and going off to college are shameful in their own right just as incontinence is in the 4-year-old. Grinker hypothesizes inherent standards of functioning in the maturing person that can lead to shame feelings as early as the first year of life, for example, in response to motoric difficulty. Though it seems plausible that frustration over tasks not mastered could occur this early, it seems doubtful that well developed instances of what adults call shame occur even before the clear investment in a cohesive self has been accomplished. In contrast with Alexander, Grinker is sensitive to the growth-defeating potential of shame feelings when such feelings push a person to strive for unattainable ends. Grinker attributes the suicide of one of his patients to intense shame over inescapable developmental failure. The dilemma of some inalterably impaired individuals is that one cannot change but one cannot tolerate being what one is. Because the healthy child retains the promise of future development, he or she generally can tolerate current self-dissatisfaction.

In thinking next about Piers and Singer's (1953) discussion of shame, one must remember that they intend "shame" to designate the full range of feeling experiences that reflect states of disparity between the perceived actual self and the ideal self. According to Piers and Singer, experienced shame is but one of several forms that shame can take. Despite this definitional complication, it seems accurate to say that Piers and Singer believe that experienced shame can occur in response to any discrepancy between one's ideals and one's actual behavior. Such a disparity between ego ideal and perceived actual self can occur in any area of functioning, be it sexual performance, moral integrity, capacity to run fast, or ability to outcon an accomplished crook. Piers and Singer differ from some earlier writers by departing from the notion that shame is a response to external criticism and guilt a response to internal criticism. They distinguish shame and guilt by identifying shame as a failure to reach one's ego ideal (a falling short) and guilt as an active violation of a principle that one values. Both shame and guilt respond to internal standards, but the relevant standards differ.

Lynd's (1958) theory accords with Piers and Singer's, both in her belief that shame can occur in response to a great variety of human situations, not just genital deficiency or body deficiencies of other types, and in the belief that shame is a failure vis-à-vis internal standards. Lynd stands alone among shame discussants in her emphasis on loss of solidarity with cultural values as a source of shame. She stresses the relationship between confusion and shame through her belief that any significant loss of the feeling that one's world makes sense or that one's participation in that world makes sense is experienced not just as confusion and distress, but as shame, as if the lack of order signified a personal failing. Her argument is interesting but perhaps overstated. External disorder creates the potential for shame because one may identify with the lack of solidity in one's environment, but one cannot assume that external disorder invariably generates such an identification and consequent shame reaction. Certainly the ability of mature individuals to distinguish between self and circumstance protects them from immediate identification with chaotic surroundings. Under extreme circumstances, this ability may break down.

Lewis (1971) associates shame feeling with a great variety of situations, all of which hold in common the failure to achieve a personal goal that has been established out of loving admiration for one's parents. She has studied closely actual shame experiences so that she is able to recognize and analyze the subtle variations in shame experience as well as the similarities. Lewis published an intensive study of shame and guilt in which she presented transcripts of early therapy hours conducted with patients hypothesized to be shame-prone and patients hypothesized to be guilt-prone. She sought to verify a theory that field-dependent people are shame-prone relative to field-independent people, who are guilt-prone. She presents many transcripts of patient hours and she identifies and discusses acknowledged, labeled shame feelings as well as states she refers to as "overt, unidentified shame" (states some might call unconscious shame) and "bypassed shame." Among other thoughtful hypotheses, Lewis advances the theory that the organization of the self in the shame-prone and guilt-prone person differs predictably. I will not attempt an adequate summary of Lewis' book here. Its richness lies in the comments made about dozens of clinical passages rather than in any single point of theory that she advances.

As a shared contribution, Piers and Singer, Lynd, Lewis, and others identify shame as a response to any variety of situation that a person judges to be evidence of personal failure. Although they understand that shame feelings often are put to defensive use, frequently in combination with guilt, they do not mistake the complex contents or dynamic involvements of the shame experience for the basic definition of the experience. Their shame definitions form a good foundation for a study such as the present one, which focuses on shame experience in the dynamic context of the individual life. Lewis should be given special recognition as one writer who pursues her inquiry well beyond the simple defining of shame as reflective of felt inferiority. She scrutinizes moment-to-moment ebbs, flows, and modifications of shame feeling in much the same way I have tried to do when analyzing my data. The primary difference between her research approach and mine is that Lewis was most interested in identifying defensive responses to moments of shame experience occurring in psychotherapy interviews, whereas I chose to seek out people who would talk with me *directly* about their shame history. The projects overlap in that I was interested in shame that was actually evoked during my interviews, but the analysis of those moments was not my primary focus, as it was for Lewis. In summary, Lewis was attuned to how a person, talking about his or her current life problems with a therapist, passed into and out of ego states that Lewis identified as shame, even though the patient did not always label them in that way. I was most interested in what the nonpatient interviewee could tell me directly or indirectly about his or her shame history; what the person could show me of his or her current shame experience, labeled or unlabeled; and what the person's active conceptualizing about his or her shame experience told me about shame and about other aspects of that person's self-organization. Lewis' orientation toward data collection and analysis and my own orientation promote different but complementary discussions of shame experience.

3 Research Method

A research project focused on shame states provided the data for this monograph. Data collection consisted of extensive interviewing with ten volunteer subjects. The purpose of the interviews was to elucidate the role of shame and related states in the lives of a number of individuals. The interviews were to explore the meaning, for each individual, of the words shame, humiliation, and embarrassment (and in some cases, related words such as guilt and self-consciousness). The interviews would engage the subjects in efforts to attach feeling labels to personal experience. The interviews also would explore the subjects' understanding of the role of shame (and related states) in their past and present lives. Whenever possible, the interviewer would elicit detailed descriptions of any state that appeared to be shame-related, even though the subject might not call the state "shame." More general interviewing and history-taking would provide a context from which to assess the significance of each subject's shame experience. The interviewer would follow cues embedded in the emerging interview data, and would remain mindful of points of interest suggested by the literature on shame. The aim of the research was not to decide between theory A and theory B. Rather, the researcher sought to generate relevant data and to offer conceptualizing possibilities that could become part of an ongoing discourse about an area of study—a discourse that takes place through successive research projects, through discussion between colleagues, and within an individual clinician's mind as he or she thinks about the shame experiences presented by patients or seen within the clinician's own life.

Interviews followed no prescribed form, but all of the topics mentioned earlier were discussed at some point during the meetings with each subject. Each set of interviews began with a statement of the interviewer's interest both in shame feelings and in the person's history and current life. Depending on the course of the first few minutes of interaction, the interviewer then either asked the subject what had led him or her to respond to the posted sign seeking volunteers for the study or asked the subject to tell the interviewer about himself or herself in whatever way felt comfortable. Or the interviewer might ask a question derived from some initial comment or question by the subject. For example, I might have followed up on a subject's uncertainty as to what I meant by "shame" on the posted advertisement, or I might have inquired about a subject's puzzlement concerning the difference between shame and guilt. From that point forward, interviews were guided by the goal of investigating as thoroughly as possible the major areas of interest already enumerated.

Only 10 participants were chosen, in part because of limitations on time and on funds for transcription of interview tapes, but also because the 38 hours of interviewing provided as much data as reasonably could be digested by one person. More data threatened to impose an overwhelming analytic task. Since the study was intended as a contribution to an ongoing research process rather than as an attempt to settle a particular question, 10 subjects provided a reasonable body of data to consider as a unit.

Participants were told in advance of the interviewing that there would be four to six meetings, but the decision to terminate with each participant came when I felt I had learned as much as I could about that person's shame experience while respecting the limits of the research alliance. In some cases the end point came because the participant closed up emotionally in some way. Either he or she appeared uninterested in the interviews or appeared concerned about giving up more time to them. Or the subject's comments, though perhaps cooperative in tone, were increasingly defended in content. In one case (Josephine), the interviewing was terminated after four sessions because the participant began to display such great distress and such a strong wish for therapeutic help that it seemed impossible to continue within a research alliance, rather than a consultation format. In other cases, the participant was not especially resistant to meaningful continuation of the process, but I felt I had learned as much as I could without drawing the person into a more profoundly self-evaluative, possibly unsettling process than I had intended. One participant (Cal) dropped out after only one interview by not calling back when he said he would do so. Another participant (Frank) lived a great distance from the interviewing site. He had been interviewed three times, with much time between interviews, when he canceled an appointment. He expressed an interest in continuing at a later date and we made several subsequent attempts to arrange an appointment, but each time he called again to reschedule. My vacation then intervened and he did not call again as promised. In both these incomplete cases the interviews had been difficult in a variety of ways, and presumably the participants were ambivalent about additional meetings. All eight other interviewees continued in the research until I indicated the termination time had come.

Criteria for research validity depend on the claims one makes regarding conclusions drawn from a study. In contrast to most research projects, this study does not attempt to use data to prove a specific point about shame experience. Instead, the data are meant to serve as a counterbalance to a tendency in the literature to bypass the process of describing in detail an emotional phenomenon. This short-circuiting takes place in the interest of increased freedom to manipulate a particular phenomenon in a field of others as if it were a known, defined entity. The research reported here aims toward a valid *depiction* of certain states of feeling and of their role in the lives of a number of men and women.

To those who would argue that the conclusions drawn from this study cannot be generalized since the subjects are a small, self-selected sample, I would respond first that I am not seeking to set up, by adherence to statistical rules, a situation that would allow me to claim that what holds true for my subjects as a group holds true for a larger group. I want only to understand and describe significant aspects of each subject's functioning so that his or her shame experience becomes coherent to me and to the reader in its multiple ties to other aspects of the person's experience. The principles of cohesion of the data within each case and the insights achieved into how best to conceptualize these kinds of data may be the findings the generalizability of which would be of greatest interest. The presence or absence of some particular static feature in six-of-ten or eight-of-ten cases has less significance. Ultimately, the reader will be the one to assess general applicability of the data as he or she takes the pictures drawn here into his or her own world of experience and makes comparisons and draws contrasts. The well presented case should form a template against which other cases can be compared. In this research context, validity depends on the researcher's clinical inference skills, which are his or her basic research instrument, and on the presentation of the interview data, the inference process, and the inferential conclusions in such a way that each reader is well appraised of the data and of the interpretive principles brought to bear upon them. As a modest check of inference validity, several experienced clinicians[1] other than myself read a substantial portion of the interview data and discussed their views of it with me.

Again departing from the usual approach to achieving validity, I did not choose my research subjects so that they fell into two groups to be contrasted. It might seem that such a practice would have been desirable, but I felt that it was not because it would have required the grouping of subjects according to some arbitrarily chosen shame aspect, thus elevating to great importance in my data analysis some feature that I had no sound reason to believe was a meaningful discriminator between people. For example, I might have chosen subjects in two groups, one complaining of frequent, painful shame experience, and the other claiming that they never experienced shame. That distinction between the two groups would have been designated in advance as the distinction of most interest. People in the no-shame group would be assumed to be more like each other than like the much-shame people. Since I had no prior reason for thinking any one such grouping to be more significant than any other, and since I wanted, whenever possible, to discover natural groupings rather than to assume them, I felt that my insight with respect to the shame experience would best be extended by maximizing certain differences between subjects so that true regularities might emerge through their insistent appearance in diverse contexts. Such an approach appeared less likely than the two-group approach to produce false generalizations. It would have been an awkward and misleading alloy of traditional experimental method and exploratory interviewing to form two groups and hold them to be of significance while leaving within each group vast numbers of uncontrolled variables that would receive considerably less attention as possible explanations of differences.

Half the subjects were male; half were female. Posted signs advertised for people over 18 who seldom or never experienced shame; for people who experienced mild, occasional shame; and for people who experienced frequent, intense shame. Other signs asked for people interested in an interviewing study focused on patterns of feeling experience, especially shame and superiority feelings. Each of the signs posted brought a response, so that I did in fact interview people who identified themselves as never experiencing shame, people who com-

---

[1] I wish to thank Howard Wolowitz, Ph.D., Suraleah Michaels, Ph.D. (a doctoral candidate when she assisted with the research), Dr. George Rosenwald's study group on interviewing research, and Dr. Richard Hertel's research study group, all of whom read portions of the interview data or listened to tape recordings.

plained of constant shame, and people who placed themselves between these extremes. I also interviewed two young women (Polly and Pristine) from among Introductory Psychology students who volunteered for interviews focused on shame experience. All interviews were transcribed into typed copy so that they could be studied carefully and repeatedly.

Certain strengths and weaknesses of the research method emerged during the course of the study. On the plus side, the interviews provided a rare opportunity to engage others in consideration of what certain feeling words mean to them and in discussion of the structure and personal meaning of their experiences in the areas designated. Psychotherapy interviewing seldom provides a comparable opportunity because the therapist is not in a position to let a personal interest in a certain phenomenon take precedence over understanding the individual's current concerns. The open-ended interviewing method also had enormous advantages over fixed sets of questions. It allowed the interviewer to engage the subject's interest in the researcher's area of investigation so that over the weeks of interviewing the subject would enlist his or her memory and creativity in the service of the project. The interviewee generally would come to each session having given thought to some question raised in the previous interview—for example, a question about the meaning of the words "shame" and "guilt," or a question about what his or her failure ever to experience shame might signify. Thus each subject became an active contributor to the research process both by adding his or her formal conceptualizations to those of other subjects, the researcher, and past writers on the topic, and by engaging emotionally around the topic so that the researcher could observe the qualities of interest, anxiety, hostility, or embarrassment stirred in response to the subject's confrontation with the research topic.

On the negative side of the balance, many of the interesting questions that arose in the course of the interviewing could not be pursued vigorously because they related to areas of major conflict and vulnerability for the subjects. Attempts to inquire too directly were interrupted either by the researcher's concern about stressing the subject excessively, or by the subject's extreme defensiveness. These constraints were greater than they would be in the course of a psychotherapy. In the psychotherapy situation, the therapist would expect to elicit significant anxiety but would be available in the future to help the person understand and mitigate his or her discomfort. Pressure to be cautious was especially constraining with subjects who flatly denied shame experiences. Those subjects often taxed my ingenuity as I tried to devise ways of learning about the meaning of shame in their lives without having them directly discuss the question or describe personal shame experiences. In some such cases, I was able to begin with relatively intellectual discussion of meanings of words or to begin by eliciting hypothetical shame situations or shame experiences observed in others. The interviewee then showed a gradually increased sense of personal relatedness to the topic at hand. At other times the personal connection to the topic at hand seemed to dry up after an interviewee had mentioned one or two rather bland, unelaborated shame experiences. Problems also arose with subjects who were only too aware of the personal importance shame had in their lives. In these cases, as the person's private help-seeking agenda asserted itself more and more forcefully, it grew difficult to continue to interview with a primary focus on research goals. I attempted to keep myself and my subjects well oriented to the differences between research interviewing and therapeutic interviewing and I tried to keep attuned to whether the subject remained able to collaborate on the research project or whether he or she was so taken over by personal needs that the interviews had become an urgent pursuit of counseling. Each set of interviews brought with it some feeling of frustration because many more questions were generated than could be answered. But this kind of frustration is an inevitable companion of research that attempts commerce with complex personality formations, rather than attempting to establish a general principle that holds true with statistical significance across subjects.

A nagging concern must attend efforts to draw clinical inferences from exploratory research interviews. The method of data collection has been less investigated than, for example, psychoanalytic interviewing or psychological testing, and it is inherently more risky to make psychodynamic inferences from a method of inquiry that is less well researched and defined. It seems quite likely that many psychological principles that apply to psychoanalytic investigations apply as well to interviews such as those I conducted (e.g., the principle that slips of the tongue have psychological signifiance often discoverable by careful inquiry or by attention to associated material within the interview), but there remains the concern that a less explored method may influence the data in ways that go unnoticed. For example, the patients' beliefs that they are contributing to research might bolster self-esteem, reduce certain manifestations of shame, and highlight paradigms related to giving help. Or the interviewers' withholding of personal information might have a meaning for the research subjects different from its meaning for the analytic patient. Some of these methodological effects will be clearly audible in the data, but others may be soft-spoken. Whenever applying psychoanalytic principles I attempted to use care in assessing the impact my method might have on the relevance of those principles.

The method of presentation of the results also posed difficult problems. A reader ought not to be asked to take on faith a researcher's conclusions nor should a reader be expected to accept blindly the quality of the investigator's inference skills. Too often, psychological case studies or books on theory ask the reader to accept a plausible set of inferences without giving him or her the opportunity to evaluate the data on which the conclusions were based. Such presentations are highly problematic in that they leave the reader equipped neither to approve nor to reject an author's thesis. Intelligent debate about the work is discouraged. Despite the obvious deficiency of presentations that fail to make public their data base, the prevalence of such writing is understandable when one considers the difficulty of presenting massive amounts of clinical data without losing the reader's attention or losing the thrust of one's own commentary. I have tried to include enough data to ground my thinking but not so much that direction disappears from the presentation.

4 Meanings and Uses of Feeling Words

Our language is rich with words to name feelings. Yet our inner feeling experiences generally occur without our knowing any need or making any effort to label them. Labels tend to be applied to feeling experiences well into their development, or after the experience has ended, as part of an attempt to communicate, understand, identify, or alter them. Giving a label to a feeling often requires directed thought. Though in some instances people know at once what label designates their feeling, the choice of an adequate label is not always obvious and the individual may not be able to assign a feeling label at all or may assign a label only after some consideration. Because words like shame or embarrassment are not effortlessly applied to experience in the way that the designation, door, for example, is easily applied to an object, we cannot assume that to study "shame" is to study an absolutely clear, well-boundaried category of experiences.

To cope with this problem of words without stable meanings one can describe states one has felt or observed rather than defining what the labeled category, "shame," or the labeled category, "guilt," means. One then can designate the described states by the words that one personally feels belong with them. If someone else feels that the writer is mislabeling a state as shame rather than embarrassment, or guilt rather than shame, that will not be of great importance as long as the reader can recognize the state itself from the descriptions given. Thus, one depends more on descriptions than on labels and the reader can evaluate the dynamics attributed to described states, not the dynamics attributed to labeled categories. I should add to the foregoing comments that I am not so tentative about the relationship between states and words as I might appear. In fact, I am nearly immovable in my belief that I know what certain affect-words mean when "properly" used. I attribute my conviction, however unjustified, to two sources. First, my research objects generally (though not always) seemed to share my understanding of feeling words, enough so that I suspect these words are quite similarly used in context from person to person, though some people have great difficulty generating formal definitions of them. There seems to be enough common ground in the use of feeling words that one at times can feel correct in saying, "Mr. Jones misunderstands the meaning of 'shame' and 'guilt.'" And one can feel justified in looking for dynamic and cultural causes for the misuse of language. I suspect that a second reason for my faith in my understanding of feeling labels is that I, like most people, use these labels with such frequency and ease, and as such basic categorizations of my experience, that I am nearly beyond the point of seriously questioning whether my use of the words is accurate by others' standards. Experimental data would have to be mightily powerful to shake my conviction that I use feeling words "correctly." Given the strength of that bias, it seems best to proceed by attending to states, not words, and then by specifying my own preferred label for the state described. This method may help to discourage the mischief that sometimes occurs in the literature when a writer assumes that everyone knows exactly what is meant when the writer talks about depression, guilt, or shame.

Definitions that people give to feeling words are related to, but not carefully descriptive of, the actual experiences of the designated states. A person might say that shame (by definition) means to feel inferior, or to feel no self-esteem, or to feel hate for something that one did. A person who is asked to describe a shame experience rather than to define the word shame may answer at precisely this same level of abstraction. The person may say, "I felt inferior; my self-esteem was crushed." But if one were to press for an exact description of the moment itself, as one might have reason to do in psychotherapy, an articulate subject would produce a strikingly different level of description. The description to follow demonstrates the extent to which the formal, abbreviated definition of an emotion is achieved by abstracting from a mass of experiential detail:

I was sitting there with the interviewer and I felt my pants were wet on the left side of the seat. First I just thought, what can I do? What is this? I didn't know if I sat in something or what but it didn't matter. I just kept imagining standing up and the interviewer had to walk me to the door and there was this wet blotch on my grey pants. My mind was on that image and how I could stay behind him to the door. Then he asked me why I felt qualified for the job and I felt suddenly I was lying, faking it, like I was just this boy with the wet pants. I couldn't talk right. My voice was getting smaller like I was just talking inside myself and I didn't really want him to hear what I was saying because it wasn't any good and he would know it. My body was stiff, tense, trying just to control everything. And all I could think of was to get out of there, escape, be back by myself where I could get myself together, but there was the thought again, how will I get to the door. I kept trying to tell myself, you can just tell him you sat in something. Anyone could have after all. It doesn't mean anything about you. But he looked so humorless and all I could think of was to make a foolish joke.

If one first elicited this description of an experience and then asked the person to label his feeling, he might label it shame, or embarrassment, or self-consciousness, or humiliation, or nervousness, or he might say he didn't know what to call it. His decision might depend on what fragment of the total sequence of images and body feelings came to mind when he tried to do the labeling. And it might depend on additional factors such as which words he found acceptable to apply to himself. Some people are willing to say they feel embarrassed, because they regard embarrassment as trivial, but they are not willing to say they feel ashamed because that labeling implies for them that they are in fact shameful or defective.

In looking at five related groups of states, which I would call shame, embarrassment, humiliation, self-consciousness, and guilt, I will refer to the subjects' summarizing statements about these feeling states, that is, to their greatly simplified statements such as, "Shame means you feel inferior." When possible I also will include descriptions of basic elements of the complex, shifting "raw experience." In interviewing subjects it was much easier to elicit the skeletal definitional statements than to elicit descriptions of actual moments of experience. At times, the state in question was experienced, not just recalled, during the course of the interviews. But when the state that is of interest is an uncomfortable one such as shame or embarrassment, it generally is difficult for the subject who is experiencing such feelings to describe them to a relative stranger. Thus I could observe but not always inquire. Regarding the subjects' summarizing statements, I found that these were quite imperfect as are the ones I have tried myself to generate while studying this topic. One tends to begin the effort at definition by holding in mind a particular experience of the emotion and generating a definition based on that experience. Later, other experiences come to mind that point to inadequacies in the definition originally generated. The definition that stands up to all cases is difficult to achieve. It was common for a research subject to say, "I don't really know the difference between shame and guilt." Later the person might describe an experience and I might ask, "Did you feel guilty?" and he or she would say something like, "No, I didn't feel guilty because I didn't do it on purpose and I felt I had no control, so I just felt ashamed that I'd done it." Such a comment conveys a clear and well conceptualized distinction between shame and guilt. But the subject is unable to produce this distinction when asked to define shame and guilt.

Motivational factors affect the defining and use of affect words. One research subject said, "Shame is different from guilt because shame is profound, it's deep, whereas guilt is trivial; you get over it easily." Two sessions later this woman was sobbing over the awful feeling associated with fantasies of leaving someone who depended on her. One sensed that her definition of guilt as trivial was affected by the need to keep an incipient feeling of guilt from gaining strength. In psychoanalytic terms, we would say that the cognitive effort at definition was influenced by denial; the person needed to say, "I know nothing about the pain of guilt—guilt is nothing." A young woman who came to a psychiatric clinic suffering from a pathological grief reaction misused affect words in ways that suggested a blurring of boundaries between the self and the lost object. She asked, "Why should I be guilty at her [for dying]?" when one expected her to ask, "Why should I be angry at her? (I'd feel guilty if I were)," or to say (or feel), "She should feel guilty for dying and leaving me." She spoke of her deceased mother's response to her colostomy and said that her mother felt "guilty" about wearing the colostomy bag. One would expect that the mother felt ashamed, while her daughter may have felt guilty. Though ostensibly a purely cognitive effort, the definitional process is influenced by motivational factors. It is also affected by the restricted nature of the person's current frame of reference. One cannot, like a computer, rapidly review all those experiences one would likely label as shame and extract the common core of them all. One can only look at the two or three or four that come to mind readily in one's current ego state. Thus the researcher has a difficult time discovering whether a subject's definition of shame or of guilt differs consistently and profoundly from his or her own definition or whether the subject's comments reflect a transient defensive posture or a failure to scan a sufficient number of experiences from which to generate an enduring definition.

FEELING INFERIOR (STATES OFTEN CALLED SHAME)

A group of feelings about the self all carry the conviction that one is small or inferior or defective. Along with this conviction comes an intense sense of displeasure about one's status and a wish to be

changed: to be smarter, stronger, neater, more ethical, or more beautiful. The core of the feeling experience is distress concerning a state of
the self that the person feels defines the self as no good or as not good
enough. To capture the state, one can think of a young boy standing
before an admired parent who berates the child as stupid, thoughtless,
or clumsy. The child may speak up in angry self-defense or he may
experience a kind of inner crumbling of his self-image, an acquiescence
to the parent's indictments, a through and through sense that he is no
good and cannot even look into his parent's eyes, which suddenly
frighten or overwhelm him because he has collapsed inside and become
weak. Nor can he speak because his voice has evaporated. He must
shy away from contact and aggressive response, actually and in fantasy. He wants to disappear or hide, not to fight, because the self is
experienced as not strong enough or valuable enough to proceed into
the world. The child may fend off such feelings with forced efforts at
aggressiveness, but the efforts feel phony; no real self-esteem backs
them up. I will refer to such feelings either by describing them or by
labeling them shame as a shorthand.

In more specific terms, what I call shame consists of an experiencing
of the self as diminished. The "experiencing of the self" might be
purely physical: a robust, active girl feels herself shrinking down and
inward, she is frozen before the parent's eyes and voice. Or the experiencing of the self might consist mainly of an image. The image might
be a personally significant image of the self, for example, as wearing
outdated clothes like one's frumpy mother wore. Or it might be an
image of another's face, which in its contempt or disgust fixes one's
status; the other person's expression of feeling makes one feel like
one's alcoholic father when one's mother disdained him. The ashamed
person feels that he or she cannot escape from the significant self-
image even though longing to do so, just as one cannot escape the
parent who compels one to "stand and take it."

Some writers have argued that shame requires an audience to one's
misdeeds. One research subject, Aba, made this claim. Piers and
Singer (1953) disagree and state that shame follows from a failure to
live up to one's ego ideal. In this respect, I use the word shame as
Piers and Singer do. According to this usage, no audience need be part
of the shame experience. Not even a clear fantasy of an audience is
required. But the particular type of misery-about-the-self that gives
shame its distinctive feel does seem to depend on some sense, however
vague, of the self standing before another or potentially visible to
another. Even when the only clear image constituting the experience is
the image of what the self has done or failed to do, plus the internal
sense of wishing to hide from the sight of one's deed, a contribution to

the feeling tone is made from an impression that might be paraphrased, "My God, what if my father, or teacher, or girlfriend were to see this?" Even more essential to the feeling is the sense that someone else, either the owner of the shaming eyes or voice or someone with whom one could be compared, would not have done this thing or been this way. He or she would have been brighter, braver, or more grown up. So one's defect stands in the context of others as superior and others as witnesses.

In the psychoanalytic literature, frequently it is argued that shame is a reaction-formation against exhibitionism. In nontechnical language this means that shame is experienced when the conscience indicts an incipient wish to exhibit oneself. Shame about one's sexuality is then experienced instead of pleasure. The excited quality of the shame experience betrays the initiating exhibitionistic impulse. Certainly some cases follow this pattern. Shame is forced upon the person because the conscience has spoken out fiercely against an exhibitionistic wish, thus leaving one to feel shame over what one wanted to exhibit proudly. Generally this dynamic appears when the person experiences exhibitionism as dangerous to someone else because of its competitive, aggressive aspect. And the exhibitionism may be dangerous to oneself because one assumes that retaliation will follow. Some people are constantly ashamed not because they have undergone narcissistic trauma in childhood but because they fear the destructive consequences of any kind of competitive self-assertion, with or without sexual connotations. Whenever they would speak forcefully, or purchase something for themselves, or run instead of walk, they begin to berate themselves as inferior and they feel profoundly ashamed. What sets in motion the pernicious chain of events is anxiety or guilt about aggressiveness. I will have more to say later about interactions between shame and aggression. They are extremely important in diagnosis and treatment. However, the prevalence and importance of shame experiences that derive from aggression-conflict and exhibitionistic conflict should not lead us to define shame as essentially and invariably a reaction against impulse expression. Although shame often functions as a reaction-formation (or some other form of reaction against impulse), the sense of the self as diminished remains the core of what I am calling the shame experience. And the characteristically ashamed sense of self also occurs outside the context of flight from impulses.

Exhibitionism is always in the picture when shame appears because shame robs a person of normal exhibitionistic capacity and pleasure, but this association between shame and exhibitionism does not imply that exhibitionism must fall victim to *conscience* as a prelude to shame. Shame may follow from failures vis-à-vis the ego ideal, not from violations of conscience. The exclusive emphasis on conscience as an antecedent to shame probably results from the historic psychoanalytic concern with id-superego conflict in the oedipal period and from the importance of superego-derived shame in the neuroses. The exclusive emphasis on conscience also may follow from a failure to distinguish between shame and embarrassment in much psychoanalytic literature. Much of what has been called shame, I would call embarrassment. Though I recognize the two states, or groups of states, as related, they are worth distinguishing. Once this distinction is made, embarrassment may prove more regularly related to offenses-of-exhibitionism than is shame.

The research subjects' comments that follow highlight some of the concrete physical features of shame and the images of self and other that contribute to it. Questions regarding the at times complex dynamics of these shame experiences will be deferred until chapters 5 through 7. A young man, here called William, describes the experience he calls shame:

S:[1] It would be like I'm on a lower level, not actually depressed but disappointed, so that there's no, I don't feel like beating my head against the wall, or I don't feel flushed or perspire or something like that. It's pretty much a thought.

If I'm walking somewhere I'd be looking down, probably looking at the ground more than around me . . .[2] If I were sitting somewhere I would probably have trouble concentrating and I would be sort of daydreaming or just whatever my eyes, whatever my eyes were aiming—I'd just more or less be looking through whatever they're, chances are I wouldn't see someone.

Asked how he would draw a cartoon character who reflected a change into an ashamed state by a change in physical state, William said he would change the character in these ways:

S: Small, smaller in size . . I was almost tempted to say, "make them uglier" as opposed to, umm, perhaps I will say that because then that would have a tendency—smallness in the sense of their own, of how they feel about themselves, and ugly in the sense of, like warning others. Or, not so much warning others, but just staving off others. [As if to say],[3] this person is

---

[1] S refers to words of the subject and I to words of the interviewer.

[2] Three dots (. . .) or four dots (. . . .) indicate that material from the verbatim transcript of an interview has been deleted from a quoted passage.

[3] Words in brackets [] were inserted by the author when a subject's comments seemed unclear without such an addition.

not a, not a "beautiful person." They're not everything that you would want them to be.

Katherine describes the facial expression she associates with shame:

S: I get a mental image of what somebody's face will look like when they feel shame. . . . Generally just a subdued expression. . . . It wouldn't ever be a full face, it would be like something that would be turned to the side, and kind of downcast, but with the eyes straight forward. . . .
I: Do you associate blushing, that kind of—
S: No. . . .
I: Do you associate blushing with embarrassment as opposed to shame?
S: Yes, much more so than shame.

In her second interview, Katherine offers this description:

S: I was always pretty sassy, that's what everybody, everybody said I was sassy, so to me, when I felt ashamed about something, I would, you know, get this humble feeling (laugh) . . . for about 2 days you don't . . . take a stand on a particular issue, you don't get into the arguments, the philosophical things, you just were supposed to be remembering something on your own . . . something that just recently happened that should give you enough to think about for a while. It kind of takes your pride down a notch.

In their descriptions of shame, Katherine and William emphasize constriction of the self and withdrawal from confident interactions with the environment. While such alterations in self-experience at times may suggest a need for self-punishment in the face of prohibited exhibitionistic impulses, they can occur in response to other forms of assault on the self or in response to a perceived failure of the self. Frank describes his recurrent shame:

S: They're not voluntary things I bring to mind. Maybe I'm working, I'm drinking coffee or whatever, and all of a sudden something just, you know, pops into my mind. It might have happened a year ago, 10 years ago, you know, everybody's forgotten it but me. And I've forgot consciously but subconsciously all of a sudden it just comes to mind and, you know, maybe sometimes whatever it is affects me so bad that I just—you know—"Oh my God!"—you know—and I actually hide my head in my hand and say it out loud.

Frank's description of cringing at the recollection of certain images of the self has an intense, excited quality to it. The excitement may suggest that, in masochistic fashion, Frank finds it necessary to experience as excruciating those excited, interested, or engaged states of activity of the self that most people experience as pleasurable; he can only find pleasure in the context of pain. Further discussion of shame and masochism will be deferred until later chapters. The central concern here is not the dynamics that lead to the shame experience, but the nature of the experience itself. In Frank's case, he describes a confrontation with an image of the self that distresses him so deeply that he barely can tolerate facing it. He experiences a profound and aroused disruption of self-regard, a disruption so great that it can lead to efforts magically to restructure the self-image through poorly planned actions or through fantasy.

When a person feels ashamed of a thought that occurs while talking with another person, certain characteristic patterns of expression may appear. A fleeting shame image often is marked by a quick laugh. If the person attempts to talk about the thought that has brought a feeling of shame, speech may at first be fragmented as a struggle takes place between the impulse to disclose and the impulse to conceal. The person may proceed to say what he or she needs to in fragmented fashion, but frequently, if a firm decision can be made in favor of proceeding with the disclosure, fragmented speech gives way to unusually aggressive speech. Frank has given an example of shame; the example does not satisfy him and he is toying with the idea of introducing another example. The interviewer asks, "Did you have another example that seemed—that you liked better?":

S: Well, I did, but I, I'm not sure whether I want to get into that. I was trying to bring up something that's a little deeper I guess, in shame. I don't know but that, you know, somewheres through this, I'll probably go *too* deep, and—well, let's get something off, can I get something off that's, I don't know how this'll affect our relationship or this whole thing and so— ahh, okay, my, I guess I, I bring a lot of shame from—two years ago, that's when my wife and I separated. So I guess we go back and talk about that right now (voice suddenly raised, loud and emphatic).

Once Frank decides to make his revelation, he proceeds aggressively. "Well, to shock you right off. . . ." he says, and he makes his disclosure.

At times the aggression associated with a shameful revelation is directed at the audience who the speaker assumes will be critical of what he or she is going to reveal. Or the aggression simply may function as a way of pushing past internal resistance to self-disclosure. The initial fragmentation and the later aggressiveness may revolve around a particular word or phrase that, for the speaker, captures the core of his or her shame. The person may be initially unable to speak the word. When the word or phrase is finally spoken, if the conflict surrounding it is still intense, the person may put forth the word contentiously and with great emphasis and hostility as if to embarrass the listener with the word. Another common aid to articulating shameful images is to identify with the potential ridiculer. For example, a research subject named Matilda spoke with energetic self-contempt about her "godawful poetry" and she labeled as "crap" the sexual thoughts about which she felt ashamed.

A theoretical proposal advanced by Shevrin (1970) has a place here because it represents an effort to define the aspect of each emotional state that gives the state its distinct, experienced quality. Shevrin's paper wrestles with the question of what makes one emotion qualitatively different from all others. I have grappled with that question at the phenomenological or experiential level and have arrived at certain conclusions about the core phenomena of shame. My definition of the core of shame depends on the presence of characteristic self-images, image of others, and body imagery. Shevrin suggests that the unique essence of each moment of feeling might be something he calls a "distinctive temporal organization" or a "rhythm" and he suggests that this same rhythm might be evident both in the physiological processes associated with an emotional state (e.g., the rhythm of neuronal firing) and in the felt emotion. Thus the concept of rhythm might bridge the gap between physiology and experience—body and mind. Shevrin's hypothesis follows from Langer's (1967) idea that feeling, as experienced, represents the supraliminal *phase* of a nervous system process that occurs at both supraliminal and subliminal (unconscious) levels. Feeling is not a process separate from nervous system events. It is the continuation of a nervous system event into a high-intensity (i.e., conscious) phase. Questions can be raised about this proposition, for example, how more specifically might one define "rhythm," but my interest here is only in considering whether anything I observed as central to the shame experience might be seen as a rhythmic element of consciousness.

The only rhythmic element of shame that I can identify is the characteristic experience of shrinking away from others and pulling inward and downward. That experience is rhythmic in that it is a motoric event or imagery that has a certain pace and direction. But it is difficult to imagine translating this shrinking and pulling into a rhythm defined more narrowly as a recurring pattern of emphasis. If one wishes to transpose affect life into musical terms, it seems that elements other than rhythm are needed, for example, tonal qualities, pitch, and patterns of ascending and descending tone and intensity. Even using all these elements we probably can simulate only moods, for example, sadness, wariness, or delight, and not the more ideationally dominated emotions such as shame, guilt, or disgust. The latter

depend on specific images of human and nonhuman objects, with associated learned meanings. For instance, the image of a judge is a
possible component of guilt. My overall impression then is that certain
rhythmic elements of an emotional state might be identified, for example, impulses to move the body at a certain pace and in a certain
direction, or those impulses to "move the self" that involve a unified
experience of mind and body. I am thinking here of the shame impulse
to hide, which is more than a hiding of the body. But impulses of this
type may not constitute the core and total composition of an emotion.
Thinking of the emotion, guilt, we might imagine that guilt would
share with shame the rhythm of shrinking inward, but associated with
the inward shrinking of guilt, and explaining it, would be a sense of the
self as having destructive powers that must be held in or kept from
contacting others. The guilty person shrinks inward not to hide but to
contain aggression. Whether the sense of the self as aggressive and
needing to impose self-restraint could be captured in a distinctive
rhythm that would be experienced as guilt and evidenced at a noncon-
scious level as rhythmic physiologic activity, I cannot say. Such a
rhythm is difficult to imagine; however, that does not rule out the
possibility of its conceptual validity. It may be that my analysis of
shame rhythms focuses excessively on macroscopic aspects of the experience, which do not point the way to key rhythms, or that the
labeled affect-category, shame, distracts our attention from certain
fundamental rhythms that cut across traditional affect-categories.

FEELING "UNDONE" AND UNCOMFORTABLY VISIBLE
(STATES OFTEN CALLED EMBARRASSMENT)

If the rhythm of shame is a pulling inward and groundward, a hiding
and concealing, the rhythm of what I call embarrassment might be
described as the self trying to pull inward or to diffuse itself into
nonexistence in response to a sudden feeling that an aspect of self has
been opened up to view without one's consent or participation. One
retreats inward or into diffusion in order to dissociate oneself from a
suddenly visible self-aspect that feels as if it has become visible without one's willing it to be so, perhaps without one's acknowledging that
this thing suddenly made visible is oneself at all. Embarrassment is a
state of *non-coherence* or *dis-integration* because the self is moving in
two directions—outward and into view and inward out of anxiety
about the outward motion. One may feel red in the face and glowing
and in that respect one seems to be moving outward, visible and showing. But at the same time one may avert one's gaze, hide one leg

behind the other, and cease talking. What I am calling shame and embarrassment cannot be differentiated perfectly. They have elements in common. When they occur together, which happens often, a person may name his or her emotional state either shame or embarrassment. I make a distinction between the states not from so great an interest in the associated words and their significance, but out of a wish to differentiate certain elements of experience.

The states I am calling shame are predominantly or exclusively painful experiences and, as indicated, they center on a sense of the self as diminished. "Embarrassment" will refer to an excited or aroused state that easily can match shame in intensity of pain, but it also may be an emotionally trivial experience or a partially pleasant experience. The definitional center of embarrassment is not pain or pleasure but arousal and the sense of being off-kilter or thrown out of balance. Because of this *dis-integrated* quality of embarrassment, it is an uncomfortable state, but it may be pleasurably uncomfortable like sexual tension can be. Some of the dictionary synonyms for embarrassment highlight differences between embarrassment and shame. Words like "disconcert," "discomfit," and "rattle" emphasize the disruption in composure that characterizes embarrassment. As with shame, embarrassment can be experienced with or without an audience present but it seems to require at least an inarticulate *sense* of audience and a *sense* of being visible—actually or potentially—while in one's exposed state.

If one looks at the dynamics of states of embarrassment, one finds a range of relationships between the person and that aspect of feeling or functioning that feels suddenly visible to self and others. Often the visible aspect is something the person at some level wishes to make known, but conscience forbids straightforward exhibitionism. The person is surprised when the carefully restrained trait or wish suddenly leaks out of containment. The person denies any wish for the self-aspect to be seen and experiences himself or herself as uncomfortable. These experiences of less than fully intentional exposure, which then must be disowned or complained of, are among the situations that produce theoretical statements that shame (here relabeled embarrassment—the literature tends not to differentiate the two) is a reaction-formation against exhibitionism, because in these states the exhibitionistic excitement is apparent to the onlooker.

By the definition proposed here, embarrassment does not shade into shame until one's discomfort over exposure is joined by a clearly negative idea about the status of the self. For example, a man whose parapraxis exposes an "embarrassing" sexual wish does not become "ashamed of himself" unless he begins to tell himself that only people with a stupid lack of verbal skill make such slips, or that no one would ever want a sexual relationship with him because he is so inept. If no such ideas enter into the experience, it remains an experience of embarrassment, not one of shame. Many people recover quickly from such unsettling experiences and dismiss them from mind. They conceive of such moments of embarrassment as trivial. William comments:

S: [If I told a bad joke], I would probably instantly turn red[4] and probably perspire and fidget and try to come up with something more or less to save face, whether it'd be another joke which was guaranteed to bring laughter or just rationalize the one I had said, something like that.

I: Would you call that shame, or not?

S: No, I don't think so.

I: What would you call that? Or *would* you call it something?

S: Just a form of embarrassment . . . an example like that would just be— just simple embarrassment, 'cause it's nothing, it'll have no consequence whatsoever. Nothing. No lasting effect.

When embarrassment activates severe psychological conflict, memories of the embarrassing moment may keep reasserting themselves. These unresolvable embarrassments suggest either that strong shame ideas attend the embarrassment situation and give it great importance, or that intense and psychologically active conflict gives special significance to the moment of tension between showing and not showing.

The discomfited state need not involve either a powerful shame-idea

---

[4]Blushing appears to be one of a group of physiological responses, including increased heart rate and sweating (Lewis, 1971), which evolution has clustered together. The inherited clustering of responses does not remove them from the province of psychological interpretation because physiological responses become meaningful to a person once experienced in an interpersonal context. Shamelike responses range from those with a physical form much influenced by inheritance to those that are essentially thoughts about self and situation. The same range of forms can be seen with other emotion-groups, for example, with those states called disgust, which appear to have derived their basic form from the physical responses of nausea or vomiting. The rejecting, dissociating aspect of these physical responses and the felt aversion that accompanies them are recognized in interpersonal or moral situations having nothing to do with actual ingestion. The parallels between actual nausea and other feelings of rejection are sufficient to determine the choice to label the nonvisceral responses as disgust. Similarly, many experiences labeled as shame or embarrassment bear some relation to the inherited physical experience of anxious flushing and rapid heart rate in a social situation. However, the meaning of feeling labels is in no way finally determined by these inherited physical responses because language categories continue to evolve over time with input from many varieties of experience, including but not limited to physical responses like blushing or vomiting.

or a guilt-driven conflict over exhibitionism. Any self-aspect that is weakly integrated into the positive self-concept or not congruent with it can produce embarrassment. For example, a pubertal girl may experience embarrassment if attention is called to a change in her body. The young person has not had time enough to do the psychological work necessary to integrate the changed body into the self-concept. When her changed body draws attention, she is suddenly confused and uneasy. She has developed no clear attitude toward the body change. Is she to feel proud of it or ashamed? Is she to feel that she is still a child and the mature body is a mistake, something that cannot belong to her? Must she feel guilty over gratification of infantile oedipal wishes? A similar threat to psychological integrity occurs if a person is unexpectedly forced into unusual self-exposure. For example, at a party, a guest is pushed into giving a speech or being hypnotized or blindfolded. Suddenly one does not know what aspect of the self is going to show. How will one look or sound or react? There may appear a specific worry or set of worries or just a general sense of vulnerability and tension. The individual's idiosyncratic Achilles' heel will determine the focus of his or her anxiety. But the situation itself predisposes most people to some form of embarrassment. If one had planned in advance to give the speech or to undergo the hypnosis, one would have prepared mentally by imagining one's behavior, deciding on what controls to place on one's actions, and imagining a range of responses from others. Such embarrassments need not be painfully uncomfortable. They may be pleasurably uncomfortable if a person is not profoundly threatened and he or she senses that the self-exposure may have a flattering or erotic outcome.

The following examples from Slim's interviews showcase embarrassment as a state of conflict over pleasurable exhibitionism. They demonstrate shame functioning as a state of distress over the fantasied body defect that the exhibitionism is intended to deny. The state of conflict that produces embarrassment may be driven by shame or by guilt or by both. For example, a man may feel he ought not to want to expose his penis because such a wish is a violation of morality (so he ought to feel guilty) or because such a wish is a sign of a strange or perverted person (so he ought to be ashamed):

S: I don't know, at an intuitive level embarrassment is a more spontaneous thing [than shame] whereas, you know, a slip of the lip, say you walk through—here's an example of embarrassment—say I walked through Meadows Mall and when I get outside I realize my zipper's down and I say, Oh, Jes—you know, that's embarrassing and everyone must have thought I was a flasher or something. That would be embarrassing. . . .

Well, you know, if somebody would get the wrong idea about you or something (laugh). They would think that you want to expose yourself or whatever. That's just the first example that came into mind.

Next Slim describes a possible source of shame:

S: Whereas shame. . . , say if I had one arm and I was very ashamed of it and I didn't want people to see it, that would be shame. . . . That's a deliberate, a more deliberate thing, more of a deepset emotion.

In the examples of shame and embarrassment given by Slim, and in those given by other subjects, the two types of states may revolve around essentially the same emotional conflict, but they reflect distinct current responses to the problem. In Slim's case, his embarrassment suggests a lively but conflicted interest in exhibiting himself in order to deny or to repair an imagined defect. His shame represents an acknowledgment or acceptance of the defect—perhaps even an insistence on it—and an effort to hide the accepted deformity. Thus his embarrassment depends primarily on the active sexual or exhibitionistic wish. Shame depends on his negative view of the sexual defect. The two feelings are dynamically related in that the exhibitionistic wish represents the attempt to repair the shameful defect that in turn may represent a defensive self-degradation intended to deny the original sexual wish.

The following passage from Arthur Cohen's (1976) novel, *A Hero in His Time*, portrays mild embarrassment that obviously is partly pleasurable and results from a situation that stirs delightful fantasy. The passage begins when the protagonist, a Russian poet, enters an office where he has been called for a job screening. He finds the secretary alone in the office:

Her attention was distracted by something slightly to the north of Yuri's forehead. Yuri looked over his shoulder, thinking perhaps he had brought a bug with him to the offices.

"Forgive me, forgive me. It's your hair. Do you know, Isakovsy, that you have a shock of hair standing up like a scarecrow."

"Yes, I know. The wind does it. The wind has always done it. I don't mind," Yuri replied and, embarrassed, patted the top of his head, flattening the scarecrow.

"It's amusing. Yes, very amusing. You will be amusing, won't you?"

"Really? And how will I amuse you," Yuri replied, non-plused but enchanted. It seemed an odd way for a secretary (even if she was totally alone and therefore superior to everyone and no one) to conduct herself, to behave in such an informal manner before a total stranger—indeed before someone who might well become her superior. (p. 22)

Several elements of this scene deserve attention as elements common to embarrassment situations. First, the man is aware of being highly visible but he is uncertain about the nature of his visibility. How is the secretary receiving him? Has he brought in a bug that will annoy her or is it something rather more pleasant? Is her pleasure ridiculing or is it warm and affectionate? Second, he is only tenuously identified with the self-aspect that the onlooker has identified as belonging to him. She looks not at his face or his gait or his hand, but at a bit of his hair that he can neither see nor feel. Third, he believes that he lacks real control over the embarrassing behavior, and he tries to dissociate himself from it even further when he is made uncomfortable by it. The hair just stands up on its own. The wind does it, not he. The wind has always done it. He feels disconcerted, thrown off kilter, "nonplused." The reader may sense that this man's experience with his hair embarrasses him partly because it is a metaphor for getting an erection. The parallel is evident in the image of the woman's gaze being fixed—with possible pleasure, possible disapproval—on a part of Yuri's body more independent of his control, more capable of surprising him than other parts may be. The claim of dissociation between the self and some unruly, surprising, pleasure-related, embarrassing self-aspect can be a function of a real and uncontrollable lack of authority, as in the case of a parent embarrassed by a mischievous child or a polio victim embarrassed by a spastic limb. At other times, the claim of dissociation signals a defensive process, as with Slim who generates fantasies of exhibiting himself, then he argues that the exhibition is purely accidental.

FEELING FORCED DOWN INTO
A DEBASED POSITION
(STATES OFTEN CALLED HUMILIATION)

The states that I will call humiliation have as their emotional center the feeling that the person has been put into a lowered or degraded position. One is not just undone or rattled, as in embarrassment. One is brought down to an abased or lowly position. Humiliation differs from shame—as I have used the word—in that shame is a belief about the self (e.g., "I am spineless") whereas humiliation refers to the current situation or status of the self and not to an identified, enduring quality belonging to the self. At times, people speak of feeling humiliated in a context that implies that they have humiliated them-selves; they have brought themselves into an abased position. When the person who feels humiliated identifies an outside source for the feeling, he or she implies a power differential between self and other. The one who is humiliated is brought low, or placed in a degraded position, by someone seen as more powerful. The humiliator often is experienced as malicious (even if he or she in fact caused *unintended* humiliation), because the state of humiliation is resented and that hostility is likely to be projected. The person who feels frequently humiliated by others is generally a person who is inclined to engage in power struggles that have an intense, sometimes intimate quality.

Humiliation is usually a temporary alteration in status, not an alter-ation in identity. However, the person who feels humiliated often will have difficulty keeping his identity uncontaminated by the humiliated status. He may begin to equate himself with his status or to blame himself for that status. In such cases, not just anger but shame or guilt will follow from the humiliation. A victim of robbery, forcible restraint, harassment, or torture may find that his identity becomes tainted by the debased position in which he finds himself. He begins to see himself as *the kind of person who* is tied up helplessly or as *the kind of person who* has his possessions taken away and is left with an empty house. He feels ashamed because his self-image is tarnished and he may feel guilty if he holds himself responsible for his humiliated status. In-grained psychological conflicts will accelerate these stress-produced deteriorations of self-esteem. A person will begin to suffer self-esteem ruptures at previously determined faultlines in the personality. How-ever, this individual psychological factor should not be allowed to eclipse the fact that all people will have difficulty escaping from a humiliated status free of self-esteem damage. This remains true even when the loss of status rationally can be seen to be outside the indi-vidual's control.

Loss of dignity and loss of power are crucial elements of humiliation. Rage is often felt, but it may be felt as an impotent rage. Humiliation experiences are not uniquely associated with a particular developmen-tal conflict, but clinical material suggests that they may have special importance during the anal phase, at which time there exists a lively concern with who will prevail in the control of the child's body and behavior. A cautious formulation would state that humiliation experi-ences in adults often center on autonomy struggles such as those in which anal-phase children engage; however, we cannot say for certain that the anal-phase child feels humiliated when defeated. The child may feel enraged; establishment of humiliation feelings may await later emotional development.

It seems likely that humiliation may occur anew in any developmental phase even when there is no history of traumatic humiliation in the anal phase. For example, a six-year-old boy who is forced to stand nude in front of the family for a clothes fitting, while older siblings laugh at the cuteness of his genitals, would likely feel humiliated. If he has not yet developed a proud estimation of his genitals, the experience might also contribute to feelings of bodily shame. What humiliates the phallic-stage child may not humiliate the younger or older child. Self-investments change with maturation, as does intellectual mastery and the overall sense of self.

The research subjects seldom discussed humiliation. Pristine gave one of the few comparisons of shame and humiliation to emerge from the interviews:

S: I think shame is more thinking, feeling, internally. The shame is something that you've done, the shame comes from within you. Whereas I think humiliation is something that—someone makes you feel humiliated, they do something to you, whereas shame is something that's felt inside of you, that's in your inner feeling and it comes out.

FEELING CONSTANTLY AWARE OF THE SELF-IN-ACTION (STATES OFTEN CALLED SELF-CONSCIOUSNESS)

When asked about shame, subjects occasionally referred to "self-consciousness." Self-consciousness can be conceptualized as an *activity* that may be attended by a variety of feeling tones. The activity of maintaining consciousness of a mental representation of one's self has significance both as an indicator of ego strength and as an indicator of ego strain. The capacity for self-consciousness represents an ego accomplishment. The ability deliberately to become self-conscious allows one to observe body states, emotions, and personal characteristics. Certain kinds of learning about the self and controlling of the self can be accomplished only by observing the self actively. The reliably functioning observing ego is one outcome of self-consciousness that appears to be crucial to successful psychotherapy.

Self-consciousness as an indicator of ego strain generally is experienced as something plaguing the person, not as an activity voluntarily undertaken. The person is unable fully to engage the self in any activity requiring that the greater part of attention be directed away from the image of the self. One finds oneself simultaneously engaging and watching oneself engage. The inability to relinquish self-consciousness can occur in any situation that leaves a person feeling unable to trust his or her spontaneous behavior. Self-consciousness will appear if a person feels threatened by some type of ego decompensation, thus he or she must attend to the self in order to maximize effectiveness of functioning. Self-consciousness is common when an inarticulate but powerful impulse to communicate hostility or sexuality threatens to express itself or when pervasive guilt about impulse-expression forces a person to limit the pleasure that attends spontaneous and intense engagement in activity. Transient self-consciousness may appear when a person judges himself or herself to be in a socially complex situation that calls for decisions about how to present the self. The person cannot simply "be" but must actively "select" the presentation of the self. Self-consciousness also appears if a person assumes, accurately or paranoiacally, that someone else is watching critically. One then will watch oneself in order to be less passive in the face of critical surveillance. One makes the emotional assumption that one can watch oneself and see what the other is seeing. Thus, one can alter one's course when necessary.

FEELING THAT ONE HAS VIOLATED A STANDARD (STATES OFTEN CALLED GUILT)

A definition of guilt is offered here, first, because there is a longstanding preoccupation with distinguishing shame and guilt in the literature and, second, because a number of research subjects showed great difficulty differentiating shame and guilt even when they readily distinguished other states, for example, shame and embarrassment. Guilt is defined here, in the manner of Piers and Singer, as the feeling that one has violated some rule of conduct to which one attaches value. Guilt is a response to *trans-gression*, to stepping across. Writers disagree as to whether guilt invariably follows aggression, or whether it can follow from other transgressions, for example, those of a sexual nature. I use "guilt" to designate any manner of transgression. Aggression is an omnipresent antecedent only insofar as the act of violating a standard can be conceived of as an aggressive act.

People frequently feel both guilt and shame in response to the same events. This concurrence of feeling probably accounts for some of the difficulty people experience in distinguishing the two emotion labels. Although feelings of shame and guilt may arise from the same situation, their foci differ. The ashamed person is concerned with the diminution of self-esteem that follows from what he has done. He focuses attention on himself as the kind of person who would perform this or that imperfect action, and he recoils from these self-images. The guilty person is concerned with the experience of his action as wrong; he feels he should not have committed the act. Guilt is a state of tension associated with having crossed a boundary that is experienced as legitimate. It is a wish to undo the deed. To some extent, the sense of regret and the wish to undo can be attributed to a fear that punishment might follow from one's act. But such a fear is not the whole of the feeling of guilt. The guilty person has a sense of being in a false or wrong or regrettable position of violation. This feeling is more than a fear of a specific negative outcome for self or other. The idea of immorality or transgression is meaningful in itself and not simply as a negative reflection on the self.

In order to imagine the co-occurrence of shame and guilt, one might think of a boy who has committed a theft. The thief may feel guilty because he has violated a societal rule that he respects. And he may simultaneously feel ashamed because the act reduces his identity to that of a thief whom he imagines his parents, his friends, and he himself would disrespect. This variety of shame is appropriately called "moral shame" because it occurs in the context of immoral behavior, not in the context of an idiosyncratic ego ideal that has nothing to do with morality—for example, the ideal of having curly hair. People seem to find it particularly difficult to distinguish between shame and guilt when their feelings pertain to a moral imperfection. A patient had a memory of hitting a little girl and of feeling both guilty and ashamed:

S: I felt very ashamed, humiliated, guilty. . . . I guess every time in grade school when I was reprimanded for something—which were always minor things—I felt ashamed. I felt embarrassed. . . . It was a girl who was kind of a brat anyway. She turned into a bitch when she grew up, but . . . the guilt feelings came about because I felt bad for what happened to her, and I felt ashamed because of what the teacher said to me—like she made me feel like I was some kind of a bad person, not that I had—she made me feel like I did it intentionally.

The boy felt ashamed because the teacher made him feel he was the kind of person who did bad things intentionally; that is, he was ashamed of being a guilty person.

Though guilt and shame may both occur in the same situation, there are situations in which one or the other feeling predominates, depending on whether the person feels that his or her actions were voluntary or involuntary. In these instances, wrongdoing experienced as volitional produces guilt. Wrongdoing experienced as involuntary produces shame, both in relation to the action itself and to the failure of self-control. Frank complains of tormenting shame over a serious interpersonal transgression, but he denies guilt:

S: Guilt for me, I don't know, it's doing something consciously and fully controlled and I guess this is probably where I feel the difference. Maybe I'm lying to myself but I don't feel that I was really responsible for what I did.

Guilt is of course not always determined by a rational assessment of whether one's actions were deliberate. One may feel profoundly guilty and responsible in relation to wishes, feelings, or actions over which no possibility of control existed. All that is required is the feeling—not the rational evaluation—that one could have done differently had one wished to do so.

Certain feelings of profound personal badness fit neither the proposed usage of shame nor that of guilt, though people often label such feelings as shame or guilt since these are the common affect words that come closest to fitting the described states. Such feelings of badness suggest that the whole self or the deepest aspects of self are conceived of as essentially bad. The badness may be associated with transgressions, as is true in those states I have labeled guilt states. For example, one may feel that one is bad because of undue greediness or selfishness or hostility. Unlike the guilt state, the state of badness involves a belief that the self, through its actions, has become *essentially bad* in such a way that undoing or terminating the questionable actions is irrelevant to the feeling of badness. The state of badness does not fit well within the group of feelings here designated as guilt because the core concern is with the self-image, not with the actions performed or the boundaries violated. The label, shame, does not adequately define the state of badness because the "bad" person is concerned with his or her evilness and destructive power, not with smallness or weakness as compared with others or as visible to self and others.

To be relieved of such feelings of badness, a person must come to believe that some good part of the self that is worth preserving survives the bad actions. He or she then can entertain the idea that bad actions might be atoned for or undone. The bad actions may then bring simple guilt rather than pervasive narcissistic stress experienced as the conviction of profound personal badness. A research subject, Frank, who appears to suffer from feelings of being a bad person, finds it difficult to distinguish between shame and guilt. One might speculate that his confusion derives in part from his effort to label feelings of badness as shame or guilt. Neither label fits exactly and his sense of the meanings of the words and of the personal experience remains confused. The attempt to force an experience into a common affect category can perpetuate confusion about the nature of the experience. This dynamic of sustained confusion can occur in psychotherapy situations if a therapist is overly quick to label feelings of personal badness as guilt or shame. In disjointed syntax, Frank comments on his difficulty distinguishing between "shame" and "guilt":

S: For me, putting the difference between the shame and guilt are closely related. And it's something that both have bothered me to an extreme.

In a later attempt to describe his feelings directly, without use of a feeling label, Frank says of himself, "I felt kinda dirty inside."

Feelings of personal badness such as those described above often have a pervasive quality. This characteristic may derive from their dependence not on a set of values that prescribe certain behaviors and proscribe others, but on an experience of direct disapproval of the child by the parent. The parent who repeatedly condemns the angry child may promote feelings of being bad, as may the parent who condemns inherently uncontrollable behavior, for example, hunger. The child thus treated develops the feeling "I am bad" rather than the feeling "I have done wrong." The parent who manages to convey to the child that he or she is basically a good and loved individual capable at times of actions that are wrong, or annoying, or even infuriating, presumably would help the child to achieve a positive identity that allows for feelings of responsibility and periodic guilt in relation to bad behavior. Pervasive feelings of badness may also derive from guilt that centers on an aspect of the self regarded as so fundamentally important that little sense of a good self survives. For example, a child who loses a parent at an early age, who believes omnipotently that he or she has destroyed the parent, may feel himself or herself to be an essentially bad person. In this event, the feeling of badness is less circumscribed and action-focused than guilt, but it rests on a profoundly important, specific culpability.

5 Shame Themes in Interview Data

When a research subject openly states that he or she suffers from shame, such shame complaints may conceal difficulty with other feelings about which the subject does not complain; nevertheless, the direct complaint about shame can be taken as evidence for a shame problem, the dynamics of which remain to be determined. An interviewer may infer a shame problem even when a subject denies any experience of shame. In such situations, any of several explanations may apply. Interviewees deliberately may conceal shame experience because to identify a current area of shame invites the interviewer to scrutinize just that aspect of the self that the interviewee wishes to hide. In fact, one must question what emotional dynamics would prompt a person to confide shame eagerly. But not all interviewees who deny shame experience are dissembling. Often an interviewer will identify a shame problem when the subject honestly has not recognized any such difficulty. The interviewer may base his or her conclusion on the subject's speech patterns or facial expression. For example, staccato laughs may signal potentially embarrassing or shameful conflict over a sadistic or exhibitionistic impulse. Use of non-lexical language or substitution of gestures for words also may mark conflict over the acceptability of incipient thoughts. In many instances, the interviewer infers a shame problem when the content of a subject's speech points to shame themes unrecognized by the subject. For example, a man may claim to be entirely free of shame but yet show unremitting interest in discussing his brother's shame problem. Or he may display such unnatural obtuseness in discussions of shame that the interviewer suspects a need to deny acquaintance with a topic that at some level is only too familiar. The same man may respond to inquiries about bodily shame by claiming to experience none, yet while talking he covers his genitals or becomes preoccupied with smoothing out wrinkles in his pants. The inferential approaches described here have become clinically commonplace methods of identifying shame. Yet they appear to require, as their foundation, complex assumptions about unconscious processing of meaningful stimuli. At the very least they assume that behavior (e.g., verbalization) can be influenced by feeling states or thoughts that are vague and inarticulate, often are not remembered for long, and have not been conceptualized as definable, labelable affect states. Whether those mental processes that result in *communication* of shame themes, without a clearly identifiable personal *experience* of shame, are unconscious or whether they are conscious but not meaningfully integrated by the experiencer, the communication of a personally unrecognized preoccupation constitutes a complex and remarkable phenomenon.

One cannot assume that shame is experienced unless the subject either states that it is or describes an actual feeling that the interviewer recognizes as shame. The inferential routes that have been described only allow for identification of "shame themes" or "shame problems," not shame experiences. A shame theme can be defined as an ongoing preoccupation with shame experience; such a concern may evidence itself even in the absence of acknowledged shame feeling. The discussions in this chapter focus on subjects' shame themes (and humiliation and embarrassment themes). Chapter 8 will focus on subjects'[1] acknowledged experiences in the shame area. Each subject presented in this chapter will serve as the stimulus for discussion of one or more topics in shame theory.

POLLY: BEING NOBODY SPECIAL, BEING UNWELCOME AND UNWANTED

Pressures Toward Conformity

A college student, here to be called Polly, volunteered to be interviewed. During the interviews, she assumed a joking demeanor, but the joking had a bland, joyless quality. When serious emotion surfaced, Polly seemed greatly discomforted and helpless. Polly did not identify many traits or behaviors of which she felt "ashamed," but a great

---

[1]Chapter 7 contains a brief discussion of Polly's emphasis on embarrassment experience rather than shame.

many situations "embarrassed" her. Polly's embarrassment situations generally implied a potential for shame. Her comments made clear that were she to focus attention on the behavior or self-aspect that embarrassed her—an activity she appeared to avoid—she likely would have felt ashamed of certain of its features.[1] Polly's shame themes center on the belief that she is a person of no consequence. She suffers from fears that she lacks talent, attractiveness, and other indicators of worth. And she believes that she is useless to other people: Others do not value her presence or welcome her affection for them. Polly's shame problems raise an etiological question. Does her belief that she is boring and insignificant derive primarily from the type of parenting deficiencies that Kohut (1971, 1977) called "mirroring failure"? That is, does she feel ashamed of herself and lacking in positive self-regard because her parents failed to instill in her a feeling that she is loved and valued? Or does her belief mainly represent a defense against, and byproduct of, specific hostile, competitive, or exhibitionistic wishes that she regards as unacceptable to her conscience? Or are both sources of low self-esteem implicated?

My understanding of the data of Polly's case, some of which follow, regards the defect in self-esteem as a primary problem, not simply an offshoot of neurotic inhibition. In other words, the sadness and despair Polly feels when she looks at herself in the mirror or thinks about her personal characteristics is assumed to be genetically related to similar feelings experienced when her parents, the original mirror of the developing self, showed little evidence that Polly was pleasing to them. Stated briefly, the leading alternate hypotheses for explaining Polly's embarrassment and chronic self-dissatisfaction both would feature shame as a feeling state that grows strong under specific dynamic conditions, yet the presence of shame does not point to a profound negative view of the self, nor must the shame feelings be addressed directly in order to alter the dynamic balance that maintains the shame experience. One such hypothesis would state that Polly's shame is a reaction-formation against exhibitionistic wishes regarded as unacceptable because they represent an unprincipled and dangerous competition with Mother. The child who runs aground on this shoal need not be a narcissistically vulnerable child, yet the end point of the defensive retreat from exhibitionism may be an effluence of embarrassment or shame responses to exhibitionistically stimulating situations; so the patient who presents for psychotherapy likely will complain of low self-esteem. A treatment that focuses on how one's parents made one feel unimportant obviously will do this patient no good. A second, related hypothesis regarding Polly's low self-esteem would state that shame flourishes when narcissistic rage cannot be tolerated following a narcissistic injury. Since one cannot fend off the blow with anger, one must accept it and accept the associated view of the self as defective. The inhibition of anger is the pin that holds the dynamic shame-producing structure in place and the inhibition of anger will be the primary point of intervention. Shame traumatizes because it produces intolerable rage, not because it produces intolerable strain on self-esteem. This last point may be obscured clinically for long periods because the patient who has felt traumatized by narcissistic rage may as an adult experience shame as traumatizing when it cannot be avoided. This occurs not because shame was the original trauma, but because the adult, defending against the feared narcissistic rage, does not allow himself or herself to combat narcissistic injury, thus he or she can feel truly overwhelmed by agonizing shame or worthlessness if a narcissistically injurious situation cannot be avoided. In anticipating my discussion of Polly's interviews, I would emphasize that it is always difficult to differentiate between those self-esteem deficits secondary to inhibition (either of feelings such as envy and competitiveness or of narcissistic rage) and those following directly from the narcissistic blow associated with failures of parental empathy; the effort at such distinctions continues throughout a psychotherapy. But I will cautiously argue that, for Polly, her painful experiences of disappointment in herself appear to reflect memories of feeling like a disappointment in her parents' eyes. Difficulties with aggression may add to her feelings of worthlessness, but appear not to fully account for them.

Five interrelated shame themes that appear prominently in Polly's interviews will be illustrated and discussed. The five themes are interrelated, however separate themes are needed in order to demarcate Polly's shifts in focus from shameful qualities of the self (e.g., fatness, stupidity) to shame-causing responses from others (e.g., being ignored, being ridiculed). Although the sense of self and the sense of the other's response interact constantly, accurate description of any particular moment of experience depends on separation of the two aspects. At any given moment, either a self-oriented or an other-oriented conceptualization of the experience will prevail. And the moment will be experienced differently depending on whether it feels like a moment of self-indictment or a moment of criticism by another person.

The Shame Themes

1. She feels she is an unremarkable person, a nobody-special. She feels stupid, boring, uninteresting, lacking in willpower and initiative, and lacking in talent.

2. She feels deficient in that she fails to appraise herself realistically. She retains high hopes of being a famous, glamorous person despite suspicions that she is in fact untalented. The resultant shame theme is that of being a fool who does not know or will not face how unremarkable a person she is. She allows other people to see her exhibit her deficiencies while she naively thinks she is exhibiting her charms. Like the emperor in the famous tale, she is so foolish that she does not know her true state.

3. She feels others will abandon her or withdraw from her if she does not make great efforts to hold them. They will abandon her because she is unremarkable and boring, but the imagery central to this shame theme is not just the self-as-boring, as in theme #1; it is the self-as-left-for-worthless.

4. She holds the image of herself caring for another person who pulls away or remains indifferent. This theme obviously relates to those above, but it differs slightly in that the central imagery is of being so unwanted, so pathetic or desperate, that she clings to someone who has no love or need for her.

5. She is needy and has dependent feelings when she feels she should be independent and dispassionate. Here the central imagery is the self as a crying baby. Plumbing this theme to its depth, one might find theme #4, in that babyishness is often experienced as shameful because one's mother does not wish to respond to one's needs. But the two themes will be kept separate because their imagery differs somewhat. The core of theme #5 is not the image of the self longing for another, as in theme #4. The core of theme #5 is simply an image of the self, for example, an image of being pathetically teary-eyed and out of control of one's feelings.

Polly's shame list reveals the close association between her sense that she is defective in some specific way and her feeling that no one responds to her with interest. To be boring is a trait belonging to the individual, but often it is assessed or identified by looking not at one's own behavior but at another's response. Polly's ongoing adult sense that she is boring and inconsequential may represent the perpetuation of a similar childhood experience of the self, or it may represent an indirect outcome of some other form of strain experienced during childhood (e.g., a parent who overreacted to the child's anger and thus promoted inhibition of self-protective narcissistic rage). All that we know for certain at this early juncture in the examination of the data is that Polly currently experiences herself as insignificant and uninteresting, and she depends on others' responses to enhance her feelings of worth:

S: I don't know how that evening ended. I sort of felt like they didn't enjoy it (laugh). I don't know, it was nice of them to come visit, but I didn't think— I don't know, I felt like maybe they—they left feeling, you know, they left and were going to say, "Oh God, what—you know, that was really stupid, you know." I don't know, like I felt obligated to keep some kind of conversation going, when I shouldn't have. But I did, and I was a little embarrassed really at each point when the conversation would end. Then I'd have to find another, you know, conversation to go on.

I wanted them to have a good time, so that they'd come back. . . . If they were really bored and, you know, we really didn't talk or anything, we just sat there and stared at each other, I doubt if they'd ever (laughs) come back.

Elsewhere, Polly talks of her fantasies of fame. Her images of success seldom refer to any achievement of her own. Her idea of pleasure and self-worth is to "hobnob with the stars," to be one of the famous and to be welcome in the company of the prestigious. According to Kohut (1971, 1977), such dependence on external sources of self-esteem points to a failure to establish solidly internalized self-esteem, which in turn points to some failure in the parent's ability to value the child or to offer the child a strong adult with whom to identify. Thus Polly's continual orientation toward external support for self-esteem may strengthen the case for a primary self-esteem problem.

Specifically what might have led to Polly's concern that she is boring and inconsequential and to her need for famous friends and overt praise as indicators of her worth? Two characteristics of the mother-daughter relationship likely would lead Polly to suspect that she is a boring, inconsequential, and unwelcome person. First, Mother is experienced as a giving and caring person against whom one seldom could feel justified in lodging complaints. Yet her attentiveness is unconvincing; she appears to be doing what is correct rather than acting on genuinely affectionate feeling. Her presence is not reassuring or sustaining to Polly, but Polly cannot fully understand what is lacking. Second, when Mother is not acting the part of the concerned parent, she is highly critical in subtle ways. She displays a dissecting attention toward her daughter, a variety of attention that Kohut (1971) has called "fragmenting" because it insists on noticing some small feature of the person while ignoring the feelings of the whole person who is trying to make herself heard. Polly receives either a bland attentiveness or a disparaging attentiveness, and in neither case is the mother's underlying aggression clearly stated. A slightly more complex argument would add that Polly, in her state of doubt about the acceptability of her feelings and actions, ultimately went on to cultivate a conventional, compliant personality, which seemed likely to please and certain not to offend. In so doing she heightened her sense of insignificance by rendering herself actually boring. In order to find approval from outside, she stripped herself of opinions and aggression and left herself open to the complaint, issuing from self and others, that she is uninteresting.

The following passage portrays Polly's mother responding in a superficially reassuring, but subtly problematic way to an important inquiry Polly made about her birth:

S: The oldest is 10 years older than me now and Sara is 6 years older than me and Billie's 4 years older than me. I was a mistake (laughs).

I: Is that just how you think about it, or—?

S: No, I like joke around it, I joke about it. I used to, at one point when I was younger—it really didn't mean anything but it was, you know, when it was something new, I would say to her, "I was a mistake, wasn't I, you know?" 'Cause my brothers and sisters are each 2½, 3 years apart and then here I come 4 years later. And she says, "Well all of you, well none of you were planned, and we love you even more (laugh)," you know, it was funny. I mean now I, it's no big deal. None of them were planned, really. I am my father's favorite though, because I think—well, he likes babies.

Polly feels inhibited from pursuing a question that would have had importance for her and probably would have stirred some feelings of hurt and anger that she needed to experience and integrate into her self-concept. She feels she must dismiss with laughter what reduces to a question of whether her parents wanted her. As she says, she must "joke around it." This quality of needing to joke her way through life and never to show strong feeling pervades her experience and is evident in numerous references to inability to show feeling. She always must be the bright, smiling, joking one. In discussing Polly's birth, her mother gives the child little opening to express strong or unhappy feeling. The mother in effect says, "There is no issue here; there is nothing to feel upset about." She manages Polly with a platitude that discourages troubled feeling and suggests to the girl that any distress is self-generated because there is nothing in the real situation to warrant it. Polly's description of a birthday celebration conveys a similar impression of embryonic inner complaints that cannot grow into full, well-articulated feeling because the superficial niceness of her family confuses her effort to verbalize a genuine grievance. She is left with a feeling of vague depression instead of a crisp complaint.

The mother's discouragement of strong feeling apparently did not always take the form of a cheerful denial of her daughter's grounds for distress. Certain of Polly's memories portray overt punishment of the child when she moved toward stronger self-expression. These memories generally have a stubbornly "anal" feel to them as well as a thematic concern with being emotionally hungry. Polly has one early memory of Mother forcing her to sit until she eats a hated sweet potato. Polly talks of being quite stubborn at that age but she finds the memory funny because she now loves sweet potatoes. The claim of loving the once forcefed food sounds in keeping with Polly's current limp compliance with Mother's values. Polly relates another memory of licking her lips while waiting for chicken soup made by a babysitter. A friend of her youngest brother is watching, and he mistakes Polly's licking for swearing at him. He tells Polly's mother what happened and Polly is punished, despite her insistence that she did not curse. The memory represents a rare portrayal of Polly savoring the thought of some pleasure and enjoying her appetites. But Mother is not the provider of the soup. On the contrary, she allies herself with her favorite son's friend when he highlights a destructive, aggressive quality to Polly's wishes. One receives the impression that Polly's hunger, which undoubtedly had aggressive and envious *components*, was regarded as something all-bad or all-aggressive; at least Polly believed that this was so. Thus aggression gradually is disallowed and the child who perhaps already feels of questionable significance to her mother gravitates toward conventionally nice behavior that is devoid of any personal coloration. Such behavior ultimately intensifies her sense of insignificance.

The next passage reflects the full range of maternal attitudes thus far mentioned. Polly tries to dress up and look attractive and Mother either fails to notice her or she notices her but is critical of her inappropriateness. Polly's complaining response to Mother's critical attention is diffused by Mother's unexplained swing to highly complimentary words:

S: I don't usually wear skirts. I'm more of a jeans person. It was a new jeans skirt and I thought it looked pretty good, you know, and I don't think my mother (laugh) liked it. And I, I don't know, I, she just didn't think it appropriate. I thought at that time I looked good, I thought I looked okay for—I think it was maybe some holiday or something, going home for dinner. And she like [said], "You could have gotten dressed or some-

I:

thing". . . . I don't remember, but it—I don't know and I was just sort of a little disappointed because I thought I looked good and I thought she'd like it, and she didn't really think anything of it or, you know, didn't even notice or something, that sort of feeling. I tried to look good for a change here, and she didn't even notice.

I: Was it that she didn't notice or was it more that she negatively noticed, in this case?

S: I don't remember (laugh).

I: She sure didn't notice what you wanted her to notice.

S: Right, probably negative. We have very different tastes anyway (laugh), but probably negative notice. And she'll say something like, "Go change your top" or something. And I think I look okay and you know, I'll, you know, it will just be differing opinions of clothing, or fashion or whatever, not even fashion just what looks good on or something.

I: How was her taste different from your taste?

S: I don't know, just—[I bought a] really off-, pretty-colored green sweater and I brought it home and I showed it to her: "How do you like my new sweater?" And she goes, "Oh, I hate that color." I said, "Really?", you know, "I love this, it's such a cool color, why don't you like it?" She goes, "You know green never looks good on you; it makes your complexion look green." And then like the next day I'll wear it and she loves it (laugh). [She] said, "Oh, you're right, it does look good." When I was little she never dressed me in yellows and greens. 'Cause I, you know, I guess I was pale and I turned color, you know, green or whatever.

The last line of Polly's comments has tempting potential as a metaphor for her chameleon-like identity development. She does indeed seem to have little color of her own. She changes to reflect what is around her. Although Polly associates her nonentity status with specific deficiencies, and though I have associated the status with a real, ulti- mately shame-producing blandness that she has cultivated, the deep- est source of feeling like a shameful nobody may be the experience of feeling like a nobody in her mother's eyes. She is now deeply motivated to be seen and admired by many important people who will confirm her value and substance.

Polly's dieting struggles express her difficulty coping with her per- ception that Mother wished her to suppress strong feeling and to con- form to conventional values:

S: I'm disappointed in myself a lot, that I can never keep a diet (laugh). I don't really try too hard but I'm disappointed that I don't try hard enough, 'cause like in the morning, you know, I'll get all mad at myself and when you're not hungry of course you say, "Okay, I'm gonna be real good tomor- row and starve myself," and in the morning you still feel that way but then a few hours into it, you know, you just eat, I don't know, I just start, like once I eat a little something even if it's not that bad, I just give up and go,

"What's the difference?" and I get mad at myself and punish myself by eating and it's terrible. . . . I'm very disappointed in myself sometimes, about that. In fact, *all* the time (laugh).

I: What's the feeling when you sort of give it up and start to eat?

S: It's aggravating, it's like, "What's the matter with you?" you know, and yet I eat anyway. I like, I *love* peanut butter. So peanut butter is very fattening, and here I'll be good and then, "Oh, the hell with it" and I'll go take a teaspoonful of peanut butter and just sit there and eat that. And like I'll be mad at myself and I'll even like won't tell anybody (laugh) about eating the peanut butter. But I'm really mad at myself like, "What are you doing? You're eating this." Yet I'm not—I'm mad, I'm very mad at myself but I don't go throw it out or something.

In the next passage, Polly responds to inquiry into images she generated of being caught eating:

I: Would there be any rebuttal to that, if a person says, "Here you say on the one hand you want to lose but then here you are eating peanut butter?"

S: I'll say, "Oh, I know, I—, I just *like*—" you know, the rebuttal would be, "I can't, I just *like food*, it's, I don't, I don't know what's wrong with me."

I: Would you ever just get aggravated at her?

S: Oh, yeah, probably, you know, because I probably get aggravated because she can do it and I can't. . . . if she confronted me, you know, [I'd say], "I'll be fine, just leave me alone, okay. I'll diet in the way I want to diet, if I don't want to diet then I won't. I don't need you to watch over me and tell me what I can and cannot eat." That would be the kind of aggravation. Like I've had that with other—like I haven't had it with her, 'cause me and [this friend] we both are bad sometimes and we're both good sometimes. But like last year, like I was on a diet, okay, but on a different kind of, like a diet where I know what I should eat and I know what I shouldn't eat, and I allowed myself so much, allowed myself—like say one bread a day or something or I could substitute. . . . I had this girlfriend, Dee. Now Dee— a diet for her is total salad, salad for breakfast, lunch, and dinner, salad her whole life. And for me it would be more a little practical—have a meat, have a bread, have this, so here I am eating something and she'd say, "What happened to that diet?" and I'll be a little aggravated at her. Or say maybe a week later I'm off the diet and I'm eating a dessert or something and she says, "I thought you were on a diet." Then I'll get aggravated at her and say, "Don't worry, I know what I'm—leave me alone, I don't want somebody to keep reminding me if I'm already off of it or something . . . She was just more of an aggravating thorn, where I don't really want to hear what she had to say.

I: Do you feel that instead of being supportive she was more sort of contemptuous, as if always there to notice?

S: Yeah, yeah, maybe, not really supportive but more being like, pointing out the things I know I wasn't supposed to [have], like an ice cream sundae or something, then her pointing it out—"What do you think, I'm stupid? I know what I'm eating here."

One reading of these passages would align the mother with the ambivalently internalized voice telling Polly to diet. Polly wishes to diet, because she shares with her mother a high regard for a trim appearance. But she also experiences the diet as a deeply resented set of pressures to control impulses toward a vigorous, pleasure-based connection with the world. She states her conflict well when she says, "I'm gonna be really good tomorrow and starve myself." She cannot accept the diet as a genuinely healthy activity because it is too closely associated with constraints imposed from outside by another person who wishes to restrict her pleasure. The diet also becomes associated with the emotional hunger that pervades Polly's experience due to her sense that she cannot connect with others on the basis of her true feelings. Polly will experience the self as shamefully degraded whichever side of the eating conflict she embraces. Although she is not obese, continuing to eat in uninhibited fashion is repulsive to her in view of her strong identification with those who would see such eating as piggish. The shame potential of that choice is obvious. Less obvious, but equally real, is the shame potential in slavish compliance with the diet. She battles with the friend who would have her eat salad instead of peanut butter. The battle represents her effort to keep alive her own desires. Her feelings about "willpower" demonstrate the way in which Polly always is guilty of a shameful action or a shameful failure to act. "No willpower" means that she is a disgustingly piggish, shamefully indulgent person. But too much willpower also is shameful because it is experienced as Mother's will, Mother's power, and not her own. To subject herself to this willpower is to identify with the aggressor and become the boring, compliant girl who now disappoints herself so deeply. Polly retreats from the anal battles that she feels she cannot win (because Mother will never approve of her will) to a pseudofemininity oriented around making herself attractive to others who can provide the self-esteem that has not been established internally.

Father's responses to Polly, as she experiences them, are as problematic as Mother's in their impact on her self-esteem. She perceives his reactions to her as an arbitrary alternation between excessive praise and indifference. She finds it difficult to complain about either of Father's postures. Consciously she construes his indifference as benign acceptance. And she regards his indiscriminate praise as too exciting to fault. However, neither of Father's postures contributes to a reliably positive and realistic self-image. The following illustrates her sense of his withdrawal from her:

S: Oh, he never cares. No, he, whatever I want, or whatever. He doesn't care, you know.

I: So, when you came home in the blue jeans skirt he didn't react one way or the other, or—?

S: No, no. He'd never, no, he'd never. If he ever did, I don't think [I've noticed]. He never really reacts in that kind of [way], to clothing or anything like that. He might say—not to me, maybe to my mother, if once I came home looking a mess or something, blue jeans with holes, and a flannel shirt, the whole mess, sloppy outfit. He would never say anything to *me*. He might say to *her*, "Doesn't she have any better clothing?" But that would be like the only kind of comment he'd make: "What does she spend all her money on, you know, for clothing, and then she wears the junk?"

When Polly's father praises her, he praises blindly and she feels embarrassed. One can think to account for the particular affect state, embarrassment, in a number of ways. Polly wants desperately to feel that she is as wonderful and talented as Father says she is, but she fears she is not and feels that the other person listening certainly will see this and find her father's praise ludicrous. She must feel tempted actually to act the part that Father assigns to her, to glow with pleasure and pride and to present herself boldly. But to do this would immediately expose her to fears of falling flat. So she is pulled in two directions, toward exhibitionism and modesty. Father offers her a pleasure that tempts her but ultimately reminds her of her self-doubt. She feels the praise is fraudulent and dangerous:

S: His pride was just always too much sometimes. Like his pride in my playing the violin and I was terrible. I hated the lessons (laughs), and he was—, I just have like three songs I can still play to this day, but he loves to—it was just incredible: "Oh, you know, she's so smart." Relations would come over: "Oh, she's doing so well in school." In high school I hung around with like a smarter group of people, and because I hung around with that group it like rubbed off that I had to do a little better. I don't know if I hung around with a dumber group whether I would have done worse or not, because it still didn't seem that hard to me.

I: How did you feel when your dad would brag about your violin playing?

S: I don't know (laugh).

I: Or, how do you feel even now?

S: Sometimes I like it. Like I remember in high school he'd brag, he'd say, "Oh, she can do any—," I'd just be a little embarrassed but I sort of liked it too. [If he's bragging about me] I'll smile and say, "You know, not really," say put myself down in a way, try to even it out a little bit because he's making me . . . just bigger than I am . . . If he started talking about like career hopes, I'd be embarrassed because I don't, 'cause I don't want people saying my big hope and then say I flop, I don't want anybody to know that I flopped. I'd rather have people know, think, that I never tried.

Polly's hopes for the future actually mirror Father's ideas about her unlimited potential. She would like to be famous and accomplished. She maintains her dreams—with little real basis for imagining them to be attainable—but she is certain she would feel embarrassed if she failed to excel and others knew her aspirations:

S: Like when I'm 82 (laugh), they'll say, "Oh, so you were going to be the next Barbara Walters, were you?"

Her fantasy that others would ridicule her aspirations can be understood in a number of ways. It is a nod to reality, an acknowledgment that after childhood passes, there is need to temper one's fantasies and to put substance behind their scaled-down versions. If one does neither, if one remains a child who dreams of fame while doing little beyond the ordinary, then people will indeed ridicule. In Polly's case, her sense of others' cruelty, of their delight in deriding her, suggests that even as a child, when such fantasies might ordinarily have met with a generous response, she was not permitted to think of herself as special.

The fantasy of being special immediately provokes a reminder from within that she is nobody and that people will see it and say to her, "Who do you think you are?" Anger enters the picture in that Polly must have wished to attack others when they entertained hopes for personal success. Through projection, this wish would intensify her expectation that others would ridicule her. One sees the common cycle of shame producing rage which then produces hostile contempt for others. The contempt in turn generates an expectation of receiving hostile contempt and ridicule from others, which generates intensified shame, which intensifies rage, and so on.

The shame theme of entertaining unrealistically grand ideas about the self (Polly's shame theme #2) appears in several cases, and it is accompanied by a profound shame that one has been such a fool as to imagine that one could be special. One feels a fool for seeing oneself falsely. The fear of being exposed as foolishly proud or ambitious may be an outgrowth of a childhood experience of suddenly recognizing that a significant other does not share one's own admiration for one's abilities. Rather than risk being crushed like the gleefully exhibitionistic child confronted by a disapproving parent, an adult anticipates the other's view and tries either to trim his or her own views accordingly or to hide the grandiosity lest it be recognized. (The case of William, presented later in this chapter, contains further discussion of this topic.)

Polly believes that she is boring and insignificant; these beliefs likely follow from parenting that failed to provide genuine support for the child's investment in her own energetic behavior and feelings. Polly also believes that the strong feelings she directs toward other people are unwelcome and unreturned. The unappreciated feelings may be loving feelings and wishes to nurture (theme #4) or they may be hungry, dependent feelings (theme #5). Thus the energies of the self are not valuable or interesting and do not define the self as worthwhile; and these energies are not welcomed by others as expressions of legitimate human feelings to be appreciated and returned. The passages to follow illustrate the convergence of Polly's sense of insignificance and her sense that her loving and dependent feelings are unwelcome. She talks of re-encountering childhood friends and recalling a childhood experience of playing strip-poker:

S: If I brought it up, I'd be embarrassed because I'd think well maybe that person doesn't remember. *I* remember it, and by me remembering it maybe I'm making a bigger deal out of it or something because I remember it when it was really nothing or something, you know. Does that make sense? If I were to bring it up it would be like I'm placing more importance upon it or something. That person may have forgotten it or something. That person may have forgotten it and thinking, "Boy, she remembers that, it must have been—," I don't know, it must have been really important to her or something.

Polly does not wish to be caught valuing an experience that another experienced as trivial. To do so would make her pathetic. In the next passage, she responds to inquiry about a hypothetical situation in which a girl is forgotten by a childhood sweetheart whose memory she has cherished:

S: That situation that you just explained never happened (laugh), but yeah, I can put myself in it and think like, you know, it meant so much to me and this person doesn't even remember me and . . . kind of upset in one way, embarrassed in another, that if I were to bring it up, like "Remember me?", you know, "Remember??", you know, trying, "Don't you remember???", like I wasn't, you know, I was nothing; I never made that impression upon that person.

Polly imagines that her interest in a boy would be offensive to him (theme #3). He would experience her attachment as aggressive pursuit. He would wish only to flee from her and to ridicule her to his friends:

S: Maybe I'm afraid that if I call them and say "Hi," he'll think that I'm after him . . . when I'm not, when I'm—well, I'd probably call and say "Hi"— but then he thinks I'm after him, so . . . he like [would] shy away and he's not as friendly as he used—or he . . . talks with his friends: "Hey, she's after me," when I'm not, and I'd be embarrassed, I'd just be embarrassed or something. He'd think more of it than it is. And it would like end the friendship or something.

A final passage shows Polly's reaction to the idea of showing affection to her mother. The overall set of interviews suggests that Polly has retreated from self-expression because of her belief that such energetic self-aspects are unattractive to Mother. That retreat, now a part of her character, causes her to feel flooded with conflicted wishes when invited to show some feeling to her mother, whom she must experience as the source of her inner struggles and inhibitions. She describes her feeling of "embarrassment." Like most feelings thus described, Polly's embarrassment involves discomfort over having shown an aspect of one's self or one's feelings with which one is uncomfortable. Polly's embarrassment is not a reaction-formation; it is not a claim of wishing to hide something that one, at another level, wishes to show off. The embarrassment reflects tense ambivalence; the wish to show and the fear-empowered wish not to show stimulate her concurrently:

S: I never really am affectionate to my parents at all. Like my mother forces me to kiss her sometimes, like she'll pin me in a corner and say, "Kiss me hello," you know and I'll laugh it away (laughs). . . . I'll get corner—, I'll, I can't express what I feel about it, I can't express my emotions that well to them.
I: What about when your mother pinned you in a corner and said, "Kiss me hello," how did—?
S: Well, I was embarrassed, you know, "Leave me alone Ma," you know.
I: What kind of feeling is that?
S: . . . I don't know, like sometimes I wish I could just come in and just go kiss her hello. . . . Like when I go home for the weekend . . . I go kiss her hello, but you know, just for the hell of it, you know. She'll say, "Give me a kiss, give me a hug," or something. You know, "Leave me alone." I'm embarrassed I guess, I shouldn't be and I hate myself for being it sometimes, that I'm embarrassed just to go hug her, but they didn't bring me up very affect—, not affectionate. . . .
I: Could you describe any more the feeling that you have if your mother sort of forces you to show her some affection? You said you feel embarrassed—

S: Yeah, I don't know. It's like, you know, just "Leave me alone"—I don't know, I'm just embarrassed, not even embarrassed, it's like—I don't know, I just, I don't know what to—I'll finally kiss her, you know, hello—I'll kiss her and laugh it off or something, you know, like "Oh, leave me alone" or something. I don't know, I—I don't know (laugh).

I: What kind of feeling, or can you think of any words that would go with the feeling of sort of wanting to shake her off—?

S: (Interrupting I.) No, that's what I'm trying to do, that's what I'm trying to think of, I can't really think of the words to explain that, you know . . . not even embarrassment just that shying away and yet, yet in a way wishing I could just do it naturally. . . . Her impulse is every once in a while—like we'll be talking and she'll say, "Come here and give me a hug," that sort of thing. I'll go, "Oh, leave me alone," I just can't go ahead and do it without putting up a fight. You know, I don't know what emotions though, like a stubbornness, that I won't do it, even though I want to. Maybe showing a weakness or something, that I'd rather not do it. . . . It would be like I'm showing her a weakness . . . I need to be talked into doing it, when I should, when it's fine for me just to get up and go over there and hug her—I want to do it but I don't because I think, you know, it might show more emotion than I want to show. . . .

I: What would the feeling be that would be too much do you think, that you wouldn't want her to see so much of?

S: (laughs) I think just the dependency—I don't want to show the dependency. . . . I'll just get, I don't know, get too emotional (laugh) which is really dumb. 'Cause I think you *should* be able to show your emotions but I can't. Like right now I feel like crying for some reason (laugh). I don't know, it's really weird (laugh). I'm embarrassed that I can't really show my love to them. And, I don't know (laugh), now I'm getting embarrassed. I'm embarrassed to show emotion, I don't know, like right now I feel like crying, but I'm embarrassed because I'm gonna, 'cause I feel like that. I'm embarrassed when I want to hug them but I need an excuse. . . . I can't let her like see me cry or anything. I guess I want them to see me more independent, or not so dependent upon them. Which I think was like, before I said I was never really the baby, even though I'm the youngest.

A Clinical Excerpt: Differentiating Primary from Derived Shame

In considering Polly's development more fully one would need to consider the fate of the narcissistic rage that presumably followed at times from the slights she received. The data are not expressive in conveying the outcome of Polly's narcissistic rage, but one would hypothesize, from the impression she gives of her overall character, that any such rage would be repressed or otherwise defended against, and such a repressive policy toward aggression would result in an intensification of her experience of herself as lacking in vitality. Given the limited data, it is extremely difficult to assess the relative impact, on shame-proneness, of self-doubt following directly from parental disappointment and self-doubt secondary to developing a bland character oriented around the control of narcissistic rage.

When listening to patients, therapists often are presented with the problem of differentiating between irreducible narcissistic problems and narcissistic problems that are secondary to specific libidinal and aggressive conflicts: Aggression conflict may revolve around narcissistic rage or other forms, for example, rage over deprivation of desired physical comforts. Such distinctions between primary and secondary narcissistic problems must be made as part of the attempt at understanding a person's personality structure in a comprehensive manner, and they must also be made on a moment-to-moment basis as one considers how to address a patient's current concerns. As an example of the therapist's ongoing efforts to discriminate irreducible shame from derived or secondary shame, I think of an obsessional woman, Mary, who talked of feeling "blue" and "down" for much of the time since the previous Friday, the day of her last appointment. She was not certain what was bothering her, nor was she certain whether she wanted to discuss her depression because it had lifted earlier in the day and she thought she might prefer to tell me about the pleasurable event that caused her depression to ease. She finally did discuss her depression for much of the hour. Toward the end of the session she turned to a discussion of her pleasure because she "didn't want to leave depressed." She did not feel that any of the unpleasant events that she recounted actually caused her depression, but they were associated with the depressed period. Clearly they conveyed something about the significance of the depression. The unpleasant events involved the men in her life. She had received a hostile and derogatory phone call from a male colleague to whom she felt attracted. And she had found her husband unsupportive and insulting in several instances. She felt particularly humiliated when she learned that her husband had been joking about her with another woman and she wondered whether there was an attraction between the two of them. The one event that revived her and counterbalanced the negative, slighting experiences with men was an unexpected compliment on her work, given by the department head at her office. The praise was unanticipated—she had expected him to be critical or disappointed—and not only did he praise her, he called others over to see her work.

In listening to this patient during this particular hour, a number of sources and types of data were available to me. The simplest statement of the hour's presenting complaint seemed to be that the patient felt undervalued, especially by men, and often in relation to other women who might be preferred by the men. The complaint as presented and experienced by the patient has a narcissistic or self-esteem focus. One man delivers a litany of complaints about her character flaws. Another betrays her private fears to other women. She feels relieved and restored only when she finds a man who praises her in front of others. Thus the presenting complaint or theme of the hour points to a narcissistic problem in the area of feminine self-esteem.

Once the identification of the self-esteem problem has been made, the therapist must next ask what is the particular occasion for this access of shame and depression. Is the emotion a reaction to a narcissistic injury that recapitulates painful childhood slights so stressful that they initiated significant defensive developments? (If so, I would call the shame primary or irreducible shame.) Or do intervening emotional events contribute to the patient's shame (i.e., the shame is secondary or derived)? In considering the possibility of derived shame, one recent event of interest was the last treatment hour, which immediately preceded the patient's depression. The last hour had included an uncharacteristically vivid, relaxed, and open reporting of dreams and fantasies by this woman who tended to be tight-lipped about her fantasy life but who recently had taken strides toward relaxing these defenses and inhibitions. The apparent theme in this earlier hour was sibling competition and guilt. Since that theme was prominent throughout this woman's treatment, though as yet minimally explored, the identification of the theme in this particular hour was not surprising. What was, however, surprising was the vivid and relatively relaxed expression of the theme. Thus the hour could be said to have two themes, one conveyed in content, another in form. One theme was competition with a sibling, the other was the increased expressiveness, which had significance within the context of a maternal and oedipal transference. At this point, it can be noted that the predominant theme of the treatment, which had received more overt attention than had the sibling competition theme, was the issue of the patient's retreat from sexually competitive and exhibitionistic feeling and her use of obsessional mechanisms (compulsive planning, isolation, doing and undoing, interpersonal stubbornness) when in flight from overt competition. In the hour preceding the depression it seemed very likely that several images of defeated competitors might condense the patient's fears of her competitiveness toward her sibling and toward her mother, now represented by the therapist.

Given the overall context of the more recent hour, I chose to conceptualize the patient's sudden collapse of self-esteem as a secondary narcissistic problem and I commented to her that I thought she both expected and felt she deserved punishment after relaxing and allowing herself some free expression of competitive feelings. I illustrated my point by reminding her that she had misinterpreted some comments I had made last hour (she herself thought she was misinterpreting as she stated her interpretation) in a way that suggested a need for me to punish her for her attractiveness. Then, after that hour, she became depressed and began to interpret most of her interactions with men in a self-demeaning way. She made herself feel like an unattractive, slighted woman, as if her conscience said she should be that. If we assume for the moment that the interpretation of the young woman's depression is correct, beyond that what can be said of it? One plus for the interpretation is that it keeps the treatment focused on the immediate relationship between patient and therapist rather than on the patient's relationship to others, for example her husband. A second plus for the interpretation is that it focuses on that aspect of a complex dynamic structure that the therapist judges to be most essential to maintaining the psychological structure; it does not focus the patient's attention on an epiphenomenon with which she might then, for defensive reasons, concern herself. A possible minus for the interpretation is that it may be too *dynamic* for this patient at this time. It requires too much thinking about how things work and may rush too quickly past the emotional center of the patient's current experience, which is her feeling of shame and depression in relation to her husband and her feeling of exhilaration in relation to her department head. She might need more acknowledgment of her narcissistic concerns—both her sense of depletion and her elation—before she can move on to considering their underpinnings. Whether the narcissistic concerns are primary (irreducible) or secondary to guilt, they are real and painful and at this early stage of treatment, when the patient is not very familiar with depressions that follow from impulse-conflicts, it may be inadvisable to bypass her feelings of shame and depression or deal cursorily with them by explaining their cause without attending sympathetically to the patient's experience.

Another source of data from the hour might have guided me toward an intervention with a stronger self-esteem focus. Unfortunately, I only noted this interaction after the hour ended, when I was thinking about the session because I thought I had missed the point somehow. At the end of the hour, the patient had made a special point of telling me her success story "in order not to be depressed." While she was talking I felt—without fully articulating the feeling—an urge to admire her achievement. Looking back later on my own response, it seemed clear to me that the patient was communicating that she would have felt quite deflated had I not responded enthusiastically. Had I noted this response of mine more clearly, I might have recognized the patient's felt need for direct gratification of her wish for praise. One still could argue that the patient's narcissistic problem was derived from conflict. For example, she might have needed me to approve her successful interaction with the admiring supervisor in order to deny the dangerous wish to outdo me. And the impending depression, which I sensed and of which she rather explicitly warned, might have followed from the failure symbolically to re-establish rapport with Mother, the original object of her competitiveness. Her elated response to the department head in itself might have signaled superego conflict more than irreducible narcissistic difficulty, in that she might have needed a boost from an outside source only because her conscience forbade her (on account of her transgressions) to comfort and sustain herself after her colleague insulted her. In other words, she began to experience self-protective anger in response to an insult, but the anger felt intolerably aggressive and needed to be inhibited. So she succumbed to the insults. Whatever the basis of Mary's current narcissistic problem, her continued need passively to solicit praise clearly suggests that the self-esteem issue must be dealt with directly, if only because she would otherwise cling to shame and depression defensively. Having drawn that conclusion, some therapists might believe that they indeed ought to praise the patient. Others would respond to the self-esteem issue by pointing out to the patient how she communicates a wish or need to be praised. In this particular case, I would try the latter approach based on the premise that this woman has no profound problems with self-esteem; therefore, were she to reflect on her need to have me praise her, she might be able to restore herself to adequate self-regard without my supplying her with praise. She might also reflect on the need for praise and that reflective process would be of value.

Mary would seem to illustrate a pattern that is in some respects the opposite of Polly's. Because of oedipal guilt in relation to a conscientious, self-effacing mother (among other superego determinants), Mary flees opportunities to present herself as feminine and sexually attractive. She feels profoundly guilty when she entertains hostile or competitive thoughts toward other women, and she retreats into safer obsessional stubbornness about time and money. In contrast, Polly appears to have lost some of the developmentally crucial struggles of the anal period. Her response is to avoid normal expressions of willfulness and to take refuge in a stereotyped femininity, which promises her a personal identity and a route to liaisons with other people. With respect to cognitive style, romantic preoccupation, and underlying competitiveness with men, Polly might be described as stylistically "hysterical" (Shapiro, 1965); however, the data do not point to triangular oedipal conflicts as the central concern for this young woman. Therefore, she would not be properly classified as an hysterical neurotic according to some diagnostic approaches (Krohn, 1978).

JOSEPHINE: SUCH A WIMPY, WHINING GIRL

Familial Values and Cultural Values

Grinker (1955) argues that profound shame can follow from recognition that one has not reached or cannot reach the standards of behavior appropriate to one's age. Such standards may be communicated by society or, Grinker believes, they may be standards innate to the organism. For example, a young child may have inherent standards for motoric behavior. One can question whether innate standards exist that produce shame independent of societal reinforcement. But the existence of shame-generative societal standards seems beyond doubt. Grinker's notion of behavioral standards unique to each developmental stage implies that shame can take root de novo at any time. Though the older person will have a shame and self-esteem history that will affect all new shame experiences, a late-appearing shame over failure at a newly reached developmental task ought not to be reduced to a mere afterimage of an infantile shame experience.

Every individual responds both to societal ideals and to familial ideals. The two (or more) sets of standards constantly interact to confirm, disconfirm, or distort each other. A young woman, here called Josephine, illustrates the distorting of societal standards by superficially similar familial ideals. Josephine is a woman in her late twenties who initially presented herself in a contentious manner, stating for example that she volunteered for the research because someone should tell psychologists that their theories are bull. Her affect and degree of contact with the interviewer was quite changeable and her emotion tended to call attention to itself by its dramatic and shifting nature. By the end of the research contact, she was caught up in an internal struggle between her need to remain aloof and contemptuous and her feeling of urgently needing help with unruly emotions and uncontrolled drug use.

American society values a trait it calls "independence." An adult is expected to form his or her own opinions and to hold to them despite pressure from others' divergent opinions. An adult should function responsibly without constant advice and support from others. Clinging, selfish behavior and emotional outbursts should be outgrown by adulthood. Josephine judges herself to be a failure in relation to the societal standards of independence. And she feels ashamed. The belief that one has failed in relation to the society's developmental standard is an adequate basis for shame. But in Josephine's case, shame appears to be overdetermined. Her mother holds a standard of independence in comparison with which the societal expectation shines like a pale flare in the distance. The mother's standard, which was both verbalized and enacted, was imposed on a young child. Because of the child's age, the expectation was inherently unfulfillable. And the child could not even strive for the standard without creating severe inner conflict over relinquishing the age-appropriate dependent behaviors she was asked to despise. The mother's unattainable standards appear to have developed from a conflict of her own over dependence and independence, self-control and emotionality. Thus the standards were energetically but inconsistently applied to herself and to her child; the inconsistency led to complications to be discussed later. In striving toward her mother's concept of independence, Josephine feels she should be tough and emotionally cool. She despairs because she is childish and emotional:

S: I like to do different things. I don't like to go shopping. I don't like to use my credit cards that I don't even have. . . . I like rough people, people who wear a lot of leather (laugh), people who like to use drugs and like really loud music.

The man I live with, his nickname is Champ—I'll call him Champ with you. Like Champ, he's not a very emotional person. He rejects psychology and psychological therapy (laugh). He rejects that very much and—if I have a problem I will talk it over with him but it usually doesn't take long for him to explain it to me and go, "Well there, okay?" [The implication is: "That's settled now, isn't it?"]

I get ashamed when I get crying and whiny, when I feel like I can't control my emotions, like sometimes I feel ashamed when it feels like I can't control my appetite. If I eat too much I will feel ashamed.

Josephine experienced both of her parents as outspoken and dramatic people. Mother insisted that people not be limp or weak if they were to earn her respect. One had to be dramatic but in a tough, flamboyant, adult way, not as a child who has dramatic upsets. Josephine says of her mother:

S: She used to put me down a lot. She knifed me, man, she knifed me in the heart once. She told me that I didn't have any character—what a—what a thing to say!

Being a small child, Josephine could not show character in the adult way that Mother demanded. Her histrionic displays of emotion seem to have represented an effort to be dramatic like Mother, but they backfired because they were childish and without character in Mother's estimation (or so Josephine felt). Josephine's efforts were further confused by her occasional suspicion that Mother herself actually was not so cool or tough. Mother's histrionics were not in fact of a different order than her own. They did not so clearly possess more character than Josephine's childish outbursts. Mother was to an extent a fraud who demanded of Josephine what she herself only pretended to. Josephine even conveys the sense that Mother needed her daughter to be the crying, whining, dependent child who fell apart and crawled to Mother for help. And Josephine obliged. She denied her occasional perception that Mother was not so tough, not so flawless in character. She sacrificed her self-image in order to protect Mother (who needed to believe in her own toughness), to protect her own image of Mother, and to protect the sadomasochistic intimacy they shared.

On Giving In

Mary illustrated shame that is largely secondary to guilt in a woman of obsessional character with significant conflicts at the phallic-oedipal level of development. Polly exemplified primary shame or irreducible shame, the seeds for which most likely were laid in the anal phase even if the shame emotion did not appear until later. Josephine will illustrate shame and guilt problems with their earliest roots in the oral and anal phases.

Polly's shame themes centered on the idea that she is not lovable. Polly believes that she is unloved and that her own love is not welcomed by others because there is something wrong with her. Either she is bland or boring, or the qualities she has are despised. Josephine illustrates a variation on this theme. She regards as shameful the love and dependency that she feels. Her love is contemptible not solely because *she* offers it; it is contemptible in its very nature and no one of worth would have such abased feelings.

Josephine torments herself with the idea that self-respecting people never allow imbalances of giving to develop in their relationships. One never asks to receive support simply because one feels a need for it. Nor does one give freely without first determining that the giving will be matched by precisely equivalent getting. The person who gives freely is a fool, a "sucker" who allows others to see that she experiences loving or dependent feelings that are strong enough to motivate generous behavior even in the absence of prior proof of parity of giving. The person who gives freely will be publicly known as someone so dependent on others, so desperate for love, that she gives in craven hope of receiving. Comparing Josephine to Polly within a developmental framework, we might say that both women appear to have had difficulty establishing a sense of their own authority over the self in the anal period. However, their resolutions of anal period difficulties differed. Polly moved toward identification with passively feminine images. She abandoned the struggle for self-expression and sustained herself instead by her attractiveness to others. Josephine alternates between fierce refusal to relinquish authority and the need to submit masochistically to others.

Josephine cannot conceive of cooperation that is anything other than masochistic submission. One only gives in because one has been overpowered or because one is a baby or a "sucker" who has no backbone. To want something from someone else is the most profoundly shameful feeling imaginable. The genesis of such a conviction is open to speculation; Josephine's mother's attitude toward independence has already received attention as one contributor to Josephine's anxiety. Listening to Josephine, one thinks of a little girl in the separation-individuation phase whose mother in effect says to her: "Why must you be such a baby as to still need my support? Why can't you take care of yourself now?" Even the child's gifts to the mother meet with disdain. They are evidence of a loving and dependent attachment, which is regarded as pathetic. The young child whose parents comfortably accept the child's admiration and dependency will, at times, shamelessly imitate beloved adults, proclaiming that he or she wants to eat just what Father is eating, to wear just what Mother wears. For some children, acting on such impulses provokes a derogatory response from the environment. The child is made to feel that loving and admiring wishes are contemptible. One should be tough and independent, a person of character. To want or to hope or to admire makes one a pathetic baby.

Josephine conveys the impression that her mother communicated contempt for "suckers" who give and take too freely. But at the same time Mother made Josephine a sucker in relation to Mother herself. So Josephine feels both contempt for her own generosity and dread that her generosity will be exploited. The indictment of a person as a sucker is particularly telling. To want to take something from another, to take food, warmth, and sustenance, makes one a fool who has given up one's autonomy and opened oneself to exploitation. Josephine fears she will be used and abused by the other person, forced to compromise her independence, to "swallow shit" in order to retain the other person's emotional support. She experiences shame and self-contempt when she lets herself be used, and she fears she will succumb to exploitation that will obliterate her autonomous self:

S: I guess the thing that makes me feel the most ashamed personally doesn't have to do with any activity, like stealing or lying. It has to do more with, with myself. I will feel real ashamed and feel sick if I take shit from my boss or if I have a conversation—with a man, that is—and I don't get anything out of it; I mean if I talk to a man and, you know, feed his fantasy or whatever, and the outcome is that I get a bottle of champagne or I get to go out and have a bunch of free drinks and just listen to some jerk, right? If there is profit for me, I won't feel ashamed. I remember one instance—this is a good example for you. We were having some, this is where I used to work, this woman was my supervisor. Woman! She was just a girl, she was younger than me, but she was the supervisor of the office. Some of the times I figured, I tried to make friends with her, I tried to influence her, to have a better diet, to get more exercise, all this kind of bullshit. One day we were having like a party or something in this room and it was just a *party*, it was a function, right? And I got off work at 5:00, and it was like 4:55, and I had rapped to everybody there, and I was really sick (laugh) of the party, and I wanted to leave. I didn't like these people, by and large. She gave me a hard time. She embarrassed me. It was like, "It's not 5:00 yet, where, where are you going?" You know? And I didn't say anything about it (voice very loud). I didn't say, "Fuck you" (loud), you know, I didn't, I didn't deal with it, I just let her put me down like that, and I felt really sick, I just felt real, I guess [a] combination of things, I can still recall it, I was so angry but really not so much at her, as myself. . . . Well I just, I got out of there, I waited until 5:00 and I took off out of there, and I just thought, my God, what is happening to me! What am I in for, if I will let this happen. And then I just started fantasizing killing her and then I fantasized winning a big prize and winning a million dollars and inviting every single person I knew to this big millionnaire's—, but not inviting this young woman, and rubbing her face in it somehow. I just started thinking about all these things, and I rode my bicycle home and just thought, God, what's happening to me? That I let this kind of stuff go, and I was ashamed. I was real upset, really disturbed.
I: So you were ashamed because that felt like quite a weakness to you. . . ?
S: Yeah, yeah, that I let this happen. That right at that moment I didn't say, "Look, there's no difference between 4:55 and 5:00, there's no difference". . . . But I didn't say anything. I just sat down. I did what she said. And I guess I was ashamed of myself for being so easily ordered about, or I was ashamed of myself because I don't want to lose my job. . . . I'd worked in this office for 3 years and I thought, you know, "Josephine, if you eat any more shit, it's going to poison you." And I guess, I'm not only ashamed but sort of afraid that they've got me. I still feel like that sometimes: They've got me now; I'm in my secure job and if I'll be good each

year I'll get a raise and I may be up for a promotion or something, and they've got me now, where they want me, because I will listen to them and I'll be good and I'll just swallow all this shit, even though I know that it will poison me. I'll keep swallowing it because I want my income, and I want my security, and I want my health insurance, and . . . those things make me feel pretty bad.

Josephine is obsessed by a conviction that the wish to be reasonably comfortable inevitably leads to shameful enslavement and loss of personal integrity. She expressed this idea many times, for example, in the context of a fantasy that therapists try to stimulate collapse in their patients so that the patient will then depend entirely on the therapist. Out of her fear of being a shameful sucker, Josephine is tempted to stop cooking for her boyfriend, even though she loves to cook. She is concerned that she is giving more than she is getting, that she is being used. She is careful to seek psychotherapy from agencies that will accept her insurance, not just because such a plan is practical, but because she wants to make sure she isn't giving too much to her employer through her work. She wants to be certain she is getting back more than she gives. When Josephine begins to feel close to someone and experiences wishes to give love to that person, she often contrives to steal something from him or her as if to make clear that she is not giving her love while trusting blindly to the other's wish to give in return. She ruptures the relationship of trust through her thefts, and in effect she says to the person, "I will not trust your generosity and be made a sucker; I will take what I need." When she once overextended herself with a man and fell in love with him she felt, "Maybe I'm a little ashamed that I was sort of a sucker or something."

The Question of Oral Shame

The oral imagery and oral impulses associated with Josephine's shame probably have not passed unnoticed. Josephine feels ashamed of impulses to cling to others, to cry, to seek comfort, to overeat, to drink in order to quiet her fears, and to swallow pills (unless she can think of the pills as a dangerous gamble rather than as comfort). One must be careful here not to take the oral mode of the activities that stimulate Josephine's shame as proof that shame occurs in the child in the oral phase of development. Josephine's "oral shame" is not shame over oral indulgence per se. In fact, she sometimes glorifies oral behaviors, such as risky pill popping. Her shame focuses on the immaturity—the phase-inappropriateness—of her behavior and on the disparity between her behavior and her mother's values. Capacity to concern oneself with maturity and with another's values probably cannot be attributed to the child in the oral phase. More probably, shame will occur in the older child who displays these characteristically early traits and has now become concerned with her self-concept. Since Josephine's "oral" shame suggests application of later, learned standards to lingering behavior, the oral focus of her shame offers no support for Grinker's (1955) claim that the very young child has inborn standards of maturation, the departure from which will automatically stimulate shame.

Josephine's experiences of shame probably did not begin in the oral phase, perhaps not until the phallic phase, nevertheless, her shame is not well described as sexual shame: That is, she is not primarily ashamed of specifically sexual deficiencies; she is ashamed of her immaturity, her dependency, and her failures of self-control. The sine qua non of shame is the investment in particular, valued images of the self. Perhaps one reason that some writers associate shame with exclusively sexual (i.e., genital sexual) conflict is that the investment in clear images of the self occurs at about the same time as the clear investment in maleness or femaleness, and one's sexuality tends to be represented as an aspect, though not necessarily the central aspect, of the developing self-images. Also, primarily nonsexual shame will have sexual implications. For example, shame over dependency will make a boy feel emasculated even though he has no specific shame about the size of his penis. Finally, much shame *is* clearly focused on genital sexuality and these common and distinct instances of sexual shame may further contribute to the strong association between shame and sexual problems.

Sexual Shame in a Woman

Josephine is ashamed of many behaviors that have little to do with sexual behavior, but she does experience shame in relation to her sexual activity and her appearance. Josephine's sexual shame appears to follow neither the Freudian theory of shame as a reaction-formation against unacceptable desire nor the pattern of shame as an expression of feelings of genital inferiority, a pattern that Mayman (1974) describes. Josephine's sexual shame reflects her pervasive shame over giving much and getting little, thus becoming a sucker in her own eyes. The interviews make clear that Josephine's mother brought her contempt for weakness into the sexual arena, in full force. According to Josephine, her mother regarded as "a lot of crap" adolescent girls' interests in making themselves attractive with clothing and cosmetics. Mother told her daughter about intercourse, but as Josephine describes the exchange she gives the impression that her mother dealt with her own anxiety counterphobically by giving all the facts in a tough, crude, highly explicit fashion. As Josephine looks back on her mother's instructions to her, she is impressed by her mother's directness, but saddened by Mother's omission of any mention of warm feeling associated with sexual intimacy. Josephine learned to associate the feminine with the ridiculous, immature, and hysterical. For example, she says:

S: I would like to, you know, deal with things and be calm and not be umm—I'll say it, and not be like a female, okay? Not to exhibit hysterical reactions and a lot of crying and stuff, but I'm inclined to do these things.

As perceived by Josephine, Mother shows extreme intolerance of sexuality, especially when sexuality is seen as the woman's being a "jerk" by foolishly giving to an exploitative man:

S: [In high school] I wanted to look pretty, I wanted to look, to be a cute girl, you know. But I was sort of lucky, 'cause by the time high school started the fashion was like a Twiggy, and sort of the flatchested look and stuff, and models were like that, so even though I was sort of short and not really built like a model or anything, I was sort of glad to be sort of small-busted and also, at that time, like ninth grade, I realized that girls who were developed had even a sort of a tougher time, that people talked about 'em and teased 'em, and you know, tried to get 'em to wear tight clothes (laugh).
I: What did you imagine that would be like?
S: I figured that would be sort of worse. You know, like I didn't feel like I was very cute or attractive or anything but—oh, there was this one girl in my school, on one morning everyone was going to school, all the store windows, all the streets, it was plastered all over, "Carry gives, Carry gives." And I mean, there were a lot of jokes, what is [it], "Carry gives green stamps?" "Carry gives" (laugh) you know. But obviously the meaning was, that she *gives*. And that was horrible, like I sort of could relate to her and I felt really sorry for her.
I: Well, how did you imagine she would be feeling?
S: Oh, the first thing I wondered was like if her parents, what her parents would do when [they] saw this all over the town. . . .
I: Were you thinking particularly about the mother, or father, or—?
S: Mother. You know, I mean, I figured what would my mother do if she saw this. She would kill me.

Evident in the early part of this passage is an incipient shame over being insufficiently feminine (the type of shame Mayman [1974] describes). But the sense of shame and vulnerability associated with embracing femininity is so great that the potential shame of insufficient femininity is not elaborated. Boyishness is welcomed as a haven. To be a feminine girl is to be a sucker. The girl gives too freely and thus enrages her mother.

In the following passage, Josephine again communicates her shame over weakness and poor self-control. And here such shame is specifically associated with femininity, with being a girl who is a jerk in Mother's eyes due to her willingness to let a boy touch her sexually and due also to her inability to bear up stoically after she has been touched:

S: I had a boyfriend and we were fooling around and—he like, I don't think he really like penetrated me or did anything to me, but he did something to me that was strange, right? I mean, like there was some contact. . . . I was really scared. And. . . . I told my mother. I was so scared I didn't know what to do and, I don't know, isn't it funny, you'd think I would have told one of my girlfriends or something. I guess I knew how mad and how horrible my mom would be about it but, well maybe I also had a lot of faith in her to help me, you know, to understand that something weird happened. What, what'd she do? She hauled me down to her gynecologist and he checked me out and he told her everything was okay and the next day I got a period and it was forgotten about.

I: Well, how did you feel about this whole sequence of things, the way she reacted, going to the gynecologist—?

S: Oh, I don't know. On the one hand—it was a very split-up feeling—on the one hand, I was so glad 'cause I could tell her, but then maybe as soon as I had told her and she started wailing on me I was sorry that I had.

I: Well did she yell, get very upset?

S: I remember one sentence. I remember her kind of screaming at me, "Did he put it *in* you?"

I: She wasn't mincing words at that point.

S: No. She never minces words and she never did. I mean we, she minces words now, I don't know.

I: Well how did you feel about her saying that?

S: I think she was, I think she didn't like me telling her. Does that make sense? I think that she would have rather I didn't tell her, because I created such an upset in her. And maybe she sort of got out of having to deal with it by taking me to the doctor.

What follows is a later discussion of the same experience:

S: I just sort of remember, I can see like slices of just talk, you now, me being a wimp and crying and shit and trying to put the problem all on her, wanting her to make it all better, instead of taking responsibility or being tough or being cool about what I had done or not done or just been an asshole about, right? So I was being wimpy and shit. My mother was probably pretty fucking disgusted with me, and then I think she tried to make me feel better. She felt sorry for me because I was just such a weak, creepy kid . . . that's what I'm ashamed of you know, that clawing, whining, paralyzed side of my personality that just you know, I'm going to try to change and not be such a wimpy, whining girl. I want to get it together on my own.

The discussion of Josephine's sexual shame points to differences between Josephine's sexual shame and Polly's. Each woman's shame bears the mark of her broader self-doubts. Josephine is most concerned that feminine behavior will make her a contemptible sucker. For this reason, she is comfortable with the more aggressive aspects of sex but avoids the gentler aspects. For example, she does not like to sleep with a man after she has had intercourse with him. Polly is ashamed that she is sexually inexperienced. She is a virgin, a sexual nothing. And she fears that if she gave herself sexually, her partner would see she is fat, unattractive, and unexciting. She thinks that her partner might gossip about her appearance in her most vulnerable state and that he would have little interest in pursuing a relationship with her.

MATILDA: NOT WOMAN ENOUGH; MAN ENOUGH NEITHER

Questions About Anal and Phallic Shame

Erikson (1963) regards shame as a key affect of the anal phase of development. Others, for example Mayman (1974), believe that self-esteem failure in the phallic phase first ushers in shame. Freud's (1905/1953, 1908/1953, 1909/1953 1925/1953, 1926/1953) writing on shame as a reaction-formation against genital exhibitionism links shame with phallic-oedipal development. Caution is in order when we link an affect with a developmental phase. This kind of pairing tends to promote an unrealistically unitary view of an affect as a single state with a clear point of emergence. However, it does seem legitimate to argue that specifiable maturational events must predate the emergence of certain feeling states. For example, it is hard to conceive of any state remotely resembling adult shame in a 3 month old child. The concept of self, central to adult shame states, would not be sufficiently developed at so young an age. At this age there might exist feelings that could be placed on a developmental continuum with adult shame. Frustration with failure at attempted motor tasks might belong to such a continuum. Knapp (1967) hypothesizes that stranger anxiety is a precursor of shame:

> As an emotion, shame probably has innate roots. The retreating, clinging behavior seen in the first year and called "stranger *anxiety*" appears to be a

response with a strong inhibitory component, which is a precursor of later shyness, embarrassment and shame. Despite the label "anxiety" we should note differences between this behavior and the wild excitement or efforts at flight which characterize primitive panic. The "stranger anxiety" is more a shrinking and immobilization, an attempt to merge with the protective background. (p. 520)

The appearance in a 2 year old of feelings similar to adult shame would not be altogether surprising, nonetheless, it cannot be taken for granted. In discussing shame and humiliation in Chapter 4, I pointed to ways in which humiliation, with its primary emphasis on loss of power rather than loss of self-esteem, seems to be a more likely affect experience for the 2 year old than shame does. This argument is quite speculative but what might be said in support of it is that humiliation, as defined earlier, generally is an experience rooted in an interpersonal transaction in which one person dominates another. As defined, shame is essentially a self-reflective experience and one that can occur in the absence of a shaming other person. Given the nature of the interpersonal experience that defines humiliation, it seems likely that humiliation or related experiences would occur developmentally earlier than shame.

Several research subjects showed clear shame themes centered both on anal concerns and on phallic concerns. These cases are of interest in documenting adult shame responses to anal traits, but they do not prove that the child of 2 years felt ashamed. The child might have felt frustrated, enraged, or humiliated in situations that only later, after further maturation and defense formation, came to be regarded as sources of shame. The point to be made here parallels that made in reference to Josephine's "oral" shame. Her oral behaviors presumably became shameful only when she labeled them as infantile and phase-inappropriate. She would not have done this in the oral phase. The following shame themes were derived from four interviews with Matilda, a woman in her late twenties who said that her irrepressible curiosity had led her to volunteer for the research. She is a lively woman who appeared to have a need to be active and in charge in order to avoid feeling vulnerable to others' actions and to their opinions of her. She used her active style in order to try gamely to respond to the interviewer's questions, despite her obvious discomfort and annoyance with personal questions that embarrassed her:

1. She feels deficient in general attractiveness, especially in feminine social graces and feminine appearance.
2. She feels she has qualities that actively conflict with one important image she holds of femininity. The suspect qualities are not

deficiencies but are active, aggressive failings: she is crude, dirty, stubborn, and defiant.

3. She feels incompetent and unable to do things well, and she compensates by investment in supercompetence. One example, which could stand for many that appeared in the protocol, is a memory of not being able to learn to ride a bicycle and feeling "tremendously embarrassed" and "terribly humiliated."

4. She feels that she might want someone but be unwanted herself. "Unwanted" has a predominantly sexual meaning in this context.

The second entry in Matilda's shame-themes list introduces her shame of the anal traits of "crudeness, dirtiness, stubbornness, and defiance." The anal traits have been subsumed under phallic-narcissistic shame. That is, anality is shameful because Daddy's little girl of 4 or 5 is expected *no longer to be* stubborn and messy. She is expected to be sweet, cooperative, and capable. Despite this organization of the shame-themes list, the actual description by Matilda of shameful anal traits leaves unanswered the question of whether she felt ashamed of these traits around age 2, during the anal phase, or whether the shame appeared later when she regressed to anality or failed to progress beyond it to the degree she felt was expected in her family. What can be stated with certainty is that Matilda feels ashamed because she is not successfully feminine. Her anal traits interact with her feminine failures in at least two ways. When she is anally out of control, for example messy or verbally nasty, her anality intensifies her belief that she is not feminine. When she uses anal-retentive traits in order to function in an orderly and effective (characterologically obsessive-convulsive) way, her anality enhances her self-esteem and diminishes the pain of failed femininity. Matilda feels much more confident of success when she pursues the anal virtues of orderliness, punctuality, and diligence than when she tries to be delicate, receptive, and attractive. Thus she generally invests herself in the anal virtues, some of which seem admirably masculine to her. She becomes contemptuous of feminine assets that others display. Anality enhances or diminishes Matilda's self-esteem, depending on whether she is exploiting ego-syntonic anal character traits or betraying ego-dystonic anal impulses. Openly expressed anal sadism or messiness always remains ego-dystonic. When recognized in the self, it brings shame. When identified in others, it brings disgust.

The following passage illustrates Matilda's vulnerability to shame when she acknowledges and makes visible her wishes to be regarded as feminine. Anality enters as a defense against vulnerability. She prefers to identify with the anticipated aggressor and to become an anally judgmental, emotionally closed and harsh critic. She dismisses her feminine creations as "crap" and destroys them. She also uses the anal character defense of practicality to reduce her narcissistic vulnerability; she claims that she discarded her writings for an utterly practical reason, lack of storage space:

S: In junior high school I turned out reams and reams of really godawful poetry. . . . One of the first acts (laugh) of my adult life was to destroy all that. . . . I used to save everything I wrote, you know, absolutely everything, and I had boxes and boxes of the stuff, rooms of the stuff, and part of it was just, was just storage space and another part of it was I thought about, you know, God forbid I should get hit by a truck, uh, this was stuff that I wrote for myself. . . . You know, even when you *do* write something, it's terrifying, even if you're proud of it or you think you've done a good job or it's the best thing you've written so far—although you hope fervently that you will improve—when you take it up, when you submit it to be published, you're already letting somebody, you're already sharing this part—although it might be a piece of some sort of fantasy that you've had that you've turned into fiction, you know, what else is fiction but somebody's, some little private fantasy, and then—if it gets published, Good Lord, you've held up a part of your soul for the world to take potshots at, and that's something that you've *chosen* to expose. And the idea of somebody seeing or reading things that I had written and things that I had thought about and considered that was never my intention to share, to have exposed, I didn't like that. . . . There was of course reams and reams of the sort of things that I suppose every girl heavily into puberty turns out (laugh)—dying and desperate love for some guy that never looks at you, that kind of crap, hopelessly romantic. . . . I never wrote anything erotic if that's what [you're looking for]. . . . It just strikes me as being unfair . . . it sort of bothers me because I write knowing that—although some people have chosen to, you know, give their papers or something, but having, you know, your rough drafts and . . . it's not fair, that's not what you—you're not done with it. . . . It just didn't seem fair to have that examined and criticized and judgments made about you, as though—because nobody would ever take into consideration that that is an unfinished work.

The following passages further illustrate Matilda's sense of shameful failure as a woman and her vulnerability when she tries to be feminine. Anality again appears primarily as a means of extricating herself from the self-esteem dilemma. When necessary, she can fall back on successful anal character traits in order to establish a self-image as a clean, efficient, rather masculine person. This defensive position is appealing in part because Matilda has wishes to be masculine as well as wishes to be more feminine:

S: I'm sensitive about weight . . . I'm frequently sensitive about it, I'm frequently mistaken for a man, which isn't at all surprising because I'm not (makes noises and gestures to imply large busted) in front and I wear my hair short and a lot of my clothing is men's clothing, but still (laugh), I get mistaken for a man a lot . . . and I feel awful if somebody points out that I have made an inappropriate comment in a social setting. Two years ago I had hair down to my waist but it was a nuisance to take care of. When you wash your hair every day, you know, lead an active life, it just got to be too much of a nuisance to keep this long hair. The cost of having long hair was too great, and it didn't matter to my husband whether I was bald or, you know, Cheryl Tiegs, so I keep it short for practical reasons. . . . As far as my other clothing goes, it's uh—I feel very comfortable in jeans and t-shirts. I do not like to wear nylons because you have to be careful with them and they run easily. . . . It's been so long since I dressed up regularly that I feel like I'm a—almost an impostor (laugh) when I'm dressed up.

[I remember] one birthday party getting a doll and losing one of its gloves. Can't tell you how many days I went back out there looking for its glove. You know, your little doll is—especially when it's new, before you tried to wash its hair and ruin it (laugh), the little doll is so perfect and clean, there's nothing broken, nothing scratched, its little dress is all nice and [its] shiny little nylon gloves, they were white. She was my only doll with brown eyes, my only doll that was not brunette. Her name was Tina (laugh), I remember quite vividly. She was very special. I was so excited about it, 'cause my sisters had dolls like this, you know, here was me, *I* had one too and this is great, first day losing one of her gloves.

In the following passages, anality appears in its messy, expressive form rather than its defensive form. As such, it must draw fire from Matilda. Anality is indicted as disgusting rather than shameful because it is not seen as a current feature of the self. It is something at a distance: It is an aspect of others or an aspect of herself as a child. Matilda's indictments of anal messiness occur in contexts that suggest some conceptual fusion between anal messiness and genital messiness. It remains unclear whether genital messiness becomes shameful because it is like (shameful) anal messiness or vice versa. Perhaps the evolution of meaning proceeds in both directions:

S: I must have been disgusting as a child.
I: Why do you say that. . . ?
S: Because you smell if you don't wash your hair (laugh).
I: You also said that you thought of yourself as kind of a bratty kid. . . .
S: I'm sure I was a real pest. Mom just says I was impossible to get a hold of when she wanted to wash my hair. I imagine I was just a real pouty, bratty little—I can imagine myself pouting a lot and refusing to do things.

S: I can forgive people for being disorganized although I may find it irritat-
     ing, but dirty—well it's tacky to say it but there are friends of mine who
     (laugh) I won't go eat at their house, I won't eat off their borrowed—one
     woman had this really neat pan that I borrow occasionally and the first
     thing I do is wash it (laugh).

I: She just leaves things sticky or—?

S: Yeah, my Mom always taught me that you—two rooms, if you had to let
     the whole rest of the house go to Hell—of course Mom would never say
     that, go to pot—um, the bathroom and kitchen should be clean. And you
     go into some of these bathrooms and the ledge of the bathtub . . . really
     obviously has not been dusted in a very long time (laugh). . . . You sort of
     wonder whether or not anything else is clean.

I: And so what kind of feeling do you have about it, that if you walked in—?

S: Sort of disgusted.

I: Um-hm, would that be the feeling with the kitchen things too, with the
     pan?

S: Yeah, really disgusted. . . . My husband was living with this old roommate
     before I was his roommate and I wouldn't sit on their toilet seat (laugh), it
     was terrible. . . . And the bathroom is (laugh)—you go into somebody's
     house you expect it to be a little bit cleaner than a gas station. News-
     papers on the floor, so what? But a dirty toilet seat, that's something else.

In the second of the two passages quoted, Matilda is disgusted with
something outside herself that would bring shame were it her own
behavior. The passage demonstrates one form of relationship between
shame and disgust: Both can express disapproval of an aspect of the
self. The passage suggests an additional relationship between shame
and disgust. Matilda's disgust, and potentially her shame, sounds like
a reaction-formation established in the face of forbidden genital or anal
interests. In Matilda's case, as in Mary's, shame (and for Matilda,
disgust, too) functions both as a straightforward registration of traits
that signify feminine inadequacy (e.g., her obesity and her masculinity) and also as a reaction-formation against the wish proudly to exhibit to others certain traits or behaviors.

Idealization as a Precondition of Shame

It has been easy to document Matilda's feelings of inadequate femininity and her shame over such a deficiency. Understanding the causes for
her convictions and for her shame as a response to them is more
difficult. Direct teaching within the family is the simplest explanation
for Matilda's beliefs about herself. Parents often teach a child that he
or she is deficient in some respect. Or the child might develop such an
idea by comparing himself or herself with older siblings or with the

parents themselves. More complex explanations of Matilda's shame include defense-oriented conceptualizations and identity-oriented conceptualizations. A sample defense-oriented explanation would argue that oedipal guilt (or a condensation of oedipal guilt and pregenital guilt) forced Matilda to negate evidence of her femininity and to exaggerate indications of her feminine failures. In one passage, she describes her father's envious and provocative comment that Matilda's husband "has it lucky" with respect to his sex life. The passage lends some credence to the defense-oriented explanation of Matilda's shame, as do Matilda's many comments about her mother's saintliness; the image of the saint would appear to cut two ways in that saintly women are admirable but not sexy. One identity aspect correlated with shame is evident in Matilda's interviews. She idealizes the parent with whom she compares herself. To the extent that Matilda idealizes her mother but views herself without such distinction, she has placed herself in a position of vulnerability to shame:

S: My mother, she's—God, she's a saint. . . . She's a delightful woman, she has always done her damnedest to be all, the ideal mother, and it may not have always been my particular idea of exactly what was (sigh)—she has always sincerely tried to do everything right, not in a paranoid or frenzied fashion but seemed to fit very easily and very, very well into the role of mother and wife, and was a very giving, hard working, generous person. . . . Mom is a—mom is a lady, she's a lady, a classy woman. . . . Mom is, my mother, I do admire her a great deal. She is, she wouldn't say shit if she stepped on it. . . . In the first place Mother would never step on it! . . . She's very calm, and she's very reasoned. She's a very loving, very giving, caring person. I just, I really admire her a great deal. Um, she always makes me feel somehow that I'm too big and have too many angles and am dirtier than I ought to be. [She's] a wonderful, wonderful woman.

I: Does she make you feel bad in those ways just by comparison, or are there ways she really can *put* you there?

S: Oh no, no, Mother would never do that. She's just . . . a very classy person. I cannot imagine my mother opening her mouth and saying something really stupid that would hurt somebody.

Idealization plays a role in many shame pictures. In childhood, idealizations are inevitable due to the parents' emotional indispensability and to their status, intelligence, and ability relative to the child. If the child feels intimately affiliated with the parents, the parents' strength feels like the child's own, and it serves as a strong protection against shame. The child does not feel that he or she must be able to perform every task or defeat every enemy. Early on, it is enough that Dad or Mom can beat up the offender or fix the broken toy. The child's identification with the idealized parent partially explains the trauma of learning that one is adopted. Suddenly the parents whose strength constitutes a large portion of one's pride and identity can feel as if they are not a part of one's self. Their strength can no longer be used so comfortably. The child whose parent is distant, actively rejecting, or actively rejected by the child will be shame-vulnerable, both with respect to the specific things he cannot do on his own and because he feels bad that he has no one to do them for him. The absence of the protector is itself accepted to be a sign of defectiveness. Various coping routes are taken. Inflated attitudes about the self can serve to deny shame and anxiety about vulnerability. Or the child may work frantically to develop certain skills. The resulting areas of competence then are kept in view at all times. The areas of incompetence and the parental unavailability are excluded from attention. Or the child, and later the adult, may engage in an unending search for an idealized self-object in ways that Kohut (1971) examines. When the parent who should lend strength actively shames the child, identification with the aggressor may provide the child relief from distress. Such identification allows the child the needed affiliation with parental strength, although the affiliation is accomplished only through a trick of consciousness that allows one to shame oneself as if one were another.

Early challenges to self-esteem occur for the normal child whose wishes oppose those of the parents. The child must not only defend his or her wishes but must now do so without the added strength of the idealized parent who suddenly has become the opponent. The child must retain the strength of the remembered, loved parent even while facing the parent who now actively, articulately opposes the child's will. A second normal developmental sequence takes the child from the period when shame is itself imagined to be an experience peculiar to childish inadequacy, to the point where the child recognizes shame as a normal experience to be faced and considered, not permanently outgrown. This recognition obviously cannot predate registration of the parents' own imperfections.

A child with two appropriately affectionate parents still may encounter shame-difficulty if the parents have major conflict between them. Such conflict undermines the child's capacity to feel strengthened through affiliation with one or the other parent. Each parent's values and capacities are cast into doubt and the child is left with no definite source of strength. Instead, he has a pervasive shame that both of the parents with whom he identifies are defective. Or the child may opt to retain an embattled idealization of one parent while vigorously rejecting the other parent. The latter route eventually creates its own trouble, not only because guilt wreaks havoc but also because the child is deprived of important identifications and relationships, no matter whether he or she berates the parent of the same sex or the parent of the opposite sex. If the child later tries to reown an identification with the once rejected parent, he or she must face anxiety about whether the parent has any good aspects that can be integrated, as well as guilt for earlier having despised the parent. Psychoanalytic case studies tend to explore failings of the individual parent in relation to the child and to neglect the interplay between the two parents' values and behavior patterns.

A child's premature recognition that a parent is himself or herself ashamed (e.g., Slim's mother) also jeopardizes self-esteem. Idealization is aborted before the child's own strengths (and intellectual sophistication) have developed to a point where he or she can recognize that it is possible to live securely and with self-esteem despite imperfections. The child is left with great doubt about how he or she will manage, knowing that his or her own current skills are not sufficient and suspecting that the parent's abilities are not great either.

Idealization of parents is shame-generative in early childhood, but it is often shame-generative in adulthood (see Frank, Matilda, and Josephine). The adult who continues to idealize a parent, or parent figure, can escape shame only through a regression or a longstanding developmental deviation that allows one to remain undifferentiated from the parent and thus not in competition, or through a circumscription of identity that keeps one from competing with the parent in the area of the parent's supposed perfection. Several research subjects idealized one or both parents. While some explicitly denied competitive feeling directed toward the idealized parent, shame themes appeared centering on points of inferiority to that parent. At times, subjects retained idealizations out of a need to deny current hostile feeling toward the parent, or out of a need to deny that past hostility had a damaging effect on the parent. Powerful teaching within the childhood family also may sustain idealizations by forcing the growing child to risk a severe, frightening break with parents and siblings in order to revise a dominant family viewpoint. Many forms of separation anxiety, all resulting from feared loss of perfect childhood love objects, can sustain idealizations. So can the fear that one is worthless unless merged with an idealized parent or parent-figure (Kohut, 1971). Whatever the source of an adult's idealizations, they always become shame-productive once one experiences oneself as separate from and subject to comparison with the idealized other.

Embarrassment and Unsuccessful Integration of Feelings

We have seen that Matilda cannot easily think of herself as an attractive woman. At times she avoids concerning herself with attractiveness by investing energy only in activities to be evaluated on grounds of diligence, not beauty or charm or cleverness. However, she does not altogether harden herself against responsiveness to sexual stimulation. She responds with considerable emotion when sexual topics are introduced, but the emotions, especially the pleasurable excitement and the impulses to look and exhibit, are not well integrated into Matilda's self-concept. When these feelings are stimulated, they appear to erupt into existence on their own, without the full consent and supervision of a self-organization that in effect says, "I own these feelings, they are part of my self." Such states of nonintegrated feeling match the state described in Chapter 4 and designated as embarrassment. When confronted with sexual topics, Matilda responds with emotion that combines excited pleasure with discomfort regarding how to own the feelings or integrate them into her self-concept. In the passage to follow, she displays her embarrassment while simultaneously describing it:

S: I changed my clothes in the bathroom for a couple of years [to avoid changing in front of Gregory Peck's poster hanging over the bed].[2]
I: Well, what was the feeling?
S: Well, I mean, my God, Gregory Peck! And here I am gonna strip naked in front of him; I couldn't do that (laugh)! It would simply be inappropriate. I don't really think I could strip down in front of anybody's picture on the wall. . . just, I mean, I think that probably one of the most vulnerable states to be in, in your entire—and all—is naked, all your imperfections there, you know, without the benefit of clothing, to lift up or to push in, or emphasis or de-emphasize, you're just standing there naked with no place to hide (laugh). In front of him, no, I couldn't do it.

This description of a male film star, given by an adult woman, suggests that she retains a childlike, idealized view of her father as a physically and emotionally perfect person who is not messily human like she is. Her idealization of her mother contributes to shame because she must compare herself to Mother. The idealization of Father can also lead to shame, for example, when she extends it to her husband and sees him as contemptuous of her imperfections. But in her fantasy life, she need

---

[2]Gregory Peck is not the actual object of Matilda's admiration and he unfortunately does not have all the traits of the original who is a logical, dispassionate man devoted to reason yet quietly conveying a good heart.

not be the equal of the idealized father. She can enjoy him as a highly erotic love object who stirs sexual wishes. She cannot easily own these wishes but neither must she fully disavow them. The following passage points to a fantasy that the perfect erotic father will want to admire and enjoy her:

S: Having all your imperfections displayed right out there, no place to hide, nothing to hide behind, just there in front of somebody who has perfect control and perfect body and perfect everything, and there you are, such a dumpy old frumpy person. . . . Oh, I could be somewhat unclothed in front of it, it wouldn't bother me to, as long as there was between my crotch and [indicates area from crotch to breasts] covered (laugh). I did my situps and all that kind of stuff . . . It turned out to be a good thing that I wasn't changing my clothes in the bedroom because it turned out that my neighbors were, or one of them, was a little bit weird (laugh). Used to climb up on top of the roof and look in my bedroom, so it's just as well. And maybe all the times that I thought the poster was watching me, you know, was not particularly, not necessarily wrong (laugh).

The uncomfortably excited quality of Matilda's response to the attentive movie star may remind the reader of Polly's embarrassment when her father compliments her violin playing, and thus he stimulates an exhibitionistic fantasy that is weakly integrated into her identity, although the two women probably differ in reasons for not comfortably accepting their exhibitionism. A later discussion of narcissistic repair strategies will further illustrate Matilda's maintenance of sexual wishes through a special fantasy world that is out of commerce with daily reality.

All pleasure experiences that stimulate conflicted exhibitionistic wishes leave Matilda uneasy. The pleasurable excitement she describes in the following passage appears to be a close kin to embarrassment. The passage illustrates the relationship between embarrassment and other states of mild disorganization and overstimulation occurring in response to pleasure that is weakly integrated into the identity. She is asked about her feelings in response to a particular type of accomplishment:

S: Wonderful (laugh). You just float on air, it's just great. You just feel like you can conquer the world when someone that you think does well with something says, "Hey kid, you're doing all right on this one." You really feel like, "ahhh" [vocalized non-word], it's really good. It's wonderful.

Asked whether she might do something or talk with someone at that point, she answers:

S: I don't know about talking with anybody. I'm likely to just sit down for a while . . . I have to wait for it to wear off a little bit (laugh) before I can concentrate on anything else. You just sit there like a pumpkin in the corner and grin (laugh).

PRISTINE: DIRTY SEX, DIRTY AGGRESSION

Sexual Shame with Roots in Narcissistic Stress and Aggression-Conflict

Pristine is a college student who volunteered to participate in the research. She is a pretty, petite young woman who appeared to try hard to be poised, sophisticated and charming. For the most part she succeeded but she gave the impression of needing to expend considerable energy to control herself. When her anger was incited in relation to something she was discussing, she quickly lost her sweet, even demeanor and became excited, vindictive, and without mercy for those she saw as deliberately abusing her. Pristine acknowledges little shame experience (though she is often "self-conscious," a state to be discussed later). She did label as shameful an early adolescent episode of being teased and pinched by boys. She also acknowledged feeling ashamed of her father whom she described as a lewd, uncouth, alcoholic man whose demeaning and poorly controlled behavior contrasts with her own and her mother's propriety. When juxtaposed with Pristine's current attitude toward sexual activity, these two acknowledged shame experiences strongly suggest Pristine's continuing potential to feel ashamed of herself as a dirty, improper person, especially as a person dirtied through sexual interaction. Asked about sexual attitudes, Pristine spoke of her wishes for men to "put her on a pedestal." She likes the idea that a man would refrain from touching her because he respects her and feels that to touch her would be to dirty her. She is gratified when men demonstrate great caution and anxiety in their sexual approaches. She experiences minimal sexual arousal, but instead seems to find an attenuated excitement in controlling and manipulating a man's sexual response. Though Pristine acknowledges only a wish to be idealized and not an overt fear of being dirtied, her wishes for men to regard her as too clean to touch, and her memories of shame when pinched and teased in adolescence, strongly suggest a potential to feel that she is shamefully dirty due to sexual interests. Other data suggest that she also can feel shamefully unimportant to a man. That is, she feels herself to be a mere object over which men excite themselves in order to gratify base needs. She is not a lady of importance and respectability with whom men would exercise caution and deference. She is a dirty little girl who is of little real consequence. Beneath considerable pretense about her sophistication, generosity, and gentility lies a concern that she is a bad girl, a slut who is sinful and also worthless or insignificant.

Pristine's potential to feel ashamed that she is sexually dirty and personally insignificant originates in several provices. Turning back to Pristine's adolescent experience of being touched and teased by young boys, we might ask what would have been necessary in order for her to experience this type of attention as flattering and pleasantly exciting rather than shaming. She would have needed a solid sense of her own attractiveness and value and a relaxed attitude toward her own aggression. These feelings would have allowed her to confront the teasing head-on, to tease back and thus, by presenting herself as strong and attractive, to engage the boys positively and to expose the admiring interest that probably underlay their teasing. Instead, in response to the teasing she caves in. She accepts the demeaning component of the communication and feels violated by the attention. Presumably, Pristine caved in partly because she did not carry into the teasing situation a sufficiently strong sense of her attractiveness and worth with which to convert the situation into a pleasurable or at least a tolerable one. Part of the explanation would appear to reside in her relationship to her father. She remembers her father as someone likely to demean her, to make her feel unimportant, stupid, and unattractive. Those of her relationships to men that seem transference-laden suggest that Pristine also experienced her father as a tease. He would stimulate her interest in him and give her reason to believe that she might be the favored woman in his life; then he would disappoint her. She would be left not only with the frustration of her wishes, but with the shame associated with recognizing that she was more interested in him than he was in her. In her current relationships to men, Pristine often teases them sexually then turns away. She told the interviewer of her reaction when her boyfriend needed an operation. The surgery made it necessary for him to abstain from sex for approximately a month and made it painful for him to get an erection. She had always discouraged his sexual advances and never had she had intercourse with him, but she planned to kiss and caress him after his surgery as a "joke" because she knew that he couldn't have sex with her then and that arousal would be uncomfortable for him. Pristine's pleasure in this prank suggests that, for her, the person who is excited but frustrated, the one who is left with undischargeable sexual excitement, is vulnerable and humiliated. Pristine's image of the person who is left with romantic excitement and arousal, which the other declines to satisfy, is similar to Polly's images of loving others who find her uninteresting, and to Josephine's imagery of being a sucker who wants to give to a mother who regards the girl's overtures with contempt. The similarity among the themes suggests that Pristine's teasing themes, like Polly's and Josephine's themes of rejection, may derive in part from early mother-child interactions even though the themes now appear most prominently in relation to men. The central issue appears to be the management of wishes to give to others and to be given to by them. Rather than seeing their affection or arousal as gifts that bring pleasure to self and other, Polly, Josephine, and Pristine regard their own wishes toward others as humiliating, childish needs that the other will view with contempt or amusement.

Pristine's sense of herself as someone actively demeaned by an exciting father and as one whose sexual and affectionate wishes are not reciprocated is an adequate explanation for her experience of sexual attention as demeaning. Given her belief that open expressions of delight over a man's attention bring humiliating rejection by him, her inability to experience the positive, exciting side of a young boy's teasing is understandable. But her belief that she will be dirtied by sex also requires explanation. Her relationship to her father again is relevant. Her father emerges as an aggressive, alcoholic man whose occasional attention to his daughter was so rough and intrusive that she might easily have experienced him as wanting to soil or degrade or dirty her. The idea of dirtiness appears in part to be a concretization of the experience of aggressive or hate-filled relatedness. Hatefulness toward another person often means a wish to degrade or to soil them. Pristine must also have wanted to behave in a hostile, "dirty" manner toward the father who so disappointed her. The threat of recalling these emotions must be strong in current heterosexual interactions, thus she is further motivated to insist on her own purity when in those situations. Finally, the identity of the dirty, aggressive girl might at times have tempted Pristine in that it brought her close, through identification, to a father she spurned but also loved and preferred at times to Mother. Feelings of fondness and erotic excitement in response to Father emerged clearly in a number of early memories and adolescent fantasies.

If Pristine at times experienced her father as hating her and wishing to dirty her, and if she entertained similar impulses toward him, the resulting sense of vulnerability to dirtiness would have added to an earlier source of feeling dirty in Pristine's life. Powerful envy and hate experienced primarily in the context of the mother-daughter relationship already had left Pristine convinced that she was a bad or dirty person. Thus the registration of aggression emanating from Father to self and the prior experience of the self as hateful both contribute to a sense of the self as potentially dirty.

Pristine routinely copes with aggression through projection. She sees other people (especially her sister and her father) as compromised by despicable emotions such as envy. Many of her descriptions of others seem transparently determined by projection and reaction-formation:

S: I was never a selfish child. And I was very quiet. My sister was very demanding. . . . She was selfish! She *was*. She was never very nice to me. We didn't even get along until I was a senior in high school, because she wasn't—she *did* demand everything . . . and I did everything for her. She was, you know, jealous. . . . She had this boy, or one of these boys would be interested in her, and she really didn't care. She just was interested in the conquest of getting their attention; she demands a lot of attention. And when she had all their attention, was the center of attention, she almost *used* people. She did, she used people (excited, vehement tone of voice from this generally sweet-toned young woman).

This passage suggests that Pristine's wishes for attention, in sexual and other forms, are attended by unacceptable hatred for those with whom she must compete. The hatred that accompanies sexual competitiveness likely provides a partial explanation for Pristine's conscious indifference to sex. Once she allows herself to become interested in men, she engages not only her fears that they will reject or humiliate her, but also her fear that her own hateful competitiveness and envy will find expression. Pristine's competitive hatred of other women, easily stirred in sexual situations, represents one agent that will dirty her. Using a psychoanalytic framework we would say that the fear of being dirtied through genital sex is a fear based on regression to an anal-sadistic conceptualization of sex as a situation in which one person dominates and soils another while in a state of rage or hatred. Pristine fears that she will be the victim of such demeaning attention because she deserves punishment for her dirty aggression. She will prove herself to be a dirty, bad person and not a sophisticated, controlled, genteel person.

Pristine's wishes for physical privacy relate to her fears that men will touch her and dirty her, but also to feelings that she is delicate and may be injured or overwhelmed by an aggressive man. Matilda's insistence on privacy (e.g., of her writing) relates to fears that a man will find her laughable rather than feminine and alluring. Each woman's comments imply that the man may be too indelicate with her and may harm her. For example, Matilda destroyed some of her writing out of a fear she might be "hit by a truck" and, following that, people might "go into her drawers" and scrutinize her incomplete, adolescent poetry without keeping in mind that the poetry was unfinished. Both women feel at times that they are delicate in ways that go unheeded by men. This sense of oneself as delicate and vulnerable to injury may well characterize most very young girls interacting with their fathers. It also may characterize pubertal girls whose fantasies of vaginal penetration by a large man are beginning to color pervasively their sense of self. For Matilda and Pristine, the early sense of delicacy appears to have fed an adult sense of excessive openness to shame-stimulating insults from men.

Intolerance for aggression within the self will intensify the woman's images of vulnerability to a brutish man. Projection of one's own aggressiveness (including aggressive sexuality) onto the physically stronger man leads to a distorted view of the woman as totally defenseless and to a view of the man as an unfeeling animal. In the face of actual sexual aggression from a man, the woman who has denied all personal aggressiveness is left with the choice either to submit to violence or to assert herself in a way that runs counter to her belief that she is entirely passive and gentle.

Women who retain a profound sense of their own delicacy and vulnerability deny their strength and aggressiveness and cling to a self-image that was realistic when they were small children dealing with adult men. The potential advantages of such a self-concept include freedom from confronting one's own aggressiveness and retention of the belief in an omnipotent father figure. The more mature woman might retain the capacity to feel periodically delicate in relation to a man—for example, during gentle, intimate moments—without retaining a pervasive sense of the self as frail, delicate, childlike, or devoid of aggression or initiative. Pristine's story, like so many others, points to constant interactions between poor aggression-management and development of narcissistic problems accompanied by shame experience or shame potential.

Self-Consciousness and Shame

Pristine claims seldom to have experienced shame other than in the situations already cited. However, she acknowledges that she is self-conscious. Her self-consciousness consists of constant awareness of the self, which is experienced as functioning under the critical scrutiny of others. Self-consciousness differs from shame, as Pristine defines that state, in that it carries less implication of a specific defect that she has identified in herself. Instead, it involves continuous vigilance regarding all aspects of her functioning and continual awareness of others watching her. Often others are assumed to watch with hostile intentions. Self-consciousness can have a range of dynamic meanings, some of which were enumerated in Chapter 4. Pristine's self-consciousness appears to result primarily from projection of impulses to watch others in a hostile or demeaning fashion. Her state of self-consciousness is as much her indictment of the other's cruelty as it is an identification of her own weaknesses:

S: There's always been a group . . . they were always against me—they always made me feel very insecure and very guilty about every action I would do because I felt that they were watching me and evaluating me and passing judgment and making negative criticism. And I've always felt under attack and threatened by that. I think that kind of goes along with the insecurity.

Pristine projects her own hostile and suspicious watching-of-others and assumes that they are the ones who watch her. And she strengthens her belief in her own goodness and cleanliness through reaction-formations, which allow her to experience herself as unselfish, sweet, and proper. The assumption that one can see through the other person and see his or her true intentions frequently accompanies projection. And the other may be experienced as seeing through the self or trying to do so. In Pristine's case, since she denies any hostile or selfish feelings, she must view others as *falsely* imagining that they see through her; that is, they see the evil they wish to see, not an evil that is actually present. But clearly Pristine's belief that she is "looked into" derives from some feeling that there is something bad inside her to be seen and that others will be successful in seeing it. Thus her self-consciousness involves a partial boundary failure, an experience of self and others who are transparent with respect to hostile intentions. She must watch herself continuously once she believes others are watching her. She must determine what they are going to see in order to institute new controls over those negative traits that she thinks are visible. If a person directs *all* his or her attention toward the other's assumed hostile watching and none toward the self in its vigilant posture, then the person goes beyond self-consciousness to paranoia.

Pristine's interviews include a focus on loving, longingful watching, in addition to the focus on hostile watching. The wish to stay in touch with an insufficiently attentive mother by watching her lovingly may even have predated and underlain the hostile watching. Whether hateful or loving, watching represents a passive form of attachment that is recognized as not injurious to the other, except where magical thinking prevails. Pristine experienced her mother as frail and as condemning of selfish, overtly aggressive people; thus passive attachment through watching might have seemed more acceptable and benign than overt demandingness. The current, continual watching of the self may represent in part a perpetuation of the mother-watching. When a child grows older and must be separated from its mother, if that loss cannot be tolerated, heightened watching of others and of the self may serve the same infantile holding on and controlling functions that early watching of Mother could serve.

Pristine kept watch over Mother, both to protect and to control. The theme of watching pervades Pristine's imagery. Pristine wishes her mother would watch her and not watch the "demanding" sister. She watches her mother moving through the world as a pretty lady, and she hopes thus to stay intimate with this loved image. But the effort goes astray in part because she cannot help but perceive that Mother does not turn her prettiness toward Pristine alone. The prettiness makes Mother a woman for men. Pristine finds herself enraged at the abandonment and enraged further because now she must compete with Mother for Pristine's other loved one, Father, and feel hopeless to succeed. Thus, Pristine's watching turns critical. She detests the pretty face she wanted to love and she thinks of it only as a face prettier than her own. Her earliest memory depicts her watching her mother. Mother is looking at herself in the mirror while she puts makeup on her eyes. The eye imagery in this case appears to relate to hostile and envious watching. The idea of being shamed by someone's watching eyes follows only indirectly in that she is shameful because she is so nasty and hostile. In the makeup memory, Mother is preparing to go out for the evening. Pristine is thinking that she would like to dress up like Mother and go out, and she is wondering how Mother puts on the makeup without poking herself in the eyes. The memory seems to carry the theme of regret that Mother is watching herself and worrying about her own beauty and her plans with Father, rather than watching Pristine or helping Pristine to feel beautiful and have pleasure. Pristine's regrets stimulate the fantasy of Mother poking herself in her pretty, but inattentive eyes.

In her adult life, Pristine always feels that all eyes are on her, critically watching. Either they dissect her, or point to her imperfections, or they watch with jealousy because she is so beautiful. The sense of others watching appears to derive in part from the wish, never abandoned, that Mother pay attention to her. Her sense of being alive seems invested in the watcher's eyes as much as it inheres in her own feelings and sensations. But of course the watching she imagines cannot be benignly admiring. She despises her watchers too much and is too critical of them for her to imagine that they could be pleased with her successes.

The sexual focus of many of Pristine's shame themes follows from her investment in sexual competition with Mother. She assumes that such hostile competition causes Mother and others to attack her beauty. The sexual focus of the themes also appears to grow out of Pristine's early investment in her beautiful mother as someone she might herself love and possess, who does not return her love and admiration. The more Pristine feels defective in relation to recollections of Father's insults or Mother's neglect, the more she buoys herself up with grandiose ideas of her own beauty and her power over men; and the more she becomes self-conscious in expectation that "whatever I say they're going to take back into their rooms and just dissect it apart, you know, try to look into me."

In thinking about the various roots of self-consciousness, basic attitudes toward the self and experiences of self-other boundaries become important. The self-conscious person does not trust that the self can function safely without constant supervision. He may fear causing harm to another if he does not carefully watch his hostility. He may also fear being harmed by an omnipotent external agent if he is not watchful. Premature failures of parental authority and omnipotence might lead a child to feel vulnerable to injury or to doing injury. Thus the instituting of self-consciousness as an internally generated parental voice initially might be experienced as supportive. Such self-consciousness becomes a torment if one never can let it abate so that one can function without actively watching oneself. The capacity to watch oneself, to be self-conscious, is an ego asset that may become a burden when used in desperation by an ego under stress from within or without.

Self-consciousness may appear during periods of transition into defense decompensation or during periods of integration of previously disowned impulses or negative identifications. If a person senses that a disowned feeling (e.g., hostility or sexual exhibitionism) is pressing for more threatening, conscious forms of representation, self-consciousness may arise as an effort to control and monitor troublesome feeling. When the old defensive posture is regained or a new one solidified (either regressively, for example through projection, or progressively, for instance through gradual acknowledgment and acceptance of feelings), self-consciousess may disappear. The more strictly the person has followed a policy of impulse-repression, the more likely that impulse-representations will be experienced as alien thoughts or feelings bursting through dangerously. In these cases of strict repression of impulse, self-consciousness is particularly likely. If consciousness of impulses is experienced as intolerable, but neurotic defenses are weak, self-consciousness will be continual. One can observe decompensatory sequences moving from initial repression of impulse-representations, to eruption of impulse-representations in thought and feeling, to self-consciousness while impulse control is attempted and partial projection appears, to psychotic disturbance of reality-testing once impulses are disavowed fully through projection.

Self-consciousness might also be expected when a person experiences profound anxieties about the dangers of interpersonal closeness. If a person fears that intimacy will result in trauma, in loss of self-definition, or in incest or injury, then self-consciousness may be instituted in order to strengthen the sense of boundary around the self. When highly self-conscious, the person cannot fall effortlessly into a relationship. He will not find himself suddenly caring about someone or vulnerable to someone. He feels in control of moving close or moving away. Although losing a rich and directly experienced sense of himself acting and being, he gains an internal image and conceptualization of the self as a product or a visualization rather than an experience. The profoundly self-conscious person who fears loss of boundary or impulse control may have difficulty sleeping because to sleep is to abandon the constant control over the definition and activity of the self.

Both self-consciousness and embarrassment have been discussed from the perspective of successful integration of varied self-aspects and failures of integration. The embarrassed person has allowed some facet of the self (often a sexual trait or feeling) to become visible. His or her affect then conveys discomfort over what has been shown. It may be disowned as accidental and not meaningful, or be owned but in an uncomfortable fashion. Self-consciousness often represents an effort to forestall the showing of emotion and ideas to others or to oneself. Through self-consciousness one attempts to control the manifestations of the self; one keeps the self from experiencing or displaying anything that would produce feelings such as embarrassment or guilt or self-hatred. To say that states of embarrassment and self-consciousness can be conceptualized in terms of integration and dis-integration of the self-experience in no way sets aside these states as unique. Numerous other states of consciousness or experience involve tension over what can be accepted within the self-concept. The more smoothly the defenses function (i.e., the less felt tension or anxiety), the greater the automaticity that characterizes the person's efforts to free himself or herself from consciousness of certain feelings. For example, the person using well established reaction-formations will experience little tension around the disavowed feelings. Embarrassment and self-consciousness are by definition states of tension and they represent felt disruptions of self-identity, which often result from struggles with unacceptable self-aspects or feelings.

SLIM: WORRYING ABOUT SEXUAL INTACTNESS

Inferring Shame Issues When Shame is Unacknowledged

Most psychodynamically oriented clinicians readily would accept that shame can be a problem for a person who vocally denies shame problems. This assertion ought not to be taken to mean that the person actually feels ashamed while thinking he or she does not (except when the person's understanding of his or her own experience breaks down at the level of labeling what is felt). The claim means that a history of experienced shame and a continuing potential for shame motivate defenses, contribute to symptoms, or contribute to fantasy, dreams, and ideational productions. As yet undefinable, ongoing, unconscious processes probably also participate in creating the situation in which a person feels no shame but continues to give clinical evidence of a shame problem. Several research subjects denied shame experience, but their comments pointed to shame problems. Such inferences require careful justification based on a judicious use of the data.

Slim is a physically active, restless young man who put himself in the position of being interviewed at length about feelings, but seemed to have minimal understanding of his feelings and minimal insight into the forces that might have led him to expose himself to extended contact with a mental health professional. Whenever possible, he oriented himself to external events rather than subjective experiences. He seemed uncomfortable during interviews and he hid himself from the interviewer with mirrored sunglasses; nevertheless something drew him back to the situation. Slim represents the most extreme case of nonacknowledgment of shame. He volunteered for 4 to 6 hours of interviewing on the subject of shame, yet he claimed to be uncertain as to how he would recognize shame if he were to feel it. A psychodynamically oriented clinician immediately would expect shame problems in an individual who claimed to be such a stranger to shame. Typically, one could not estrange oneself from a universal feeling state so fully without engaging in vigorous defensive activity. In the course of 4 hours of interviewing, Slim acknowledged only one shame experience. As an early adolescent, he had been profoundly ashamed of his curly hair. The report is noteworthy in several respects. First, the only reported shame experience is safely distant from the present. Second, the apparent object of shame appears to be symbolic of some other object, because nothing about his hair is particularly strange, and his culture places no special emphasis on the straightness of a man's hair as an object of pride or shame. Analytic theory and Slim's overall psychological concerns suggest the hypothesis that his curly hair is a displacement from pubic hair; however, Slim's description of his preoccupation provides no persuasive data either to confirm or disconfirm this hypothesis.

What other data are available that bear on Slim's relationship to shame? Though he disclaims personal shame experience and even attests to some confusion about the meaning of the word shame, he is quick to generate examples of circumstances that might cause some other person to feel ashamed. His hypothetical shame examples often center overtly on sexual problems. Those examples that have no overt focus appear to have a covert sexual focus. He says that a person might feel ashamed if he were in the public eye and it became known that he was a homosexual (overt sexual focus). Or a person might feel ashamed if he had only one arm (possible covert castration focus). Shame-related states such as embarrassment also were associated with sexual themes. Slim's comment relating shame to the experience of having one arm was juxtaposed with the statement that he would feel embarrassed if he went shopping with his zipper down and someone thought he was an exhibitionist. Slim's imagined embarrassment over his exhibitionism points to an impulse that he has not integrated into his self-image. Analytic theory would suggest the possibility that Slim probably wishes to exhibit his penis in order to assert that he is not castrated (i.e., he wishes to prove that there is no shameful defect). He cannot acknowledge ownership of the socially unacceptable exhibitionistic impulse, so its appearance by "accident" embarrasses him. A convergence of evidence from several directions suggests that shame is historically and potentially a meaningful experience for Slim. The evidence also suggests that shame is centered on the idea of a defect of masculinity.

Complex Determination of Sexual Shame in a Man

To identify a potential for deep shame represents both an investigative end point and a place to begin inquiry. To the extent that the defense against shame becomes a major organizer of personality development, identifying a subject's fear of shame is an analytic end point. Many behaviors can be better understood by recognizing their function in the flight from shame experience. The shame experience is feared as too painful or too disruptive to the self-concept. But shame-identification also marks a beginning point for exploration. In Slim's case, it requires us to ask why this man so readily generates images of a sexually damaged, ashamed self. Analytic theory suggests that we look to a poor resolution of the oedipus complex. Instead of overcoming castration anxiety through identification with a respected father, the subject reluctantly might have chosen a feminine ("castrated") identity, which could keep him from competitive interactions with Father; but this identity causes him shame. The actual case data point to a number of possible explanations of Slim's fear of sexual defect. These explanations are offered as hypotheses, not as conclusions, because the data are not sufficiently complete to generate firm conclusions.

Two members of Slim's family suffer from readily apparent personal damage. His brother is severely brain damaged. His mother is reportedly manic-depressive. Identification with his mother and with his brother must have been an omnipresent possibility for Slim. The data suggest that such an identification was both frightening and alluring. On the one hand, both his mother and his brother clearly were impaired and were stigmatized by socially undesirable conditions. In depressive phases, Slim's mother suffered obvious pain. More specifically, Slim believes that she experienced great shame over her condition. Despite their impairments, both the mother and the brother emerge as privileged in certain respects. Both periodically displayed great freedom from inhibition, and both were capable of shameless acting-out of impulses. They were capable of unselfconscious, unruly activity in which the average individual would not indulge. Identification with the mother and the brother would have mitigated Slim's guilt over being better equipped than they, and it would have allowed him to partake of the chaotic pleasures to which they had access. It would also have kept him emotionally close to two loved family members. Thus one might expect that Slim was torn between his abhorrence of personal damage and his wish to remain close to his mother and his brother and to have their license for regressive behavior.

There is considerable distance between the conclusion that Slim identified with two damaged loved ones and the conclusion that he experienced himself as sexually impaired as a consequence of those identifications. In support of the latter, extended hypothesis, there are data suggesting that Mother's manic excitement was experienced as a sometimes pitiable, sometimes stimulating *sexual* agitation. Other images link shameful phallic damage in a man to a particular quality of psychic pain associated with Mother's pain when she is emotionally beaten by an angry and sadistic husband. Slim seems to believe that Mother swings mysteriously between pain and pleasure and is somehow made vulnerable to Father's shaming and abuse due to her capacity for heightened states of pleasure and pain. His penis, too, is capable of registering intense excitement and painful sensation and seems vulnerable to the kind of physical punishment that Mother received emotionally. Both Mother and his penis emerge as traumatized and vulnerable pleasure organs. Both seem invested with nearly magical powers to stimulate delight and fury in others.

The data point to strong, repudiated homosexual wishes in Slim. They also suggest a fear that an intense relationship with a man could lead to murderous aggression between them. The images of attack and murder generally pivot on the idea of one person having something the other wants. If Slim has money, he will be attacked and robbed. If he is attacked, he may murder his attacker out of rage and panic. Murderous attacks for the purpose of theft may issue from men or women. To whatever extent Slim thinks of his penis as something that another might envy, he is vulnerable to attack. He is safer without his penis, although he is then a victim of shame. Not everyone prefers castration to danger, but for Slim the images of assault are so vivid and frightening that one can appreciate his motivation to avoid such dangers.

The inferences about Slim are admittedly speculative. Their contribution is to demonstrate that shame may not follow simply from too much shaming or from a profound, irreducible defect in self-esteem. Individuals can choose negative identities that are inherently shameful if they believe that their only alternative identity creates intolerable danger or guilt. The shame that follows from self-imposed castration (or other forms of self-limitation) is no less real or problematic than the shame that follows when a child is belittled by a parent. But the approaches to alleviating the two varieties of shame will differ.

WILLIAM: PHALLIC CONTROL AND EARLY OMNIPOTENCE

Phallic and Anal Shame Themes in a Man

William is a young man with an earnest, somewhat burdened demeanor. He approached the research interviews seriously and admittedly used them as an opportunity to explore personal feelings and problems. He employed his intellectual orientation and aptitude adaptively in that these qualities gave him enough control and emotional distance, in relation to troubling feelings, that he could allow himself to approach such feelings with genuine, if attenuated, interest. Slim's primary shame-related anxieties concerned what equipment he has or does not have and what sexual identity (male, female, heterosexual, homosexual) he can assume. Compared with Slim, William demonstrated a less profound anxiety over catastrophic body damage and masculine body integrity. But he did show an overconcern with his performance in phallically oriented activities. William's protocol is useful as a male counterpart to Matilda's protocol. Each subject is preoccupied with phallic stage achievements, both those typically associated with his or her own gender and, to a lesser extent, those typically linked with the other gender. Both subjects show compulsive traits such as concern with messiness, order, cleanliness, and emotional control. Matilda's anal conflicts emerge most persuasively in her character defenses. The same is true to an extent for William, but he demonstrates an additional preoccupation with sadistic and omnipotent control by self and others, which further supports the supposition of anal conflicts. The data to be presented suggest that anal phase frustration of strivings toward pleasurable and prideful independent functioning may predispose a child, perhaps especially a male child, to intensified anxiety concerning the adequacy of his phallic level self-control. Frustration of early (anal) efforts to exert control over the mother and to retain control over the self may lead in the phallic phase to a preoccupation with proving the self phallically powerful, if not omnipotent. These phallic strivings for unlimited power may then lead to guilt because they incorporate wishes sadistically to control a love object.

William's discussion of his motorcycle jumping illustrates his ongoing concern with phallic effectiveness. His involvement with maintaining a state of high tension in the activity also suggests that the jumping may excite him in part because of its relationship to controlling sexual excitement during masturbation:

S: [I was] riding my cycle one time and I was playin' around with it and it was up at my uncle's and they had like a little rise in their driveway and then it goes up into the field. And I was pulling wheelies off there and see how long, how far up the field I could go and just keepin' on the back tire. And I had a good one, maybe 80 feet, well this one I got it down perfect. One more, it would be the best one. And I got up there and it got so that I was leaning back too far and lost my balance and was sliding off the seat. . . . I couldn't do a damned thing about it. There was no way I could stop what was happening. I just had to let the cycle go. . . . I was trying for the last straw, the last straw to save it (laugh). . . . I knew I'd be all right, maybe a scratched knee but, but I knew that, 'cause it was so slow—I was lucky if it was a little bit faster than walking speed. But I knew that any damage was gonna be to the cycle and *that* I *didn't* want, taking pride in keeping it in good shape, still do. And a few nicks and stuff here and there—it just, it was probably more frustrating than, well, there was fear too. I mean it was "oh no, I can't do anything!" But as far as the cycle was concerned it was just an intense frustration that I couldn't do a damned thing about it, I just had to let it go. . . .

I: What about if you think back to before the accident to the time just before that when you really were doing well with what you were trying to do, could you describe the feelings?

S: Oh, that was accomplishment galore, 'cause I had tried so many times off that same mound every Sunday afternoon or weekday afternoons, after school or something. . . . You know, after so many tries and finally, finally figuring out where, how far up and how much throttle to give it just as the front wheel hit the rise, to get it up to where I needed it to be, to keep the balance.

I: Any fantasies that would go along with that?

S: Hm, I don't know, just the idea of being able to . . . Once I got it up and could find the balance point, if I come off of there and got it right I could just keep going 'til I'd run into bushes at the end of the field or something (laugh).

Like the bike-riding adolescent, the young boy depicted in the following memory has clear phallic ambitions:

S: I climbed up on a ladder in front of the house—and I guess my parents were, yeah, they weren't too far away. They were out the walk from the house. That puts them about 50 feet from where I was. I was climbing on the ladder and I had a ruler and I played like I was a carpenter and measured, oh, from the wall to the rafters or something, and fell off the ladder, hit my head on the rock. And then they had to run me down to the hospital, and they put the stitches—, but I can definitely remember climbing up on the ladder and falling off. I don't remember the impact but (laugh) it was bad enough remembering falling off (laugh)!

I: Yeah, what do you remember about that?

S: When I climbed up, the ladder was set on one. . . .rock and then there were rocks for the walk at the front door there. And I climbed up on there and I was trying to use both hands to hold the ruler and measure and I lost my balance and went over backwards. And all I saw was treetops and sky on the way down. I know with one hand I tried to catch the ladder but I think I actually held the ruler in the other hand and didn't let go even after I fell (laugh). I was worried about breaking, breaking the ruler as opposed to breaking my head (laugh)! . . .I think that that one was Dad's, and I had asked him if I could use it. I think that one was his. . . .Every once in a while *he'd* break one so then we'd get a new one. And for the most part he would never use the broken parts. That's why I'm not sure if I had one of the broken parts, a 38-inch ruler as opposed to a 72-inch ruler, or whether I had gotten his, and I think it was his 'cause usually when he stopped working and backed up, you know, near the end of the day or the afternoon, I just can't, yeah, that was the afternoon 'cause the sun was still out, like late afternoon—, he'd take his tools out of his pockets and the hammer holder off and set it down and I probably borrowed his, to use for that.

I: And do you have any recollection of how you felt before you fell. . .?

S: Well, I felt good. I felt like I was actually doing something constructive, helping I guess was probably my biggest thought. I was gonna check and make sure there really was the right numbers, I don't even know what numbers I was looking for, trouble remembering now, once in a while (laugh)! . . .too many little lines on that stick. Yeah, it was a sense of helping out. While he was taking a break I did it (laugh).

William's memory documents a child's-eye investment in manliness, but it does not portray a definite shame experience. However, William refers explicitly to his shame in adult situations that highlight phallic inadequacies. For example, when his mother belittles his atheletic performances, or when he gives an ignorant response in class, he is acutely ashamed.

Certain depictions of William's dyadic interactions with his mother suggest that his preoccupation with potency is intensified by early, probably prephallic, experiences of frustration of his attempts to control her. She appears in his memories as someone who knows all. While Father can be rigid and tough, he emerges as straightforward and seldom sadistic. In contrast, Mother is experienced as using her omnipotence to control and frustrate the boy who sets out to outsmart her. Such sadistic wishes are ego-dystonic for him and they generate guilt. The following memories, the first of a babysitter, the second of Mother, suggest early concerns with Mother's power:

S: My earliest memory. . . .let's see, about 2, with the baby sitters. . . .I can almost remember her face, parts of it. I don't know, one time I was mad or something, I don't know what the problem was, but I ran upstairs and hid. She had a hell of a time finding me. I thought I was pretty clever for that stunt. But I can remember looking—I hid under the bed—I can remember looking out from underneath the bed and watching the feet go around looking for me (laugh). And the only other one—

I: Before you go on from that, what do you almost remember about her face?

S: I can remember her dark hair, and her eyes, but the nose and the mouth and the chin are—I can't really, I couldn't really place that, but definitely the eyes and the dark hair.

I: Any feelings about her face?

S: Hmm, let's see, it was like no matter what you did or you thought, her face looked like she knew what you were gonna do or were thinking. It was like she could almost look right through ya, and tell just what you had done, whether you said anything or not.

I: Anything else about that image of being under the bed—feelings or just the way things looked to you from there?

S: No, not really. . . . excited at the time, 'cause I succeeded in disappearing. But it was also the curiosity as to what would happen after I was discovered (laugh). 'Cause you know, I didn't know how *she* would react. At least I don't think I did (laugh)!

I: To what you had done before you hid, or to your success in hiding from her?

S: Oh, my success in hiding. I don't—as best as I can remember it, I don't think I did any-, really wrong, I don't think so. I think it was just a big hide-and-seek game for me. And I found the ultimate hiding place (laugh)!

In the next memory, Mother frustrates William with her power:

S: One that flashes to mind was—this would have been quite a while later, probably humm, probably about 8. . . . I did something wrong. I don't know what it was now, I blocked it out purposely. We were outside and, I don't know whether I was going to get slapped or spanked for it, but for some reason I thought I could outrun her. I tried, but didn't make it (laugh)! That—nasty consequences, that warranted a switch and that wasn't too nifty. I don't know what I did wrong, I wish I could remember but, hum, outside, I don't know, maybe, just trying to remember, maybe I had thrown something. I don't know what it was, probably said something that got me in trouble. . . . I figured if I could outrun her then I could escape punishment, but it was inevitable for whatever I had done. But then when I was caught and punished, it was like, it caused more, whether it actually did or not, it probably did, because I can remember her saying, "Don't try to run away from me! Don't try that again." That sticks in my mind.

I: And then she hit you with something?

S: Yeah, a switch (words lost), some small sapling. We lived near the woods—there was plenty of them around (both laugh). Too many, wish all the trees were big (both laugh)—high branches, ahh.

I: Any other feelings besides being afraid?

S: Well, for an instant I thought I was clever because there was a gap between the time I decided to run and she caught me and there—I figured I had a chance but my estimate was wrong, so I didn't act very—I was clever, I thought I was going to escape the punishment. But after she caught me and I knew I was had, before she hit me, I think I was crying before I even got hit. I knew it was coming, there was no way I could escape it then.

William's phallically-oriented shame experiences often focus on failure to achieve mastery of personal performances (e.g., humor or athletic activity). Shame themes also appear in connection with his failure to control women in his life. For example, though William denied any shame when twice disappointed by a woman friend, he asserted that his philosophy was "fool me once, shame on you; fool me twice, shame on me." Comments such as these support the idea that his preoccupation with phallic accomplishments may include in its history an experience of painful inability to control a vital love object. He appears to have felt overly controlled by a powerful parent rather than feeling that he and she could share control. When the child originally experienced it, this imbalance of power may have brought humiliation, rage, or frustration rather than shame, but it might also have contributed to an enduring sense of personal weakness and to a preoccupation with exercising control. In the phallic phase, this preoccupation would have made William hypersensitive to Father's possession of greater personal power and control over Mother than William himself had.

If we look at William's experience of his Mother as someone who tenaciously guarded her authority over him and engineered his submission while at the same time she ridiculed his failures of manliness, we see a young man able to consolidate neither an identity of comfortable subordination nor an identity of confident masculinity. Perhaps due in part to superego projection, he also experienced Father as harshly critical of cockiness if it carried any implication of outsmarting Father or behaving antagonistically. Aggression in the service of perfectly upright, constructive goals was acceptable; in fact, it was expected. But aggression tainted by any trace of rebellion was detected instantaneously and punished through humiliation, as shown in the following memory:

S: It was Christmas time and we [were] shopping or something and we had gone by one of the registers. They have these registers in all the different sections, tools and toys and clothes, and we'd gone by this one and there was a stack of pencils there—I guess the salesman used to write up slips or something. I just picked up a passel of them, was gonna cart them off, stuck them in my pocket. For all I remember they may have been pencils that they were giving out or something but I just decided to take a bunch of them, and later on in the store I showed them to Dad what I had, a fistful of pencils. And with that, umm, I forget, I forget what his words were, but it was stealing, and it was wrong, and with that he marched me back and made me hold the pencils out and give them back to the salesman. And that was a source of intense shame because it was, it was embarrassment at having to give them back, but the fact that what I had done had not only embarrassed me but it had embarrassed my father, it had consequences of something gravely wrong—stealing—that was something that stuck in my mind and still stays there. Something to be ashamed of, very ashamed of. . . .

I: Do you have any recollection of your feeling as you showed your father what you had [pencils]?—before he came down on you.

S: Not a sense of pride or, or being proud of what I had done, but a sense of sharp accomplishment. I had pulled something off and nobody knew it. My showing them to him was like the culmination of that.

I: So was there an image that he might admire what you had pulled off?

S: I think I expected, maybe not an admiring . . . I'm not real sure now if I expected to be in trouble after I showed them to him or not, but the fact that I had pulled something like that off without anybody knowing it. In other words, I was sharp enough to be able to pull that stunt and nobody find out. I just wanted to demonstrate my ability at fooling others. And I probably expected recognition of my inconspicuousness. I don't know that I expected recognition in "good job, stealing pencils!"

I: So there might have been a sense that you were clever about what you did, but you shouldn't have done it anyway.

S: Right!

I: You didn't even get half of that.

S: No, I lost all (laugh)! I expected a 50% recognition and got zilch!

A number of research subjects, among them William, demonstrated a preoccupation with fantasied situations in which they proceeded confidently in exhibitionistic behavior only to learn later that everyone found them ridiculous. Both William and Polly feared this eventuality. William spoke of the shame of confidently raising his hand in class but giving a wrong response. Such false confidence would be more shameful than a hesitant delivery of incorrect information. He also described a fantasy of confidently making a speech while below him words on a screen flashed insults to his performance. Polly talked of the shame of pleasurably sharing an ambition with others, then learning that they thought her laughable to assume she could be someone so successful. William's and Polly's situations differ in some respects but they share the quality of extreme discomfort over proceeding confidently only to learn that others think one is a fool. The audience emerges as powerful and as dangerous to one's self-esteem. Self-consciousness, rather than confident exhibitionism, is the only defense against the audience's scorn. Asked to invent a cartoon image that concretized his shameful speech-making fantasy, William responded with the flashing words fantasy and with the following images of piloting an airplane:

S: Probably the smooth delivery—uh, this is a semi-bizarre [response] (laugh). [The smooth delivery would be like] an airplane—jet or kind of a prop—in a straight line not deviating from its course, all systems go, all green lights across the dash, altimeter's, everything's on target . . . that would be a visual representation of a smooth delivery, just continuing in open space ahead so that it looks just like clear sailing: nothing in its way, yet having some logical destination out there somewhere. As far as how *they* [the audience] would perceive the conversation, the airplane going along and at the point where what I say is inappropriate or wrong, the wings fall off and yet—placing myself in the role of the pilot since I'm the one that's steering the conversation—I don't realize it, I don't look at any of the gauges, I just look out the windshield and see everything's clear, there's nothing blocking my path and yet before I know it, I've lost the whole basis to what keeps me in the air, to what keeps my conversation going and pretty soon, I crash! (laugh) but I'm ignorant of that.

I can only speculate about the genesis of William's fearful associations to exhibitionism. The situations cited would seem to parallel the experience of a young child who confidently proceeds with some activity (such as singing, dancing, or talking), quite intoxicated with pleasure and the unquestioned expectation of the parent's pleasure, only to be met with sharp, derogatory remarks such as "Stop that foolishness," or "Can't you sit still?" or "You've made a mess of this room again." The unexpected failure of empathy with the child's high estimation of his or her activities comes as a shock and as a blow to self-esteem and clear conscience. William also appears to suffer from literal castration fears to which he responds with denial and omnipotence (reminiscent of his attempts at omnipotence vis-à-vis Mother. The omnipotence and denial are ultimately interrupted by their opposite, the conviction that the catastrophic castration has already befallen him. Polly's and William's fantasies are probably intensified by projection of the subjects' own critical responses to exhibitionism in others.

Attainable Ego Ideals and Insulation from Shame

William is vulnerable to shame experience under certain circumstances and often he feels less than satisfied with his abilities. Nevertheless, he appears to be a person sustained by adequate self-esteem and coherent values. He may at times have experienced his parents' values as weapons wielded against him in order to subordinate and constrain him. But his parents' values also had a constructive influence. His parents were people who could respect themselves by adhering to their values, and in most situations they welcomed him into a positive identification with them by presenting him with well defined expectations that he was able to meet. In order for him to meet these expectations he sometimes had to engage in mildly self-punitive behavior. But the pride and sense of belonging that resulted from the identification partially offset the self-constraints with which he needed to live. The identification with the aggressor that he sometimes is pressured to make is not an identification with sadists but with parents who had limited tolerance for free displays of playfulness, emotionality, or rebelliousness. By emulating his parents, he achieved an identity that limits expressiveness but allows him to live with reasonable pride and success in the world.

ABA: NO MAN'S SON

Shame Induced by Failure of Parental Warmth and Identification

In most parent-child relationships, especially during the early years, the parent experiences an intense bond of affection, protectiveness, and appreciation for the child. This parental feeling communicates itself to the child and encourages in the child the growth of feelings of intimacy and identification with the parent. When identified with a strong parent, the child can proceed into the world imbued with good feeling about himself or herself. When a parent lacks an intense affinity for a child and presents himself or herself to the child as a distant or critical force in the child's world, profound effects on the child's self-esteem and self-confidence would be expected. The child must not only contend alone with the outer world; he or she must also interpret the parent's indifference.

Aba is a young man of African birth. His biological father deserted his mother prior to the child's birth. Aba had an adoptive father, also African, from about the age of 6. Prior to that time, he looked to affectionate uncles and a loving grandfather as father figures. After his adoptive father entered his life, he was largely separated from his uncles and grandfather. In the interviewing situation, Aba was polite, warm, and slightly deferential. He had a childlike quality and was deeply engaged in the interviewing and in the interviewer's responses to his life story. Aba began the first of five interviews stating that he never experiences shame. He also claimed to have little or no feeling about his adoptive father's apparent lack of affection and respect for him. During the course of the interviewing, he increasingly identified shame and distress within his relationship to his adoptive father. The cool relationship to his stepfather, which deepened the wound of abandonment by his natural father, would seem in itself to be a source of shame that would leave the young man shame-vulnerable in relationships that require a positive masculine identity. In the passage to follow, Aba explains why he is not hurt by his father's lack of interest in him. He has described how sentimental his father's work shows him to be and he has contrasted his father's sentimental attitude toward work with his indifference toward Aba:

S: I don't really feel anything. I don't feel anything because I've gotten used to the idea that he's just that way. That's just his person-, his personality, that's the kind of person he is. And so I just accept it. Because you know, I can't relate to him, certainly not on that level, on the sentimental side of him. I can't even relate to him on the intellectual side. So I don't know, I don't even bother with it really. See it's not, when I really bother with it, it's not that I don't, it's not that I felt hurt or anything by it, but I just don't have any feelings. If I had some feelings about it, then I might feel hurt. I just don't have any feelings because I don't see him having any feelings toward me.

As Aba continues to talk about his father, he articulates the relationship between his "hurt" and his incipient shame. The more successful Father appears while excluding Aba from his successes—indeed from his life as a whole—the more Aba feels saddened but also unworthy, ashamed, and inferior. He describes a feeling that has begun to bother him:

S: Ah, that my Dad really doesn't care about what's happening to me, you know, *that* kind of a feeling—it's nothing—and it's, I feel, ah, maybe a certain kind of anger, you know, but the fact that maybe he feels that he's put himself on a—you know, it seems to me that he put himself up so high that he can't be reached. He's written all these papers, he's very well educated, he tends to tell me about that a lot without saying it in words. You know, by his remarks, etcetera. Like he said before, "What you do in high school doesn't really matter, but what you do in college does," and then when I get into college he said, "Well, law school is what really counts."

I: He told you where *he* stands and where *you* stand?

S: No, he never tells me where I stand as such. Yeah, you—what you're saying is correct but he never outright tells me that. He *shows* me, you know in different ways, like say showing me some of the books he's written or showing me the letter he got from Albert Einstein or the recommendation that he got from Robert Oppenheimer, etcetera. All these things. . . . All I can do is ah—if I really felt that, if I appreciated him as much as a father, then I could just be glad that he got those things: "Fine, That's great." But I don't feel that because he . . . he won't let me—you know, I could say he won't let me, maybe, I don't know whose fault it is, if it's anybody. But I just can't feel that I can relate to something like that and say, "Okay, that's really good, I'm proud of you." I can't ever say that to him: "I'm proud of you."

Aba takes no pride in his father because his father takes no pride in him. Pride in another, or shame for another, implies close relatedness and the sense that one shares in the loved one's successes and failures. Aba feels that his father has excluded him from his world of success and left Aba ashamed, hurt, and insecure. Although Aba came to the research presenting himself as a person who never feels shame, he partially abandoned that claim, at least in reference to shame in the past:

S: I really cried in front of [my mom] one night and I told her . . . I can't take that anymore, accepting him as my father and then having to take all this from him. It's hurting me emotionally, it would just be better if I don't think of him as my father . . . I can't be dependent on him, can't be emotionally dependent on him and get all this thing that I feel rejection . . . I felt ashamed with him, plenty of times, I felt ashamed because I felt inferior to him. Every time he said something or he made a point, he made me feel inferior to him.

Aba demonstrates precisely the interdependence of rejection and shame. He despises his own abilities because his father has greater abilities. Every child experiences inferiority in comparison with a parent, but in most cases it is not devastating because the parent, through affection and admiration for the child, lets the child feel that they are a twosome: the parent's strength is the child's to share. Aba experiences his father as wishing sharply to differentiate the two of them, not just by attention to relative ability but by lack of investment in the child. A child who does not attract the parent's interest will not feel able to share in the parent's abilities and will see his or her own undeveloped skills in the cold light of premature independence; they will appear pathetic. But the parent's lack of interest is itself the greatest shame, greater than all the paltriness of skill. In the child's eyes, the parent obviously has looked at him and found him or her not worthy of the parent's love. The child is left to deal both with the narcissistic strain and with the anger it creates.

In the passages quoted, one can see Aba struggling over the extent to which he will acknowledge shame in relation to his father. Although the acknowledgment does not come altogether easily, one might argue that, for a 25 year old man, Aba is surprisingly accepting of a rather pathetic position for himself. It would be prudent then to ask whether the shameful status of the unwanted, unaccomplished, deprived son has seemed more acceptable to Aba than some competing identity or experience. The following passage suggests that Aba finds it more acceptable to be victimized than to be angry and powerful:

S: Personality-wise I've never had any problems or even ever felt angry toward people, at anybody that would amount to anything. I've never felt that with my peers. . . .

I: Could you say any more about that? Something brought that to mind; I'm curious what.

S: The reason I said that was because I hear of friends getting mad at each other, etcetera. But I've never had any kind of a confrontation so to speak with my best friend or really any of my peers that I can recall. Any time that I've had a disagreement . . . it's been on an intellectual level, it hasn't been on an emotional level.

Were Aba more comfortable with anger, by now he might have dethroned his stepfather as the arbiter of personal worth. He might even have challenged his stepfather in a way that ultimately would have strengthened their mutual respect and sympathy. It is important here to ask why Aba continues to sidestep aggression and instead to spin the particular web of shame themes that he does. Why has he not found a way to escape continued recreation of shameful self-images?

Aba's protocol was replete with references to horrifying experiences of abandonment and of damage to love objects. He has gained a tenuous mastery over such memories. One hypothesis regarding his repression of anger is that were he to agitate his relations with his parents by moving into the forbidden areas of sexuality and adolescent rebellion—that is, were he to bid for more mature relationships that demanded his parents' tolerance for his separate but equal status—the early trauma and abandonment images might reassert power. He seems to have preferred a latency-like adjustment in which he sacrifices the pleasures of sex, outspoken individuality, and equal rank with Father. In exchange, he retains great intimacy with a once abandoning and fragile mother, and he retains a predictable, though masochistic and unsatisfactory, relationship to his father. Incipient shame and self-restraint are a price grudgingly paid for basic security in a world that once felt frightfully insecure:

S: It was just a vivid impression: they [his family members] were really working. And also the fact that they could die at any time; that went through my mind. You know, they're working hard and I'm not doing anything for 'em, and what if they die all of a sudden?

I: What was the image, what if they would die and you haven't been working—?

S: It made me feel depressed. It made me feel lonely. It just made me feel, you know, like crying. I didn't want to—I just, I don't know how to express it, I didn't want to—it's like I didn't really want to lose them. I thought that if I did my best that they might (laugh) live longer or something. You know, that kind of a feeling. Ah, it's not necessarily, didn't necessarily have any kind of realistic connections. But that—it was a vivid image. . . . When people carry the dead over there, they don't carry them in caskets, okay? . . . I used to come home and walk back from school and I would see these people being carried away. And there was a special, ah, this very sad chant, and it's just, you know, if you just can imagine the environment, it's, you know, in the evening, sun setting, and these people going carrying the dead to the river, and I was by myself coming back home and you know, waiting to come back for dinner and wondering like how hard my grandparents worked, my parents worked. And those kind of things, every single, you know, little portion that all these things, uh, have an impact, they really do.

Aba is threatened by the intensity of his grief and also by feelings of omnipotent destructiveness and omnipotent power to protect:

S: [She was wearing a long dress] and it just, uh, you know, air, I guess a current of air came by, this was in Europe.

I: Just the two of you together?

S: Yeah, we were there. And I *told* her not to keep it close, I mean I was like 3, 4 years old, I don't even know why I said that even. And I remember that much, you know, and she just, it was a nylon dress, and it just kind of lit up. I didn't know what to do. . . . She told me to go downstairs and call somebody. The landlord wasn't there. I was out in the streets screaming. I didn't know any English and I was screaming in [his native tongue], like I was crying, and nobody understood what I was saying. . . . And I'm just, I'm just, I was screaming like, "My mother is dying" and, you know, and there's nobody there. . . . And every time I saw my mom [after that] a little thing went through my mind that, you know, what if she dies, right now? And from then on I've always kind of had that thought, 'til I've become independent. It was a scary feeling for me. I used to always think, what if my mom dies, right now? What am I going to do (laugh)? It was a very real thing for me. I used to always think that. Any time I would feel depressed that would go through my mind.

FRANK: IDEALIZING AN IMPASSIVE PARENT

Constant Shame Based on Condemnation of Aggression

Shame often follows when an individual feels insufficiently forceful in his or her behavior. Whenever shame results from a person's perception that his or her behavior is weak in character, we must ask whether the weakness of behavior derives from some unavoidable limitation on the individual, for example, a physical handicap; whether it follows from excessive caution stemming from deficient self-esteem; or whether the weakness results from an inhibition of forcefulness. Shame also may attend behavior that is experienced as aggressive but uncontrolled. A research subject named Cal felt ashamed when, as a child, he brought a bird's egg to school and on route he smashed it in his pocket. He also felt ashamed when he took machines apart enthusiastically but then could not reassemble them. Imagery of energetic but disorderly anality often connotes shameful aggressiveness. William spoke of "blurting out" comments in class and thinking that his speech was "garbage" and "mush."

One may encounter shame over behavior that is overly forceful and thus lacking in gentleness. This type of shame occurs in men who greatly respect or idealize femininity, who see themselves as clumsy or destructive by comparison. Women who feel insufficiently gentle also manifest such shame. In the research sample, Katherine demonstrated resistence to an identification with her mother. She saw herself as having the same "body clock" as her father. She detested feminine things, such as bras and sanitary napkins. In childhood situations that confronted her with her femininity (e.g., receiving a gift of underwear while boys were present), she became rude and aggressive, but she then felt ashamed of her aggressiveness, which set her apart from her ladylike mother.

Frank is a middle-aged man, the oldest of the research group and the only one who came complaining of agonizing shame experiences. He came across as a tightly controlled, self-effacing, and profoundly unhappy man who experiences himself as helplessly trapped within his psychic misery. His tight, rigid presentation also had a resentment-filled character to it. Frank appears to cycle between the three types of shame described above. He is ashamed when he is weak and unassertive, for example, if he cannot stand up to his boss. He is ashamed if he is aggressive in an uncontrolled way, for instance when drunk. And he is ashamed when he is deliberately aggressive and ungentle. A significant determinant of Frank's shame is his need consciously to idealize a father whose behavior toward Frank often must have been experienced as sadistic. Frank describes his father as a perfectly controlled individual who never hugged his children or spent time with them. Rather than feel angry or deprived in response to his father's controlling, ungenerous behavior, Frank idealized his father's dispassionate approach to life. Although depicted as hard and uncaring, Father is spared Frank's aggression. Aggression is instead directed toward the self once the self has been demeaned as inadequate to satisfy Father's standards. Thus Frank torments himself for being aggressive in an uncontrolled manner that Father would not himself display. He torments himself when he is angry with his children. He tells himself that his anger is too passionate. Father would punish his children with discipline and fairness, not with emotion. When Frank refrains from punishing the children because he pities them, this too is a sign that he is weak and emotional as Father would never have been. In Frank's quest for dispassionate self-control, we see the impact of idealization of Father combined with the culture-wide admiration for assertiveness and independence.

Constant shame must offer some variety of pleasure or apparent psychological advantage in order for a person to continue to tolerate the experience. Frank's original motivation in withstanding so much painful emotion would be difficult to discern from three interviews, given his entrenched character pathology. His flight from aggression into shame once might have represented an effort to protect a vulnerable parent by denying aggression toward the parent and identifying with his or her vulnerable state. In the current situation, we see shame functioning to reduce the separation between Frank and his fantasied parents. He maintains a powerful belief, supported by childhood memories, that when he is hurt his mother and his otherwise emotionally distant father will pity and protect him. To be ashamed is to be loved and protected. Behaviors that suggest he is not so damaged or miserable are the ones that bring a tide of shame. Although normally he is profoundly inhibited even with respect to simple conversation, he has a pattern of getting drunk and becoming garrulous and fun-loving. After these episodes, acute shame descends on him. Frank believes that his temporary relinquishing of behavioral control fully explains his shame. But one could conjecture that he insists on interpreting his behavior, after the fact, as shameful disinhibition because to view his behavior positively, as enjoyment and self-assertion, would suggest that he is an autonomous, intact individual who is not in need of his parents' protection and pity. That which threatens to separate him from his parents brings the most severe attacks of shame. The drunken behavior represents a forbidden expression of aggression. Thus the shame that follows—once he has forced himself to perceive his behavior as a pathetic loss of control—constitutes a punishment for aggression.

Frank's interviews contain themes of castration and descriptions of castrated behavior, such as unprotesting acceptance of his wife's refusal to have intercourse with him. It is difficult to know where to place Frank's feelings about his genitals with respect to his overall hierarchy of motives. What can be said is that his willingness to tolerate, even to relish, "castrating" situations corresponds to his overall willingness to be shamed, humiliated, and injured. The following passage illustrates Frank's readiness calmly to accept bodily injury as a condition that brings with it solicitous attention:

S: From the [accident] scene, the next scene is wakin' up in the hospital. Uh, about—I don't know—six, seven people standing around the kid. I know Mom and Dad was there, and my teacher was there. She had a big basket of fruit for me and ah—I don't know, there's a feeling there that, I guess I can't explain whether it was happiness maybe, having all these people around my bed, seeing them there.

A second example shows the depth of Frank's investment in eliciting his mother's worried attention, even if he must be injured in order to achieve the desired end:

S: I think it made her feel real bad that she'd hit me on the leg. She was probably real sorry she'd done it . . . 'cause the image, the only image that I have is she's bent over, and her arm's down on my shoulder, and she's looking at my leg. . . . She always worried about me anyhow, all the time.

Frank is willing to tolerate his wife's disgust with his masculinity, apparently because he believes that he can sustain an intimate bond with her only by putting himself in the position of an injured, castrated person:

S: My wife just didn't care that much about sex, about having sex. If she never had it—in fact it was really something that—I guess it was right around Easter. . . . the year before we separated, we sat there one night and she said, "You know what would make me really happy?" She said, "First of all, if you and I were divorced." Um, I mean, you know, it didn't bother me 'cause I, for the last couple of years I knew my wife didn't love me and wishes, you know, I was gone [from] the house, so what she said didn't bother. It was just funny that come [true], that we were divorced, that I would, you know, pay the support, take care of—which I'm now doing—ah, she would have the kids, which she has, um, that she would have the home and security, which she got, you know, the furniture, car . . . , she got the whole works, everything. And last of all, [she wished] she would never have to have sex again in her life.

When Frank's wife leaves him briefly, his dramatic response is to attempt to rape his daughter while in a drunken and possibly psychotic state. His description of his state of mind immediately after the rape attempt and on the following day strikingly communicates his rage toward the castrating wife who he believes has made him behave impotently over the years. His comments reveal the underlying wish to triumph over her rather than submit to her. It seems that by leaving him, she breaks the unspoken pact stating that he will submit to emasculation and humiliation as long as they can remain intimate. As sobriety dawns, attended by the need to face his wife, Frank returns to his habitual pattern of shame over behaviors that highlight his potency and reduce his passivity and dependence. His habitual shame pattern is supported by the fact that his own moral code and that of his society despise his pleasurable rape behavior as shameful and unforgivable:

S: In my mind I raped her, but she said I didn't, so I don't know. That's why I guess I keep saying *attempted* rape; I don't know, to me it was rape . . . because I thought I had. . . .
I: Were there any feelings of being triumphant or getting even, that kind of—?

S: I don't think of getting even. I think of being triumphant. I think there, I know there was definite, feels that way, that, ah, "Hey, I've made it," you know, I'm, I can almost still see myself there and, I don't know, everything in a lot of ways are jumbled, but I can almost see myself right at that point where I thought I did rape Fran—I still say I did—uh, or "Hey, I've won, it's happened, Fran's going along with it, everything's gonna be great." There was a lot of pleasure in the whole thing . . . I guess the pleasure of doing what I'd set out to do that day and accomplished it. . . . It was a crazy night. Uh, she went to Nancy's [after the incident]. . . . This is a ways, you know, a ways later: She's gone, I don't know what's going on in the world, I don't really give a damn what's going on in the world, I'm still happier than hell. Uh, I spent twice that night masturbating, which seems—well, terrible. But I'm trying to show you my triumph and, you know, my victory over this whole thing . . . just the frame of mind that I was in, that "Hey, I've won, everything is great and, you know," when really everything was going to hell at the same time. . . . Then I went to bed and went to sleep. You know, when I woke up it was all over. Then I realized, you know, then I realized what I had done, the shame. . . . All this glory from last night was gone. And I knew, you know, that things would never again be the same. . . . I cried all morning, wrote a letter to my wife telling her the whole thing. . . . There's a lot in that letter to make me, you know, kind of crawl.

Dramatically evident in this passage is Frank's ambivalence about the rape attempt. He knows that morally he ought to despise his behavior, and this moral assessment pushes him to reoccupy the masochistic role in relation to his wife. But he cannot forget the feelings of immense triumph and wellbeing associated with carrying out his plan to seduce and rape.

WHAT ROLE HAS SEXUALITY?

As noted in Chapter 2, the shame literature emphasizes conflicted exhibitionistic impulses and genital inferiority feelings as major sources of shame. Some prominent writers believe that shame feelings always mark the presence of sexual complaints. The interviews conducted suggest that specifically sexual inferiority feeling need not be central to every complaint of shame. For example, shame might center on the belief that one is not valued by one's mother or on the feeling that one is overly angry or selfish. Some might argue that such complaints, if they are sources of shame, likely represent defensive transformations of feelings of inadequacy about the genitals. I know of no way absolutely to refute this argument, but I have not seen clinical evidence that it holds true. What does seem tenable is that development to the phallic-oedipal level (or to some other specifiable developmental level, e.g., anal phase dominance) must take place before shame experience emerges. Such developments would establish the intense commitment to the self-image that is a requisite of shame. The shame that then becomes possible need not center on the core issue of the dominant psychosexual stage. That is, although shame development may await the phallic phase, shame experienced in the phallic phase or later need not center on sexual identity concerns. But once the phallic phase is reached, virtually all emotion that expresses feeling about the self will reflect on the self as a specifically female or specifically male individual. If the 5 year old girl feels unloved by her father, she will feel that she, *as a girl*, is unlovable. Even though she might attribute her father's rejecting behavior to her clumsiness or stupidity, not to her gender, the self that is unlovable has now been defined as a female self. This approach suggests that not every shame complaint need be ascribed to a feeling about the genitals, but every shame complaint has ramifications for one's masculinity or feminity. Aba might feel ashamed that his father does not love him and this may be an essentially straightforward complaint, not a disguised version of negative feelings about the genitals experienced during the phallic-oedipal phase. The shame over his father's indifference then may create or potentiate feelings that he is inadequate as a male. Josephine may feel ashamed that she is babyish and this complaint will not have derived from a negative feeling about her female body. But the idea of being babyish might only have become significant once she was old enough to know that she should be a pretty, bright girl and not a whiny baby. The developmental context of the shame-complaint is her investment in age-appropriate femininity, but the complaint need not reflect a well-articulated belief that she is unattractive or unappealing.

This is an appropriate place to reintroduce the nonunitary concept of affect categories such as shame, a concept that has some explanatory power in relation to varied shame theories that have been put forward. If in common parlance "shame" designates a group of loosely related emotional experiences, it is possible that those who insist shame always signifies genital-exhibitionistic conflict and those who state otherwise are focusing their attention on somewhat different phenomena, which overlap sufficiently that both are often labeled as shame. Those who emphasize genital level conflict over exhibitionism may be thinking of experiences with an acute, painful, aroused quality. Such experiences include a subset of those I have labeled embarrassment in Chapter 4 and a subset of those labeled shame. The shame label is also applied by some to those preoccupations, about personal defects, that are quietly painful experiences not characterized by the sense of being emotionally excited and hypersensitive. These un-aroused experiences need not involve conflict over exhibitionism. They likely will signify a concern with personal deficiency, sexual or nonsexual in nature. Conflict may form the background for such shame experiences, for example if self-protective anger is too conflictual to tolerate, but the actual moment of shame will be best portrayed not as a moment of acute coonflict between two opposing trends, but as a moment of preoccupation with a perceived deficiency.

It is difficult confidently to summarize the 10 subjects' shame themes because there are many ways to describe the same clinical material; and the theoretical preconceptions brought to the interviews will significantly affect the summary statement. My effort at summary led to the impression that one male subject, Slim, and one female subject, Matilda, generated shame themes focused primarily on sexual potency or attractiveness. Though each subject may have had defensive motivation to retain a belief in sexual inferiority, nevertheless, the fact remains that sexual inadequacy appeared to be the central focus of shame. Matilda appeared to be predominantly ashamed of inadequate femininity. There were also suggestions of penis envy. Slim seemed primarily ashamed of feeling castrated. Feminine strivings were difficult to determine because Slim seems to have gratified any such strivings by close identification with Mother. Clinically, one often sees instances in which dissatisfaction with one's sexual adequacy consists of wishes to be like the opposite sex *and* of wishes to be a more potent or attractive person of one's own gender. For example, women who have difficulty making the oedipal phase identification with Mother often alternate between despair that they are not sufficiently feminine and misery because they are not male. One may speak of the masculine strivings in such cases as regression from the positive oedipal conflict; nevertheless, they have shame significance in their own right.

In three of the four remaining male cases, some form of ineffectiveness constituted a major shame theme. For one of those three men, Aba, the concern with ineffectiveness (in his case intellectual ineffectiveness) was paired with a concern about being unloved by his father. The subject's incapacity to stimulate loving feelings in his father appeared to be the most important form of ineffectiveness in his life. In the other two cases of the three, current interpersonal ineffectiveness looked less central. When such themes surfaced (e.g., being dropped by a girlfriend as a sign of being a fool), they took the form of examples of ineffectiveness with regard to tasks that pit man against man for demonstration of superior skills. William's concern with masculine effectiveness may have overlain an anxiety about powerlessness vis-à-vis a dominant mother. The data pointed to castration anxiety, perhaps in relation to Mother and Father both, but the data were less persuasive than in Slim's case. A fourth male subject, Frank, abstained from self-assertion to a degree that most people would regard as ineffective living. But the shame theme that he developed most fully did not in fact revolve around personal impotence related to these abstentions but instead indicted lapses in the abstention policy as if these were shameful failures of self-control. At least on one level this man defined effectiveness as the capacity to keep silent, remain unemotional, and remain constantly rational like his idealized father. In summary then, minimally three, perhaps four, of the male subjects showed major concerns with effectiveness, but none gave clear evidence that such concerns related primarily or exclusively to preoccupation with the size or function of the penis. In this respect, they differed from Slim whose main shame theme focused on genital inferiority.

A common cause of shame in men would appear to be flight from sadistic use of the penis or from sadistic aggression of any kind. Fear of sadistic phallic behavior produces inhibition and the subsequent belief that one is shamefully impotent or unmasculine. Identifications with women may become pronounced in place of identifications with men because men are experienced as overly aggressive. Shame then follows from the belief that one is a castrated male. In some of these cases, early problems with separation from the mother seem to pave the way for a later defensive employment of sexual confusion and partial cross-gender identification. Perverse solutions to conflict over sadistic sexuality appear to come easily to some of these men because of the strong early identifications with Mother, the troubled identification with Father, and the erotic ties to Father. Clinical experience shows that shame in men also follows from inhibition or other forms of self-castration instituted to protect against the feared actual castration by the oedipally challenged father. Guilt also protects against castration anxiety in that guilt checks the dangerous impulse to confront the rival antagonistically.

Three of the five women interviewees generated central shame themes that were not evidently focused on the sexual self. Josephine's shame complaint was much like the men's central shame complaints. She worried about her ineffectiveness. She differed from the men in that her effectiveness concern was strongly and articulately connected with her mother's idiosyncratic expectations of her. Josephine's wish for effectiveness related to an intense wish to be worthwhile, not "wimpy" or overdependent in her mother's eyes and her own eyes. Nothing in the interviews suggested that this concern was primarily a transformation of wishes for sexual effectiveness, either in male or female form. Another female subject, Polly, generated shame imagery about being a nobody who longs for love, which she feels no one will want to give her. Again, the major concern is not apparently sexual.

The fifth woman, Katherine, generated few shame themes. Those she did produce include definite indications of shame over femininity. Katherine tries to avoid activities and feelings that associate her with femininity, though she does not refrain from sexual activity. A penis-envy interpretation is possible, but stronger evidence suggests that she associates gentle femininity with the vulnerability inherent in dependent wishes toward her parents, especially Mother. Since she feels that her parents did not want her (the last in a long line of children), she has to obscure all feelings associated with longing. Otherwise, she would experience hurt, depression, and shame. Ultimately she becomes ashamed both of her failure to be feminine like her mother and of her failure to interest Mother.

The women's major shame themes are somewhat more difficult to summarize than the men's. There is more obvious concern with the shame of loving when one is not loved in return. There is concern over sexuality, but the diverse nature of the sexual concerns is more impressive than the shared features. Shameful feminine sexuality can represent such fates as a perpetuation of dirtying contact with an alcoholic father, the revealing of dependent wishes toward a lovely but indifferent mother, or the misery of futile efforts to be as lovely or sexy as an idealized mother.

The female subjects often sharply differentiate sexiness from feminine social poise and charm. At times they fail to achieve sexual attractiveness (e.g., Polly when she is fat and dull). At other times, they fall short of their ideals of feminine gentleness (Katherine, for example), but sexual activity and vigor may be maintained even when a sense of gentle femininity is weakly established. Pristine functions in the opposite fashion. Terrified of sexual activity, she retains her sense of femininity by constant attention to her poise and (asexual) social graces.

Although femininity has somewhat different meanings for each woman, all of the female subjects periodically generate themes associating femininity with vulnerability and delicacy, which meet with unpleasantly intrusive, damaging, or demanding male attention. In each case, there is a tendency to embrace boyishness as a less vulnerable position and to keep one's femininity to oneself. All the female subjects, with the possible exception of Pristine, show this pattern. At times the vulnerability in relation to men appeared to be founded on a sense of weakness vis-à-vis an aggressive mother (Josephine), which generalized to produce a pervasive fear of intense, intrusive contact; or the vulnerability to men may rest on variously determined failures of identification with Mother (Matilda) which leave the girl feeling herself to be an impostor at femininity.

6

Shame in the Dynamic Interplay Between Feeling States

The discussion of shame themes in Chapter 5 was intended to articulate the varieties of concerns that can generate repeated experiences of shame and related feelings. The aim of this chapter is to explore the dynamic interplay between shame experiences and those feeling experiences that either follow from shame or give way to it. Also of interest are the points at which a person "chooses" shame over another emotional state, or vice versa, without actually passing through one conscious, identifiable state to reach the other.

Examination of feeling-state sequences should highlight the aspects of the shame experience that make it difficult to bear and cause a person to welcome the shift to (or the initial choice of) an alternative state of feeling. The examination also should highlight painful qualities of other emotions that make them so dysphoric that shame is at times experienced as a less troubling alternative. This type of analysis is important to the study of any feeling state. Even joyous exuberance imposes some strains—for example, eventual fatigue or loss of quiet, reassuring contact with others. And depression generates some comforts—for instance, creation of a steady state in which one can feel safe and grounded, though in other respects displeased. The sequential analysis of feeling states, with special attention to defensive sequences, constitutes a regular part of the clinical inference process as applied to psychological testing materials and psychotherapy sessions. Shame experience makes an appearance in a great variety of affect sequences. The sequences to be mentioned appeared prominently in the research interviews. At times, shifts from one state to another were evident in the subject's behavior during the interview itself. At other times, the person's recounting of his or her life outside the interview made it clear that such shifts occurred. Often the data suggested that the experience of one feeling had been defensively intensified in order to attenuate some other feeling.

A feeling state also can be regarded as a statement by the self about the self. Even when this emotional statement has defensive utility, the experienced state is more than a simple avoidance of another state and is worthy of attention in its particulars. Psychoanalytic discoveries concerning the defensive function of emotion represent an invaluable contribution to the explication of psychodynamics. But these same discoveries at times tend to reduce the analysis of emotion to the analysis of feelings as exclusively functional events rather than as expressive events. A complete analysis of a feeling experience identifies both its defensive aspects and its role in expressing a current belief about the state of the self.

A feeling state may have special significance because one attaches implications to the fact that one feels what one does. Depression may be viewed as a state that makes one like an ambivalently regarded friend or irritability may be a link to a resented brother. Pride may represent an experience of the self as strong and expansive, and it may serve initially as an escape from shame. But if pride also signifies a breech of one's religious principles, the pleasure in the experience may soon be lost to the implications of personal sinfulness.

INTERACTIONS BETWEEN SEXUAL EXCITEMENT AND SHAME, EMBARRASSMENT, AND HUMILIATION

Psychoanalytic writers frequently link shame experiences with sexual excitement. The theoretical link is made by way of reaction-formation, an unconscious superego prohibition of pleasurable sexual exhibitionism. Reaction-formation determines that (defensive) shame will appear rather than excitement. The arousal component of sexual excitement is thought to be retained by way of the arousal component of shame or embarrassment. The research data for this book, used in combination with additional clinical material, tend to support the idea that one form of association between shame and sexuality is the superego-mediated flight from positively experienced exhibitionism to negatively experienced shame or embarrassment. Shame and embarrassment experiences that originate in this particular way would appear to be common in neurosis. In these cases, the individual may experience shame after distorting the significance of some personal trait. Something that potentially is a source of pride, generally sexual pride, is regarded as a shameful blemish. For example, a woman with an unpleasantly thin mother begins to regard her own attractive curves as shameful obesity. At other times, shame follows when an individual forces himself to abandon a prideful behavior, instead pursuing something he considers to be inferior. In these cases, the person generally does not recognize that he has required himself to behave shamefully out of guilt. For example, a man who is guilty about intellectual successes requires himself to speak in a shamefully disorganized manner. I would limit the use of the term reaction-formation to those instances in which an individual distorts the significance of some act or feature so that something that should be a source of narcissistic pleasure is reacted to as shameful. I have the impression that reaction-formation has been used more generally, as a designation for any experience of shame that somewhere in its genesis has roots in superego conflict over exhibitionism. Little attention is paid to the various twists and turns marking the routes taken from prideful exhibitionism to shame.

The association between sexual excitement and shame need not be made through reaction-formation or other reactions of conscience. A straightforward shame response may follow sexual excitement or exhibitionistic behavior if the underpinnings of sexual self-esteem are weak. Sexual feelings then lead to concerns about whether one is adequately womanly or manly. Sexual behavior may serve as a reminder of shame experienced in childhood when adults ridiculed the child's efforts to be charming, lovable, or impressive.

In previous chapters of this monograph, I have suggested that embarrassment reflects feelings—especially sexual or exhibitionistic excitement—that are poorly integrated into the identity. The integrative failure may rest on a variety of bases, including a guilt dynamic such as that outlined earlier. If guilt precludes sexual freedom, then sexual feelings may be experienced as alien, uncomfortable, and overexposing, and thus embarrassing. Other sources of integrative failure may occur. One may dissociate oneself from sexuality out of an infantile belief that the sexual partner will angrily damage one's genitals (or vice versa) during intercourse, or sexual feeling may be denied because the implied separation from the parents is intolerable. Sexuality may become so alien as to caused a confused embarrassment when sexual feelings emerge unexpectedly.

The aroused or stimulated quality both of shame (or embarrassment) and exhibitionistic excitement does seem to represent an important link between the two categories of experience. The feeling of arousal often associated with shame and with exhibitionistic excitement promotes rapid shifts between the two experiences, defensive relationships between them, and indistinct boundaries between them. For example, a female hysteric confronted with an older man who for her has multiple, intense, unconscious or unarticulated meanings might respond to this person's presence with a state of physical-affective arousal. Such states of intense excitement may be labeled shame as often they are labeled sexual excitement: The belief that sexual excitement is dangerous in the situation, or inappropriate to it, may obscure the suitability of that affect label to the preconceptual emotional experience. The person is left with an uncomfortably excited feeling that is difficult to label. The label shame, or embarrassment, may begin to feel appropriate not only because sexual guilt opens the door to affect labels that suggest something is wrong with the self, but also because the presence of confusing emotion that does not lead to clear, effective action may make the person feel so undone that she now has a secondary reason to believe she is ashamed: She is ashamed not just of her sexual response but of her tense, confused emotional state as well. Often, in psychotherapy, patients report shame when sexual fantasies lead to arousal, which then is interpreted in a self-demeaning rather than a self-enhancing fashion. For example, rather than allow himself the fantasy that the female therapist responds admiringly to his body, a male patient might tell himself that his body is flabby and weak; therefore, the excitement associated with fantasies of exposing it must be shame. If the struggle between proud exhibitionism and shameful exposure remains undecided, the person might feel embarrassed rather than clearly ashamed.

The relationships between humiliation and sexual excitement could probably sustain a separate volume. In the data at hand, particularly the case of Frank, the man who attempted a rape, we see repeated flights from positively experienced excitement to feelings of humiliation. Positively experienced excitement is associated with ecstatic feelings of triumph. He has gained power in relation to a critical or withholding woman. The feelings of triumph bring anxiety about retaliation, and they bring guilt because of their sadistic component. When feeling excited and triumphant, Frank ultimately becomes so threatened by fear of retaliation and fear of an intolerable alienation from the love object, over whom he has prevailed, that the triumphant feeling cannot be sustained. Humiliation would appear to enter at some of these junctures. He becomes the defeated one, not the victor, and he is humiliated by his loss (or abdication) of control.

For Frank, there is no clear evidence that the humiliation representing the flight from sadistic dominance is itself a sexually exciting state. In some clinical cases, we do see sexual excitement over the prospect of humiliation (Rangell, 1952). These situations, too, seem to give power dynamics a special role. Certain dynamic relationships between powerlessness and excitement may partly explain the erotic response to humiliation. Powerlessness certainly can generate excitement, especially physical powerlessness. Often such excitement has both a fearful and a pleasurable quality. The feelings associated with riding a roller coaster serve as an example. Fear and excitement intermingle when the overpowering force evokes both expectations of being hurt (or traumatized by excessive stimulation) and fantasies of ecstatic delight. The inefficacy of all personal responses, especially attempts at active mastery through physical activity, appears to heighten stimulation. For example, if one is tied up and tickled, the inability to escape the stimulation or to reduce it through activity intensifies apprehension and excitement. All one can do is to experience the stimulation. There is no way to modulate it. The quality of excitement will vary depending on a variety of factors including one's expectation of pleasure or of trauma. Humiliation generally involves loss of power, but loss of power is not always humiliating. Persistent sexual excitement experienced when a quality of humiliation is added to the loss of power would signify an atypical association between degradation and arousal (Rangell, 1952). In the case of Frank, who seems to court humiliation (though he gives no clear indication of intense sexual pleasure accompanying humiliation), his most intimate contacts with his father were spanking sessions conducted not at the moment of transgression but by arrangement in the child's bedroom. One thus might expect that a humiliating situation also provided intimate and passionate contact. A man in treatment often imagined that he would provoke other men to beat him. He seemed both frightened and aroused by such images. The images appeared to give him license for unrestrained aggression against male competitors. As long as he was clearly the weaker and more humiliated combatant, he could discharge his aggression furiously. He also appeared to be aroused by the image of intense homoerotic contact with the oedipal competitor.

Excitement experienced during humiliations can signify identification with the perpetrator of the humiliation. The person tied and beaten may experience so vividly the assaultive, demeaning activity of the humiliator that his experience while humiliated is one of sadistic aggression more than one of subjugation. Union with a sadistic other can bring feelings of safety achieved through intimate and dependent association with a person of great power. In other cases, sexual guilt is so profound that humiliation represents a compromise-formation. Excitement is allowed as long as a penance is exacted through degradation; inhibition precludes excitement in response to a potent or sensual partner who is loving rather than frightening. An obsessional woman raised in a religious family showed this pattern. She could allow herself sexual relationships only with men who were hypercritical of her. These criticisms represented an externalized conscience. As long as she absorbed insults and sadistic directives from the partner, she was able to sustain the relationship. For this woman, emotional abuse during sexual activity was not in itself exciting. Abuse was not a stimulant; it was only the necessary precondition for a sexual relationship.

The shared feature in most cases with prominent humiliation themes is the experience of relationships characterized by great power differentials. One person dominates the other. Humiliation and its complementary state, triumph, follow from this conceptualization of relationships.

Vulnerability to shame in sexual situations is a common experience. Less common is the turning of such fear and vulnerability into the primary source of excitement, not just the companion of excitement. Typically, shame vulnerability in sexual contexts rests in part on the relationship between excitement and novelty. That which is different-from-the-self, new, and capable of surprising is most likely to excite, but it is also most likely to surprise the self in a negative, shaming way. Thus a new sexual partner may bring an intensification both of arousal and of vulnerability to shame. Vulnerability to shame in such a situation can be reduced by strengthening the belief that self and other are alike or by devaluing the other, but generally such protective perceptions compromise excitement.

Sexual intimacy represents the great, prohibited aspiration of childhood in our culture. Guilt over sexual intimacy will in turn promote shame either by blocking efforts to invest positive feeling in one's adult sexuality or by actively enlisting shame (or humiliation) feelings as punishment for forbidden sexual activity. When guilt over sexual intimacy prevails, shame vulnerability is further increased by the reduced availability of the internal good parent as a source of reassurance regarding one's worth and goodness.

INTERACTIONS BETWEEN SHAME AND ANGER

Studying the interview data for this project, I was repeatedly impressed by apparent interactions between shame experience and anger. These interactions seem both frequent and highly consequential for character development and for symptom development. By use of the word "interactions," I mean to designate a number of phenomena. Shame and anger experiences interact when one state is the direct cause of the other, for example, when a person becomes ashamed *of* his or her anger, or angry *because* he or she has been reduced to shame. The two also interact when one state represents a sanctuary from the other state, which has presented the person with a painful self-image, a painful image of another, or a painful feeling of disorganization or overstimulation. In the interview data, we see people opting for one emotion as an apparent protection against another emotion. This occurs despite the person's denying even a transient experience of the more dreaded feeling state. Though the individual denies any acquaintance with the more noxious emotion and any fear of its development, his or her communications suggest that such a fear is psychologically influential. Finally, superego-motivated inhibitions of anger frequently result in shame feeling: When anger is inhibited, the ground becomes fertile for shame development in ways I shall later discuss in greater detail.

Shame as a Judgment Against Unacceptable Anger

William experienced progressions from aggression to shame based on the conviction that his anger was a morally inferior response. He described an experience of repeatedly asking a young woman for a date. She always had a reason not to go. Finally, she agreed to a date, but she cancelled at the last minute. William then saw her in a bar and was rude and insulting to her. Subsequently he became ashamed of his hostile behavior. As with Frank, William's ego-ideal emphasized kind, rational, controlled behavior. His hostility toward the woman violated this ideal and could not be accepted. Equally important, his sarcastic, spiteful behavior must have felt uncharacteristically childish and chaotic to him. If sustained, the behavior would have brought him dangerously close to recognition—thus far eluded—that the woman's refusal had great potential to hurt, frighten, and shame him. Independence was the backbone of this man's functioning, thus to recognize a potentially disruptive impact from another would have been a significant threat. He found it more palatable to accept his immorality and the moral shame over that fault than to accept the shame of disrupted functioning and disturbed self-esteem in response to a girl's rejection. William's early shame memories focus on shame over threats to masculinity. His later shame experiences focus on immoral aggressiveness. The latter shame-type seems to be less disruptive to him now than the former, presumably in part because a feeling of strengthened masculinity attends his preoccupation with a strong morality, even if the preoccupation follows a guilt-producing violation of his standards. Recognition of performance shortcomings brings no such covert confirmation of masculinity and good character. Thus, his shift from aggression to shame over immorality satisfies his conscience, confirms his identity as a moral person, and prevents crystallization of vague feelings that his manliness is in question.

Shame Relieved by Anger

Subjects who claim to feel no shame or very little shame (e.g., Katherine and Cal) often achieve their shame-free states by reflexively attacking anyone who stimulates an incipient shame experience. When Katherine opened frilly underpants in front of boys and felt embarrassed, she slapped the gift-giver with the underpants. She then became preoccupied with her feeling that she had been rude and aggressive. In telling the story, she acknowledged guilt over her rudeness as well as an unexplained "embarrassment" but she denied any additional feelings such as shame. A move from shame to aggression represents a shift from a passive state in which one is victimized by pain to a state in which the self mobilizes around an action. Katherine's intolerance of states of passivity that are accompanied by intense feeling appears to be associated with her longstanding feeling of estrangement from her mother. The less a child has confidence that a parent will tolerate the child's states of vulnerability and help him or her gradually to re-establish the self-respecting, active self, the greater will be the impetus to leap into reflexively aggressive states. For at least two interviewees, Cal and Matilda, caustic responses to real or imagined criticism were a major determinant of the person's predominant interactive style.

Anger De-emphasized Through Shame Emphasis

Josephine frequently felt ashamed of her own poorly controlled behavior, and she contrasted this behavior to her mother's tough, cool personality. But occasional comments suggested that she may have been zealous in her breast-beating as much from a need to highlight her mother's courage as from a simple perception of her own cowardice. Out of the need to strengthen her mother, thoughts of angrily insulting Mother quickly gave way to guilt or to shame over Josephine's own lack of control. For example, she mentioned once that as a child she had been critical of her mother. Asked about that critical sentiment, she responded:

S: Sometimes maybe I didn't think that she was in control of everything. Because she would get excited and yell at my dad and yell at me and—I feel badly now, about what I've told you.

I: Why is that?

S: I don't know, because I don't want to put her down or anything, you know.

Josephine makes but one or two references to Mother's deficient self-control. They quickly produce conflict and she backs away from them. In contrast, she continually draws attention to her own failures of self-control. She portrays herself as wimpy and portrays her mother as tough.

Josephine is moved to shame not because she is invariably ashamed about her aggression, like William was. She seems instead to be frightened by her aggression (for complex reasons to be discussed later); she prefers shame, another response that makes sense to her in the situation but is more acceptable. She bypasses the experience of aggression toward her mother and moves directly to shame.

Shame Flourishing When Anger Is Inhibited

I have suggested that Josephine emphasizes her own shameful weaknesses of will in order to deflect attention from such weaknesses in her mother. She actively pursues self-shaming in order to protect a relationship. In other cases, shame is not the antagonist to anger, pursued in order to deflect anger; it is an experience that grows with unnatural vigor when aggression cannot be used to counteract it. We can illustrate this dynamic by thinking of a woman who walks into a store and finds herself unable to ask the storekeeper for what she wants. She experiences her problem as a problem of self-esteem. She feels that she is ashamed of herself as a wishy-washy, inferior, unattractive person who should have no right to get anything she wants. Analysis reveals a profound inhibition of aggression based primarily on a fantasy of doing damage to the other person through overly demanding behavior. When the inhibition of aggression is relieved, the shame feelings spontaneously lose their potency. The belief that she is unattractive may remain intact, but it has less significance and does not inhibit action. She is able to argue with the belief, to defend herself against it actively. This type of dynamic suggests that shame is a natural potential in many situations. When aggression is tolerated, shame often can be kept at a low level. The person can combat his or her self-doubts by disputing their validity and by pressing ahead into action. But when aggression is inhibited, both in interactions with the outer world and in internal pursuit of self-esteem, shame can grow unchecked.

To the guilty person, shame often feels proper and deserved. The guilty person who inhibits aggressiveness often will experience shame, not just because of feeling no license to defend his or her self-esteem, but because guilt makes a person feel that an actual attack on the self is deserved. Shame ideas about the self then represent the deserved attack. A clinical example of this dynamic is a man who heard on a talk show that women enjoy sexually aggressive, even abusive partners. The statement upset him, ostensibly because he felt himself to be incapable of such aggression. He was convinced that his wife's first husband was more of a man than he and more capable of such aggressive sexual intercourse. He dwelt on the image of himself as a shamefully impotent, castrated, sexually pathetic man. Analysis of the fantasy revealed evidence that his chain of thought was initiated by conflict over his own powerful sadistic fantasies toward women. The comment made on the talk show created such a temptation to acknowledge and enact these feelings that he reacted against it by denying his aggressive potential and attributing it—recast as a masculine virtue—to his rival. His conviction that he was shamefully emasculated clearly served as a denial of his sadism and as a punishment for having entertained sadistic fantasy. It also appeared to serve as the germ for an alternate form of sexual satisfaction. He would become the effeminate man whose femininity would provoke other men to attack or seduce him. Thus he would be punished for his sadism but also gratified through exciting, albeit masochistic, intimacies with other men. He would also be justified in expressing sadism toward these oedipal competitors. The man's sadism toward women represented in part a regression from fantasies of a sexually available woman to fantasies of a teasing, withholding woman. He had to flee from images of an available woman because these would have tempted him into a dangerous competition with the powerful oedipal father.

Often guilty people anticipate that they will do foolish things that will stimulate others to shame or embarrass or humiliate them. In these instances, they are projecting superego activity and attributing to others those impulses to punish them (via shame) that they themselves are inclined to feel. Upon analysis, many of the "foolish" acts such people fear they inadvertently will perform appear to be aggressive rather than truly foolish. One emphasizes the foolish side of one's action rather than the aggressive aspect, because at that moment it is less threatening to see oneself as humiliated than to see oneself as hostile.

The examples given suggest that many problems presenting as profound self-esteem issues, accompanied by complaints of shame, under close examination prove to be examples of shame that flourishes when the self is disorganized by anxiety or actively assaulted by guilt-driven self-hate. Therapy cannot approach such self-esteem problems directly by providing support and empathically reviewing memories of parental ridicule or neglect. These self-esteem problems are best viewed as experiences that evolved from and continue to depend on an active conflict over aggression.

It would be wrong to conclude that an emotional problem such as that illustrated in the storekeeper example reduces to an instinctual conflict and not a narcissistic problem. The shame is real and painful and must be acknowledged as such. It cannot be dismissed as a meaningless epiphenomenon. And the underlying conflict over aggression cannot be conceptualized without reference to self-esteem. Indeed, the problematic aggression may be the consequence of narcissistic affront. If the woman in the storekeeper example feels that her aggression is dangerous and therefore must be inhibited, then she feels that *she* is dangerous. Put most severely, she may feel herself to be an animal or a monster. This then becomes a problem of self-esteem, as well as a concern over harming others. By inhibiting aggression, she tries to prevent damage to others and to avoid the experience of the monster identity. Thus one would not conclude that the inhibition of aggression does not reflect a narcissistic problem. But the narcissistic problem centers on self-hate more than on the shame over being wishy-washy and ineffective. Granted, a profound feeling of helplessness may lead to defensive, omnipotent "monstrousness," which then leads to aggression-conflict; and in such an instance the narcissistic problem might be seen as deeper than the impulse-conflict. But even in such a circumstance, aggression-management and its impact on self-esteem will be of crucial therapeutic importance.

At times it makes sense to view the interface between aggression and self-esteem as an interface between conflict and structure. Conflict around aggression (or other emotions) can lead to problems with self-esteem. These then present themselves as problems of self-structure. They present as defects of self-esteem, which are static situations. That characterization is not without validity, but it may obscure the ongoing conflict, which continues to function as the wellspring of the structure. One cannot repair the defect through direct attention to it. One must resolve the conflict that actively maintains a structure that otherwise would dissolve.

Of course, the cause and effect relationship between aggression-management and self-esteem may at times work in the reverse direction. That is, pervasive deficits of self-regard may make it difficult for an individual to feel entitled to make aggressive demands on others. Or self-esteem deficits may make a person feel too weak to tolerate the aggressive response his or her hostility might provoke. If inhibitory efforts fail, the person may express aggression chaotically, without full approval of the conscience and of the reality-appraising functions of the personality. Such chaotic expressions of aggression would lead to further decline of self-regard, as would the constant inhibition of appropriate aggression.

Shame Conceptualized as Anger Turned Against the Self

Erikson wrote of conceptualizing shame—with its self-hiding, self-reproaching aspects—as anger turned against the self. I prefer to keep the two states, anger and shame, conceptually separate because of their distinct experiential qualities. One nevertheless can recognize a variety of dynamic interactions between shame and anger. The value of Erikson's concept is that it identifies the particular situation in which an individual who feels that he or she cannot or ought not to express anger instead becomes self-critical and feels ashamed. A childish emotional logic argues that when someone accuses, someone must be in the wrong. Thus either the accuser is at fault or the accused has been justly criticized. If the fault cannot be laid with the accuser, it must be taken upon the accused self. The resulting emotion may feel like self-hate or it may feel like depression or shame. But to conceptualize shame as aggression turned against the self ignores the often distinct phenomenologies of shame and anger, each with its own analogues in nonhuman animals (e.g., appeasement behaviors as shame analogues in nonhumans [Knapp, 1967]) and each with infantile forms or precursors, in humans, that seem reasonably distinct from each other (e.g., stranger anxiety as a forerunner of shame rather than of anger). The conceptualization also makes it difficult to think about those shame experiences that represent an appropriate response to real deficiencies as well as those that seem to be self-protective and self-loving more than they are self-attacking. Such shame experiences might be described as efforts to hide the self in order to save it from further narcissistic trauma. And the conceptualization of shame as anger turned against the self tends to fuse shame and depression because depression, too, is regularly understood as introverted anger.

"Shame" and "depression" designate states that at times are not altogether distinct from one another. Nevertheless, the words seem worthy of independent definition, because at certain times their referents *are* quite distinct and, even when they are not, the shame-component of an experience is distinguishable from the depression-component. The word depression historically has been used to designate a great range of states, all of which hold in common the experience of lowered pleasure in life and reduced engagement with the ordinary world. Self-esteem generally suffers when a person is in a state of depression, either because the individual feels actively self-hateful, as in the melancholic states described by Freud and others, or because self-esteem cannot be maintained when the individual experiences himself or herself as withdrawn, pessimistic, childish, exhausted, or powerless. There are numerous forms of depression—all of which have received attention in the literature—ranging from dynamically complex states of despairing self-hatred to the simple depressed mood, often accompanied by mourning work, that may follow the completion of a project to which one has dedicated much energy.

When an ashamed person judges that he or she cannot correct a personal deficiency that diminishes self-esteem, the person may become depressed. Though depression is an unpleasant state, simple depression unaccompanied by extreme self-hate or paranoia can be restful when compared with acute shame. Thus, when a person has suffered shame that seems inescapable because the false step cannot be retracted or the defect corrected, he or she ultimately may cease to experience acute shame and may settle into depression. States of shame and depression may alternate as a person engages and disengages from a conflict. A young woman patient approaching her oral exams in history generated frightening images of utter failure. The shame images appeared to be the outcome of two trends. First, there was a need to fail rather than to shine. To succeed would be to humiliate and demoralize the oedipal rival. Second, there was a conflict over sexual identity, which dictated that she use the orals to prove that she was triumphantly masculine, not feminine. The latter goal was inherently unattainable, thus shame followed straightforwardly from images of showing that she was "nothing but a woman." As this woman approached her orals, she alternated between shame in anticipation of failure, and depression when she backed away from the conflict. In the depressed state, her anticipated disappointment about her functioning was not nearly so vividly imagined or actively combated as in the ashamed state. In the depressed mood, she felt lethargic and incapable of stirring herself to make the active response that she knew the orals would require. The depression seems to have represented passive retreat from a losing battle combined with active inhibition of efforts to succeed in the orals situation.

Grinker (1955) has discussed the influence of shame in promoting profound, even suicidal, depression. He treated a young woman who had great difficulty functioning away from her mother. Grinker encouraged the young woman not to force herself to return to college. He believes that her eventual suicide is explained by her intolerable shame over regression and her belief that progressive functioning was impossible for her. Other writers (Lynd, 1958) have discussed the growth-promoting effects of shame in contrast with guilt. Guilt is seen as inhibiting adequate behavior in the world, while shame stimulates self-improvement. It would seem that shame can produce either depression or growth, depending on whether one feels able to overcome the defect that stimulates shame. If the defect is inherently uncorrectable or is inalterable due to guilt or to an overestimation of its permanence, then depression is the likely outcome.

Shame and subsequent depression in response to developmental failure certainly ought not to be conceptualized as an invariably pathological response indicative of neurosis or narcissistic pathology. Some degree of shame or depression is appropriate when one reflects on an inability to do what others can do or be what others can be. In treating patients who suffer from deep shame, it is important to distinguish between pathological shame that is itself the primary problem the treatment must address and shame that is an expectable outgrowth of those developmental failures resulting from neurotic conflicts or interpersonal fears (e.g., profound separation anxieties). If shame is secondary to alterable developmental failures, the patient can be helped to acknowledge his or her shame and to live with it while working on the psychological problems that have interfered with normal development.

SHAME, SELF-HATE, AND SELF-DISGUST

A person who perceives what he or she takes to be a personal flaw may cringe before awful images of a pathetically shameful self or may turn toward himself or herself—as if toward another—and begin to berate the self with feelings of hate or disgust. Periodic shifts from painful shame into self-hate were observed in several research subjects. Others showed an ongoing enthusiasm for aggressive self-attack, which appeared to leave them minimally susceptible to shame. Shifts to self-hate and ongoing preferences for it both may be motivated by the vigorous activity inherent in the experience of self-hate. When ashamed, a person often feels helpless. He or she can be acutely aware of personal defects but at a loss over how to relieve the pain. The person may sink into depression or imagine constructive future activity that would recreate the self-image in a more estimable form. But often the solace the person imagines depends on the impossible deed of undoing actions or impressions of the recent past. The move into self-hate is like a move from flailing about helplessly to vigorous, steady hammering. The shift to self-hate backfires at the point when the person must put aside mastery-through-fantasy and must resume functioning in the world. The relief coming from self-attack is exposed as fraudulent because the person recognizes with sudden anguish and anxiety that the attacked, dissociated aspects are indeed self and they must be reintegrated in order for one to proceed into the world feeling whole. For example, a crippled person may prefer to make angry, contemptuous remarks about his or her bad leg rather than to imagine walking out in public ashamed of limping. But when the person must walk out, if still insisting on an attitude of self-hate and self-disgust, he or she will be likely to bruise or bang the leg on a passing obstacle and unlikely to take care in learning to adjust to the disability. A writer who reacts with shame to a critical review might take a red pencil to his or her work and feel some relief. But if fueled by too much self-hate, the editing may leave the work in fragments with nothing that is still seen as good. Matilda relies on self-attack in some areas of her life. Her self-directed aggression drives her toward perfectionism and toward sharply limited self-expression. She constantly dissociates herself from romantic feeling by using the language of humorous self-disgust. She describes her early poetic interest as "dying and desperate love for some guy that never looks at you, you know, that kind of crap."

SHAME, HATRED, DISGUST, AND CONTEMPT

A television interview brought into focus a particular dynamic relationship between shame and hatred. A policeman was addressing charges that he had killed a young boy after minimal provocation. A remarkably bland, mildly spiteful tone distinguished the man's response to the interviewer. At one point he began to describe the death of this boy as well as other deaths he had witnessed consequent to his own or others' aggression. He referred to people who die with "appropriate" reserve and to other, more emotional people whom he felt embarrassed to watch die. His comments suggested that his fear of shameful weaknesses within himself was so great that he despised and to an extent felt justified in killing others who showed such weaknesses. He experienced their displays of cowardly or uncontrolled actions as if they were his own; such displays "embarrassed" him. The intensity of the policeman's hatred toward weak others who embarrass him also points to the possibility that he once despised a parent for his or her weakness—weakness that compromised the boy's self-esteem because of his identification with the parent. The boy might then have struggled desperately to keep the self free of the shameful and hateful defects he perceived in the parent.

Several research subjects showed disgust, contempt, and hatred for others in contexts that suggested that these attitudes derived from projection onto others of traits unacceptable in the self. If owned, the traits would produce either shame or guilt, depending on their nature. For example, Josephine felt contemptuous of women who are highly dependent on others' opinions and much invested in being warmly accepted by others. Josephine vacillated between such contempt—accompanied by the conviction that she herself is tough, cool, and independent—and open shame over her own clinging dependency on others.

INTERACTIONS BETWEEN SHAME AND FEELINGS OF SUPERIORITY OR TRIUMPH

In moving defensively from shame to angry attack, or from shame to active contempt, disgust, or hatred, a person shifts attention from the disappointing or publicly humiliating quality of the self to defects in another. In contrast, the shift from shame to superiority feelings maintains attention on the character of the self. Superiority feelings may signify a state in which one tells oneself that one has *disengaged* from the other, who is seen as not being worth the bother of a sustained relationship. Or superiority may be experienced *in relation to* another person from whom one has not entirely disengaged. In the latter situation, the world remains object-filled even though there is no interaction between objects. In contrast to superiority feelings, aggressive feelings represent obvious continued engagement. Josephine described swings from feeling ashamed and deflated to feeling superior and inflated. During her interviews, she enacted the sequence apparently without awareness of it. In the passage that follows, she comments on "silly" women to whom she feels superior. She implicates her own feelings of estrangement as the wellspring of her contempt:

S: I am cool but—but maybe it would be better to not feel that way and more feel, "Hah-Hah, isn't she being silly?"

I: More a part of it, you mean?

S: Yeah, exactly, I feel out of it a lot, and maybe what I try to do to make myself feel better—since childhood I felt out of it, I feel like people don't like me—so maybe I decided, "Who cares? I'd rather be with *me* anyway, because I'm so much more interesting, I'm so much more unique."

Lewis (1977) discusses dynamics of shame and triumph in a book on shame and guilt:

A "righting" tendency often evoked by shame is the "turning of the tables." Evoked hostility presses toward triumph over or humiliation of the "other", i.e., to the vicarious experience of the other's shame. (p. 42)

For Josephine, the belief in her own superiority relieves her of feeling cast out and self-critical, but leaves her alone in the world with an awareness that she has artificially inflated her self-esteem.

INTERACTIONS BETWEEN SHAME AND OMNIPOTENCE

Omnipotence as a defense against shame and vulnerability has received considerable attention in the psychoanalytic literature. Shame can also function as a defense against the dangers of omnipotence. A man in psychotherapy was plagued by intermittent feelings that he had lost his masculinity. During these periods he generally felt agitated and depersonalized. He was frantic to engage in sexual activity in order to reassure himself that he remained masculine. But sexual encounters terrified him because of his alarming feeling that there was literally "nothing down there," a reference to his genitals. He forced himself mentally to rehearse sexual relations with every woman he encountered even casually. He felt that he might be forced at any moment to have intercourse; therefore, he should try to remind himself of what it felt like to feel masculine and to have erotic sensations. He complained of a profound sense of shame with regard to this castrated condition.

When in despair over his emasculation, this man sometimes would describe to the female therapist his feeling of losing his genitals. In telling of his plight, he would erupt involuntarily into a tickled, delighted brief laughter. He could not understand this laughter over such a serious, shameful, almost tragic matter, but he associated it with a feeling of amazement and comic resignation with regard to his perverse ability to so completely frustrate his sexual wishes and so effectively render himself a most ridiculous, castrated figure. He laughed over fantasies of going into a woman's bedroom, taking down his pants, and announcing that there was nothing there. In listening to these tales, the therapist felt that the man's outbursts of laughter related to a feeling or fantasy of magical power. As the treatment developed, a number of dynamics unfolded. The flip-side of the feeling of castration was a conviction on the patient's part that he had magical sexual power over women, which no other man had. Thus he would feel certain, in these literally "omni-potent" periods, that a beautiful woman could turn down scores of men who were eager to seduce her, but when the patient approached, she would offer herself to him without question. In these states he felt dangerous to other men (and also dangerous to women, but that is another matter). He felt he could emasculate other men at will. He could take puffed up, proud, monumental men and turn them into wilted remnants of their former selves. The burden of this power over another man's masculinity motivated him to retreat into a castrated state from which he represented a threat to no one. The castrated state also protected him from the dangers associated with being a male child in the presence of a seductive mother. He shifted from omnipotent sexuality to impotence, and from pride and aggressiveness to passivity and shame. But the feeling of omnipotence about sexuality and the anxious delight in such sadistically utilized power survived in the form of delighted laughter regarding his magic ability to transform himself into a eunuch. He himself became the object of his magical powers and he spared the other man from damage. Later developments in the treatment suggested that the feeling of omnipotence relative to other men was partly a defense against castration anxiety in an oedipal context. But the omnipotent defense against shameful castration itself became threatening (e.g., it might injure Father or provoke Father to retaliate) and was defended against, ironically, by a self-imposed realization of the dreaded castrated state.

INTERACTIONS BETWEEN SHAME AND GUILT

Both in the psychological literature and in informal conversation about feeling states, discussion of shame frequently brings spontaneous mention of guilt. Under the heading "Shame," the *Psychological Abstracts* lists only, "See Guilt." Shame and guilt often co-occur, and they hold certain elements in common. Due to these shared features, shifts between the states occur rapidly and conceptual boundaries between the feeling-categories are difficult to maintain. Shame and guilt are most similar and most easily confused when moral shame is the type in question. Shame over ineffectiveness (as opposed to shame over immorality) generally is well distinguished from guilt. In fact, the clear differences between shame and guilt when shame involves no moral issues may explain the common conviction that shame and guilt are different states even though they are sometimes hard to distinguish.

Alexander (1938) described affect sequences involving shame and guilt. My data support his descriptions and explanations of shame-guilt sequences. Guilt gives way to shame once guilt has put an end to aggressive behavior and has initiated passive behavior that the person judges to be pathetic or inferior. Shame over ineffectiveness may lead back again to guilt once shame inspires intensification of aggressive behavior. Wurmser noted cycles of shame and guilt in a claustrophobic patient:

> The most prominent boundary dilemma was the one between the guiltful expansion of power in success versus the shameful collapse of power in humiliation. In both instances, Andreas used the metaphor of "invisible lines": when his enemies violated his shame boundary he had to kill. . . . It was always the shame boundary which, if crossed by a foe, absolutely needed to be defended by bloodiest violence. But before this occurred, there was a crash of self-esteem, a stunning, paralyzing sense of humiliation which could only be repaired by revenge. (p. 321)

Repeated cycles of shame and guilt can have great significance in determining the course of a life. William displayed such a cycle in his relationships to women. Doubts about his masculine effectiveness sensitized him to apparent rebuffs by women and motivated him to act sexually forceful in congruence with images of admired, powerful men. However, due to superego projection, he also feared that women would indict him as insensitive or brutal. If a woman seemed anxious in the face of his aggressive pursuit, he immediately would retreat into passivity. In the recoiled state, he once again felt ashamed of his weakness and felt impelled to assert himself aggressively.

In discussing the relationship between moral shame and guilt, less emphasis need be placed on the possibility of a dynamic sequence in which one state promotes behavior that in turn induces the other state. Often, moral shame and guilt occur together in response to the same behavior. As defined earlier, shame involves attention directed to a specific self-image. The person recoils in shame over some defect represented in the image. The guilty person attends to his or her action, not to a self-image. "Action" includes any production for which the person holds himself or herself responsible, be it a dream, a fantasy, an accident, or a deliberate deed. As an example of the subtle distinction between guilt and moral shame, one could consider a man who has been incarcerated in a brutal prison environment. He has done nothing grossly inhumane during his incarceration, but he has witnessed others' cruelties. In the guilt state, after release, he torments himself over numerous minor acts performed or thoughts experienced while in the prison. His complaints to himself take the form, "How could I have *done* that?" The action may be vividly imagined, especially in its effect on the injured party, but the recollection of the action does not center on an elaborated image of the self. The basic image of the self is taken for granted: Of interest is the action in which the self engaged. At another moment, in a moral shame state, the man reviews the same minor cruelties by vividly imagining himself performing them. For example, he sees himself petulantly refusing to give food or a bit of blanket to another prisoner. Here he is not concerned with morality for its own sake. He is concerned with the degraded image he has of himself. Attention takes the form, "What kind of weak, inferior, childish, subhuman type of animal could have done that?" If he finds no specific personal actions to fault, attention focuses on the image of the self simply existing in the degrading, inhuman environment, as if to say, without regard to reason, "No decent person could have been in that monstrous place." One aspect of the rape victim's shame depends on this same emotional logic. The degradation inherent in the environment is experienced as so great that shame by mere association prevails, despite reason's counsel that the individual was not there by choice.[1] In the prison situation described, attention might shift rapidly between attention to one's behavior as a sign of personal inferiority (a shame signifier) and attention to one's behavior as an improper action that seeds and reseeds regret. Because guilt and moral shame are responses to the same behavior, because one response gives way to the other with only a slight shift in attention, and because both emphasize impropriety—though the emphases have different ends—guilt and moral shame are not readily distinguished by those who experience them.

Guilt and shame may be difficult to distinguish for individuals who feel either pervasively guilty or pervasively ashamed. For example, some people feel responsible for all qualities of the self, even those that are involuntary. A man who has a rash on his hands may feel ashamed to go out on a date looking unattractive and may also feel vaguely guilty. The guilt follows from the belief, which may be poorly articulated, that he is somehow responsible for the rash. The irrational sense of responsibility may follow from infantile or defensive omnipotence, from an association made between the rash and some secret sin of aggression or sexual license, or from other sources. But the constant quiet presence of guilt (or of shame, in other individuals) may obscure the conceptual boundaries between affect states.

Confusion between shame and guilt may follow from efforts to apply the terms to experiences that actually fit neither category. Experiences of the self as terribly "bad" or "evil" or "rotten" differ subtly both from shame, as already defined, and from guilt. Attention turns

---

[1] The painful emotion commonly described as survivor guilt probably includes a large component of (moral) shame. As an added complication, it is possible that guilt promotes shame as a punishment felt to be appropriate for actions perceived to be morally wrong.

to the image of the self, but not (as is typical of shame) to the self as pathetic or weak or inferior. Instead, the self is experienced as powerfully bad, contaminated, or dangerous. The status may be despised not because it signifies inferiority, but because it separates the self from humankind and horrifies the individual with inexplicable feelings. The guilt label fits poorly because attention is not on specific action that is regretted, but on the state of the self and on the regret and discomfort associated with such a state. Frank talks of a feeling that seems to be not quite guilt and not quite shame:

S: I don't know how to describe it for you, to describe it to myself. I felt kinda dirty inside. . . . maybe absolute disgust with myself. . . . I just had the feeling I was really a rotten person.

Ultimately, the recognition and description of a range of states having varying significance is more important than the categorization of a state as shame or guilt.

The shame and guilt literatures contain some discussion of shame-prone *types* and guilt-prone *types*, and some debate about which hypothetical type is more emotionally mature. Lynd (1958) contends that the tendency toward shame suggests greater emotional maturity than does the susceptibility to guilt. Her argument rests on her belief that shame-prone people have genuine sensitivity to others, whereas guilt-prone people live according to internal and external rules and not according to recognition of feeling:

But to a person who lives and views experience primarily along the guilt-righteousness axis, other persons tend to be primarily external and instrumental to himself or—another version of the same thing—he instrumental to them. This is true whether he regards them (or himself in relation to them) as indulgent or depriving agents administering pleasure or pain, as representing certain social roles, or as members of an audience who mete out approval or scorn. To a person oriented more to the shame-identity axis, other persons, They, or at least some of them, are parts of himself as he is part of them. (p. 236)

A person who lives more on the shame-identity or shame-freedom axis, and who opens himself to his emotions, faces other difficulties and other possibilities. There is not only more question of what I think of what I do and how it will effect others. Much more important, there is more ability to see the world through the eyes of another person, with another instead of myself as the center. (p. 236)

Lynd makes a valid point about one possible effect of guilt on object relations. Severe guilt may result in mechanical, obsessional functioning, which diminishes sensitivity to one's own and others' feelings.

Unfortunately, Lynd goes far beyond this simple point to generate an unfounded generalization about guilty people and ashamed people. The guilty are portrayed as essentially unconcerned with human feelings. The ashamed are portrayed as admirably united with others and sensitive to their feelings. The generalization is flawed in several respects. It ignores the development of considerable interpersonal sensitivity that may underlie the visible, rule-conscious (guilty) style. Many obsessional people with aloof, mechanical surfaces have histories of deep concern for others. Such concern remains evident to the careful observer and can be reintroduced into many areas of the person's life if extreme forms of guilt, requiring extreme defenses, are overcome. Thus, Lynd's generalization would seem to rest on a superficial assessment of the "mechanical" person's object images. In a second demonstration of that superficiality, she applauds the shame-prone person as deeply rooted in the human world. In a discussion of narcissistic personalities, Kohut (1971), too, comments about the very "close" relationships ("part-object" relationships) between a certain group of shame-prone people and their significant others. However, for Kohut, the fact that narcissistic personalities experience others as self-extensions is both the key to their shame propensity and the sign of their pathologically weak self-esteem. He contrasts the shame-prone narcissistic personality to the healthier, guilt-prone neurotic. Kohut's discussions make clear that shame-proneness, in and of itself, does not signify good human relations. Certainly the shame-prone person is sensitive to others' behaviors, but the person's perceptions often are transference-distorted and his or her concern may be highly egocentric.

Lynd's formulation carries the implication that people are *either* guilt-prone *or* shame-prone. Many people have severe shame problems *and* serious guilt problems. These states may co-exist or they may alternate in response to psychological dynamics. The frequency of such cases suggests a flaw in theories that outline dramatic, predictable object-relational differences between guilt-prone types and shame-prone types. Guilt-proneness or shame-proneness does not by itself predict the strength of a person's human relations. This argument is further supported by recognition that "shame" and "guilt" have a range of forms and will have different appearances when embedded in different personality structures. Also, both shame and guilt have different meanings depending on whether the words are used to refer to actually experienced emotion or to the propensity to develop an emotion. Lynd's descriptions of the guilty as mechanical and rule-controlled suggest obsessional people who may not *experience* much guilt. They ward off guilt through punitive self-control. But her de-

scriptions of the shame-prone bring to mind those who actually experience considerable shame. Thus, there may be an inconsistency within
her comments that confuses her argument. If she only includes the
shame-*experiencing* within the shame-prone group, she would be
likely to exclude those narcissistic personalities who constantly fend
off shame with arrogance. If she includes the shame-vulnerable, the
group Kohut describes as narcissistic personalities should be covered
by her comments.

NARCISSISTIC REPAIR STRATEGIES

Those dynamic interactions discussed thus far gave momentary relief
from a shame feeling, or they allowed the shame experience to be
bypassed altogether. Such dynamics appear in the experience of all
people, whether or not they have unusual problems with shame. Individuals who have severe, ongoing shame problems may develop regularly used patterns to support their self-esteem. These maneuvers no
longer appear as simple, transient defenses. They become significant
aspects of an individual's experience and identity. Some such strategies or structures are simply elaborations on the transient patterns
already identified. For example, a person threatened by severe shame
may organize his or her life around activities and sentiments that
express contempt toward particular others who represent externaliza-
tions of the person's own weaknesses. In this brief section, examples
will be presented of research subjects who counteract an ongoing
threat of shame by engaging in activity that reinforces self-esteem at
its most vulnerable juncture.

Matilda has received attention in several contexts. She is the young
woman who is prone to sexual embarrassment. Her embarassment
appears to result from poor integration into her identity of excited
sexual feelings and sexual competitiveness. This poor integration in
turn would appear to depend on the combined effects of guilt over
oedipal hostility and shame in response to feeling less feminine than
her sisters and mother. Her shame over deficient femininity is graphi-
cally described at numerous points. She sees herself as ugly, clumsy,
awkward, masculine, in continual struggle against dirtiness, and un-
suited to attract sexually engaging men. In her day to day life of work
and marriage, she responds to her feelings of feminine inadequacy by
embracing an asexual, if not masculine, identity of efficiency, hard
work, and productivity. She accepts that she is not feminine or attractive and tries to make herself valuable in genderless pursuits. She also
displays contempt for the values and personal habits of women who are

overly involved with their femininity. However . . . Matilda is a writer. And in her fiction and in the world of fellow writers that constitutes as great an interest as the writing itself, we see both the continued vitality of her feminine and sexual ambitions and the efforts she makes, in fantasy, to repair her feminine self-esteem. She keeps her writing world sharply separated from her everyday world. She does not show her work to her husband, her family, or her non-writing friends. When she is deeply involved in writing, she travels alone to meetings where people speak a special jargon suited to her particular type of writing. She has even divided her house into a meticulous upper floor and a messy basement that seems to represent her creative, feminine, yet ambivalently viewed underworld. In Chapter 5 we saw the everyday Matilda who renounces femininity. Here we see the secret Matilda who struggles to undo the shame damage she has sustained. She describes a portion of a story that she wrote. Details have been changed to protect confidentiality and the passage has been abridged:

> There's one [story] . . . where this bacteria gets into the air. Everybody's inhibitions fall away. . . . I figured everybody is gonna be terrifically embarrassed because they've all made asses of themselves in front of everybody else. . . . [The manager] runs into [the waitress] . . . and she hollers at him for knocking everything out of her hands, and he apologizes, forgetting that he outranks her, and then she bursts into tears. . . . and it turns out that she is, um, she took off all of her clothes and was dancing naked in the lobby and now everybody's teasing her, calling her Bitty Breasts and Funny Figure (laugh). He tries to explain to her that this is not a problem, that she's a very attractive female. [How can] you try and kiss a woman who's got these big forcefields [i.e., breasts] out here. . . . Basically they end up in bed and afterwards everything is fine.

Matilda's description of this story is one of many passages suggesting that the overriding concern of her secret writing world is the repair of shame damage. In this world she is a sexually interested, though insecure, woman and not an impostor. She isolates these restorative activities from her daily life out of her sense of vulnerability to ridicule were she to let her loved ones (or herself) know that she longs to be more attractive.

Despite her sexual conflicts, Matilda has a relatively liberal policy toward her sexual fantasy. She allows such fantasy to emerge in weakly disguised form as long as she fails to recognize the significance it has in counterbalancing images of herself as unfeminine. Pristine's sexual conflicts center on the belief that she will be touched sexually by men in ways that dirty, humiliate, and degrade her. She allows herself no such flamboyant expression of sexual wishes as Matilda permits.

Her sexual behavior is quite limited and her fantasy is circumscribed. Sexuality has been ruled out of her life to a great extent. Pristine does retain a fantasy of a proper, clean, quiet, marital sexual relationship. It remains to be seen whether such an image, carefully tended, will allow her some sexual satisfaction after marriage or whether it will collapse under the pressure of real sexual activity. With respect to her current situation, we can say that shame and humiliation are circumvented by avoiding sexual activity and by constructing an unrealistic image of herself as a perfectly pure, lovely lady uncompromised by vile sexual or aggressive impulses. Thus the essential shame protection is the identity circumscription.

Aba also shows a circumscription of identity that may result from his shame that he is fatherless. He has trouble thinking of himself as an adult man and he avoids overtures toward women in order not to risk embarrassment over failures to conduct himself properly with them. An additional, more active effort at self-esteem repair comes through repeated efforts to engage older men as sources of praise for his performances. A cherished fantasy involves performing athletically before crowds of people. Following the game, the prime minister searches him out in order to congratulate him. Aba seeks external confirmation of his worth in the manner described by Kohut, however, he does not display consistent arrogance or failure of empathy for others. On the contrary, he seems to be an openhearted person with a childlike orientation toward praise and a readiness to give praise and support to others whom he sees as needy.

7

Individual Patterns of Shame Experience

Discussions of shame in the previous chapters have tended to fuse (a) shame experiences that the person clearly feels and acknowledges, and (b) shame potentials or shame themes. Little has been made of the patterns of actually experienced emotion that differentiate individuals. The three case presentations to follow represent attempts to describe the individual's actual experience in the shame domain and to demonstrate how the person's predominant shame patterns correspond to other aspects of his or her affect life and identity formation. Of special interest are formal congruities between the individual's shame life and other areas of the person's experience.

FRANK: KEEPING A MOTHERLY EYE ON ONESELF

Frank stood out among the subjects as the one individual who experienced profound pessimism about his life and about life in general. Other subjects suffered from deeply painful feelings, but only Frank seemed weighted down with all the miseries of the universe. Frank's pain consisted primarily of depression and shame. Often he could not differentiate his shame from guilt. Frank's masochism has already been discussed as a dynamic that contributes to his readiness to experience shame and guilt (Chapters 5 and 6). Of interest here are the formal aspects of Frank's shame experience and their relationship to other formal aspects of his affect life. As experienced by Frank, shame involves close and active attention to the status of the self. His shame consists of an attentive internal review of how the self and body are faring in the world:

S: I guess the only way I can define [shame] is . . . doing something, oh, for instance there's a few times in my life where I feel like going out and getting bombed, getting drunk. Okay, the next morning, the feeling of shame, of knowing that, hey, what I'd done last night should have never happened . . . I'm ashamed of that, because I let myself go too far . . . I know usually as a matter of habit—and this has been going on for years and I don't even know when it really started—my mornings are filled with nothing but what happened yesterday. And usually 90% of what happened yesterday I'm ashamed of, ashamed or feel guilty about. I guess that's why I have such a hard time separating the two of them.

I guess the shame of it is just the daily living and feelings that you have—that *I* have—when it appears. Not what I consciously think of or whether I don't, uh, you know, like in, ah, go hide in a hole or something, uh, which wouldn't help me, I'd still be thinking about it. All of a sudden this comes to mind and I just hang my head and like to uh disappear or something.

Most shame, you know, you get, you get a feeling in your chest, or I get a—I should say *I*—*I* get a feeling in my chest, just a really terrible, rotten feeling.

Frank's experience of shame is almost continual. Whenever he is out in the world and often when he is home alone, he is engaged in a shame-filled monitoring of himself. Putting aside specific dynamics of maso-chism, we can argue that certain *formal* aspects of Frank's shame—its omnipresence, its focus on the self, its protective function vis-à-vis the self—can be understood in the context of Frank's overall personality structure.

Frank presents himself to others and experiences himself as a motherless child. He deeply values memories of being a hurt child who became the focus of concerned parental attention. For a variety of reasons related to distrust of self and others (e.g., fear of his own sadism), he cannot engage with other people in an overtly dependent manner. But through his shame he can relate to himself as a needy child. While engaged in monitoring the shameful self, he regresses to activity that is both autoerotic and self-protective. And despite its painful quality, the shame experience is cathected like a valued self-function or an object relationship: it is something he owns and knows intimately.

One might speculate that under optimal circumstances, a young child relates to painful emotion as a condition of the self that can be altered through reassuring contact with Mother: a sad or distressed self becomes a relaxed and receptive self. Or the child may relate to painful emotion as something to be brought to Mother and thus disposed of or made to disappear. The child wishes to get rid of the feeling, to give it away to Mother who will deal with it. Once he or she can bring it to Mother and be comforted by her, the child can be done with the feeling state and can invest in the pleasurable interaction with Mother or in a pleasurable cathexis of self or another. If a problem in the relationship keeps the child from dissipating pain by communicating it to Mother, he or she might attempt psychologically to bury the pain and to proceed as if it does not exist. But the child might also learn to attend especially closely to the pain either with the motive of mastering it on his or her own or out of a need to preserve it until Mother can be found so that she will respond to it and offer comforting contact. To hold onto the pain is to hold fast to the fantasy of finding Mother's comfort. To let go the pain is to abandon hope of contact with Mother and hope of real resolution of the painful state. When pain must be preserved for later resolution, a new type of relationship to painful emotion may appear. The child, or older person, may learn to focus attention on his or her pain or to become interested in its structure and functions. The person eventually may find that the pain itself can give pleasure because it has a rich structure and an intense quality, akin to excitement, or because the act of attending to it feels reassuring as a substitute for attention from others. Thus a relationship develops to one's own pain that invests it positively in a way alien to the secure child who rushes to Mother, receives comfort, and runs back to play once delivered from discomfort. Such a relationship to pain and to the inner world in general may lead to creative activity or it may lead only to autistic responses to stress or to the preservation of pain as interesting, safe, valuable, or strangely comforting. The individual who becomes closely attuned to the nuances of his or her own painful inner experience, and who finds a kind of stability and comfort in the intimate association with painful experience, may come to fear that the interpersonal world and the world of action will be paltry, empty, or uncontrollable compared with the inner world of rich dysphoria.

In Frank's case, it appears that the repeated act of shaming himself corresponds to an overall tendency to attend closely to the self as a parent might attend to a child. The shame also calls out to the listener as a plea for support. Frank came to the research with a complaint about his ex-therapist who "is overlooking shame and guilt, and everything comes back to anger [according to the therapist], which I can't really agree with." Frank wants for the therapist to soothe his pain as a parent soothes a child. He does not want the therapist to attend to anger. Shame and guilt reach out to the parent for protection, but anger disrupts parent-child symbiosis.

The domination of Frank's world by an endlessly renewed feeling state implies that his world revolves around a particular constellation of developmental failures, which seldom releases its grip on him, even for a moment. The continual presence of a sharply restricted range of feeling states suggests some variety of ego vulnerability that motivates the person to live within a limited variety of familiar inner states. The dominant feeling state comes to represent a major aspect of the person's identity. He thinks of himself as a miserable victim of shame and guilt and he resents anyone who suggests that he is an angry person. The presence of a chronic affect state also requires our scrutiny as a possible means of perpetuating an earlier environment that Frank is loath to leave behind. At times, a feeling state can be thought of as an environment, or inner medium in which one dwells, or as an object to which one relates. Such dynamics seem most in evidence in the case of strong moods, like depression or bliss, which color all events. If a crucial early relationship or event is associated in memory with the creation of a particular mood or feeling state, the old world can be perpetuated through the recreation of that feeling, be it a feeling of peaceful, gloomy darkness, or giddy excitement, or some variety of shame that connects the person to a scolding and concerned parent. For example, if Frank needs to remain in close contact with his mother, and if he experienced his early relationship to his mother as a series of shifts from aggression to shame to re-acceptance, then the revitalization of past affect states keeps alive the tie to the mother. The data in Frank's case only suggest this interpretation, but I make the point in order to call attention to the plausibility of this variety of analysis, especially in the case of rich mood states like depression that seem to wrap a person in a desired environment.[1] What we definitely

---

[1] Faulkner's (1946) character, Quentin III, appears in *The Sound and the Fury* as one who relates to emotional states of grief and despair, and to the associated images of blackness and death, as representations of a pure, intimate, and eternal union with the associated mother-image who is both erotic and enveloping. Faulkner describes Quentin in words such as these:

Who loved not the idea of the incest which he would not commit, but some presbyterian concept of its eternal punishment: he, not God, could by that means cast himself and his sister both into hell, where he could guard her forever and keep her forevermore intact amid the eternal fires. But who loved death above all, who loved only death, loved and lived in a deliberate and almost perverted anticipation of death as a lover loves and deliberately refrains from the waiting willing friendly tender incredible body of his beloved. (p. 411)

Quentin's thoughts constantly play with the themes of death, blackness, and intensely intimate, incestuous sexuality:

If it could just be a hell beyond that: the clean flame the two of us more than dead. Then you will have only me then the two of us amid the pointing and the horror beyond

can see in Frank's case is a vivid, valued image of himself as injured and subsequently bathed in the sudden warmth of maternal concern. This dynamic pervades Frank's memories as can be seen in the two memories quoted on pages 116 and 117. Frank's behavior during the interviews further demonstrated that he encourages the recreation of the old integument of maternal concern, even though receipt of such intense concern may prove to him that he is pitifully damaged as a man.

SLIM: RUNNING FROM STIMULATION, RUNNING FOR STIMULATION

Slim was discussed in Chapter 5 as the interviewee with the most clearly defined and unvaried shame themes. The majority of his allusions to personal defect or to shame development refer to a particular sexual problem such as homosexuality or exhibitionism. It seems quite clear that he fears genital damage, although the history of that fear and what aspects of experience beyond the physical it might symbolize are less clear.

Although shame themes appear frequently and vividly in Slim's protocols—for example, he talks of intense shame that others might develop—Slim denies any actual shame experience of his own. He does acknowledge some "embarrassment" accompanied by frequent blushing. He discusses embarrassment as an inconsequential response to a trivial event such as a "slip of the lip" or a failure to zip his fly. His embarrassment relates to the *nature* of what is accidentally shown, e.g., his penis, and to the *implications* surrounding the act of showing, e.g., that he wishes to show his penis because he is "a pervert." The embarrassment generally occurs in the context of an effort to enhance feelings of sexual intactness.

Certain striking qualities of Slim's self-presentation and of his description of his childhood object world suggest additional explanations for why his self-doubts appear as frequent attacks of "insignificant" blushing and embarrassment and why he initially reacts to the word "shame"—with its connotations of serious feelings of inadequacy—as if

---

the clean flame (p. 144). . . . When I was little there was a picture in one of our books, a dark place into which a single weak ray of light came slanting upon two faces lifted out of the shadow. . . . I'd have to turn back to it until the dungeon was Mother herself she and Father upward into weak light holding hands and us lost somewhere below even them without even a ray of light. Then the honeysuckle would begin to come into the room in waves building and building until I would have to pant to get any air at all out of it. (p. 215)

he had never heard the word, let alone experienced the feeling. Scrutiny of Slim's personality organization and of a typical embarrassment episode reveals formal correspondences between the two organizations of experience.

Slim has a concretely defined, action-centered concept of self. He lives in the action sphere of races won or lost, skills learned or forgotten, injuries inflicted or sustained. Slim is a bicycle racer by avocation, and he seems too constantly in flight to have time to think. He cannot worry about who he is or what he values or feels. He must worry about where he is going, how he will get there, what pits there are in the road, and whether anyone is chasing him or waiting to attack if he should fall. Slim tries desperately to remain in this action world, on his feet or his machine. As an adolescent, he imagined that, "Whatever my occupation would be, part of it would be driving a motorcycle":

S: It's a neat machine for me; it's a respect for a machine, as a machine itself, a glorification of technical brilliance. . . It's a real sense of freedom; they just go real fast. I like them, uh, especially at that time, I like things, big racy things that went fast (laugh), roller coasters.

Slim wants no part of those feelings—like thoughtful shame or depression or love—that define the self and place it in vulnerable connection with the object world. Slim associates such feelings with his mother, who he believes feels constant shame. When he stumbles onto similarities between himself and his mother, for example, in their feelings of weakness when in discord with his father, he avoids articulating the parallel. And though he acknowledges his mother's frequent, profound shame, he refuses to be affected by her pain. He claims her cries go "in one ear and out the other." He tries to think of himself as like his tough father or like his mother in her energetic phases, when life with her must have been like a "racy thing," a "roller coaster." Slim accepts feelings that have the form of his action world, feelings that come as quick attacks that he can regard as meaningless, highly physical bursts of intense and powerful activity. For example, he readily engages in violent fighting. But he often cannot say why he does so, or he gives an explanation of the provocation that many would consider an inadequate stimulus for extreme violence. Slim is not someone who prefers a flat, colorless world, who experiences feeling only because it erupts against his will. He enjoys feeling, but it must be intense and powerful so that he can experience himself as managing a driving energy. And he must be able to think of the feeling as an event that arises from the external stimulus, not from the self. Embarrassment, in its formal aspects, fits with his pervasive action style. It is intense, physical, and transient. It can be experienced as a strong but meaningless response to an external event. The response has no serious implications with respect to the self.

When Slim speculates about "shame" in the fourth interview, by which time he has begun to find the word more meaningful, he wonders if shame is "a necessary outlet." The emotion is described like a flow of energy from an overloaded circuit, not like an experience of specific thoughts or feelings about the self. When Slim wants to emphasize the strength of a feeling, he does so by specifying a quantity or by repeating a simple phrase about the event. He tells *how many* students were in his new school in order to explain its impact on him. He states over and over that something was "really big" or "really bad" in order to indicate how he felt about it. Those who have a well developed, valued self-concept or a greater tolerance for subtle feeling often prefer to struggle toward progressively richer articulation of the feeling itself, but Slim emphasizes only the size or duration of the external event that triggers his feeling.

Trauma appears to be a likely explanation for Slim's orientation toward responsive action rather than deliberation. During childhood, he was confronted with family members who represented living proof that catastrophic physical, intellectual, and emotional damage does afflict people. Not only were these alarming presences there to haunt him; he had to rely on them to sustain him. People on whom he depended were prone to physical violence, as well as to dramatic fluctuations in general competence and emotional state. In later childhood, he himself had a serious illness and major surgery. Listening to his history, one feels little surprise that Slim seems constantly in flight from thought and feeling, from physical and emotional attack, and from personal collapse or collapse of people in his environment.

Slim behaves as if the less substance he has, the less vulnerable he will be to attack. A self with specific, deeply valued feelings becomes a liability because, whatever a person feels, someone is likely to attack him for it. And whatever he has, someone is likely to kill him trying to take it away. It is best to slip by unnoticed, though plagued by residual, poorly understood wishes to exhibit oneself.

Slim shares with Polly a disposition toward embarrassment experience, as opposed to shame experience. Polly's and Slim's personality organizations differ in many respects, but the two interviewees hold in common their hazy articulation of a personal identity. Both Polly and Slim are highly reactive to external events and to external influences on self-esteem. Their embarrassment-proneness appears to correspond to their outward orientation. They are responsively oriented individuals rather than individuals who actively generate ideas about the self (see Josephine or William for a contrasting pattern). Since neither has explored and conceptualized the range of feelings that constitute the self, each is easily surprised by reactions from others that point to some feeling of affection or anxiety or sexual interest that has come into public view. Each seems to view the self for the first time when the self has made an impact on another. The self is suddenly caught sight of in the other's response. For example, Polly sees herself (i.e., her ineffectiveness and futile efforts to engage others) in the boredom or discomfort of her house guests. In fantasy, Slim sees himself (i.e., his exhibitionistic wishes) in the shock of an onlooker who spots him walking in public with his pants unzipped. Each is surprised by the audience's response, and embarrassed because of not privately considering and defining the self in a way that would bring him or her to the audience with established attitudes of pride or shame about the self.

Blushing, unsettled embarrassment states often are highly excited states that retain a pleasurable quality or at least a connection to a pleasurable fantasy, despite intense pain that also may characterize them. The confusing pleasure-pain aspect of embarrassment seems of special significance in Slim's case. Numerous images from the protocols suggest that, during his childhood, he experienced stimulation that created giddy pleasure. Such pleasure either alternated with severe pain or itself changed into pain as the pleasure became sufficiently overstimulating to frighten and disorganize a young child. Slim describes a world of intense emotional and physical stimulation. In the following passage, we see a mother who allows stimulation to upset her young child's equilibrium:

S: She'd be driving around in the car . . . when the noise in the car would get really bad and the kids would be jumping on the back seats and pulling each others' hair . . . She'd just turn the radio up (laugh), or if the car started to make some smoke . . . and it started to overheat and there was water coming out of the front, and steam and stuff, and the kids were going [crazy], she'd just turn up the radio (laugh) . . . In retrospect that's a neat coping mechanism.

I: How about at the time?

S: Oh, it was just too noisy. The whole car was too noisy, too much activity for me.

Within Slim's world there was little help in understanding his sensations, and there were few quiet and predictable relationships. He lived in a world of extremes. His mother alternated between states of manic excitement and of black depression, between states of devastation and those of omnipotence in which she presented herself as a magician capable of making a broken machine race with a well-placed patch of chewing gum. Slim describes his own childhood home as a mess, but his friends' mothers covered their furniture in plastic. The plastic covering and the chaos seem to symbolize his own mother's extremes. He prefers the mess to the plastic-covered furnishings, and he can imagine no middle ground. Things are chaotically alive or they are dead like his mother was when depression immobilized her. His earliest memories include images of strange women who speak in languages that are meaningless to him and who organize their expectations of him according to bizarre social rules to which he adapts compliantly without any understanding of the significance of the rules. He cannot interpret the quality or nature of the excitement in people around him. Playful teasing often turns to brutal attack. He hears people giggle when they are out of view, and thus he cannot tell what is being done to them. Things that look painful turn pleasurable and things that look sweet turn sour. He takes a gulp of his aunt's tomato juice and cannot understand why it looks good but tastes bitter, until later he learns it contained invisible vodka. And he learns also that his aunt was a secret alcoholic. His parents' relationship puzzles him enormously, especially with respect to the infliction of pain or stimulation:

S: They argue a lot with each other, you know (laugh).
I: What does that sound like?
S: It's just like puppy dogs playing; they're just teasing each other . . .
I: Does it seem like teasing with a little bit of *an edge?*
S: Yeah, it's just teasing with a little bit of truth to it. In other words, if you really sat and listened to it, you could get upset. Nobody really does. They don't even really listen to each other (laugh). It's an unusual marriage, they're really unusual . . . I would seriously think if—say if I were a marriage counselor, I would seriously [predict] that these people wouldn't live together any longer and that the divorce would be imminent, but it's not; they never want to get divorced. They just want to continue in this.

Irrationality appears to have been the norm in Slim's childhood.

Two qualities of Slim's current feeling-world look like derivatives of his childhood experiences with unpredictably fluctuating stimulation. He dreads situations in which another person inflicts pain. For example, he is panicked by minor medical procedures and dental drilling. A local anaesthetic is no help. He claims it does not reduce the pain. He pleads with the dentist or doctor to knock him out completely. When commenting about an operation he underwent, he describes well the disorientation he associates with externally inflicted pain, and he conveys his apprehension that parenting figures will not limit the pain to bearable intensity:

S: Right after surgery I just totally lost the concept of what time it was, and what day it was, what hour it was . . . the only thing that really became important was getting the shot when it started to hurt . . . and I was afraid the nurses wouldn't react quick enough.

Also interpretable in the light of early stimulation patterns is Slim's orientation toward *maintaining* high levels of physical and emotional stimulation as long as he feels either that he has control over the fluctuating intensity or that he can remain unaffected by the stimulation if he renders it emotionally meaningless. He presumably is attempting to master past trauma by managing powerful stimulants, for example, speeding conveyances or frightening physical assaults. But he also associates such stimulation with joyous excitement, which probably attended some of his childhood experiences of stimulation. He fantasizes about performing miracles on a paramedic squad where he can master body damage fears by reconnecting amputated limbs, and he simultaneously can get high on stimulants like fast action, cutting, bleeding, nudity, and noise, which are reminiscent of Mother's chaotic activity during manic periods.

Slim's pursuit of emotionally intense experience—with mixed pain and pleasure qualities—is consonant with his propensity for attacks of highly stimulated "embarrassment." The embarrassment, which he tolerates so much more easily than he tolerates shame, is formally similar to other aspects of his experiential world. The embarrassment is intense and physical. It suggests to him that he is in the presence of a powerful stimulus without forcing him to recognize that anything of great significance is going on within the self.

JOSEPHINE: FEEDING ON FEELING

Josephine is among those research subjects most prone to identifiable experiences of shame. Indeed, her shame has such intensity that the experiencing of shame itself becomes a source of additional shame because the emotional state represents an instance of what Josephine considers to be pitifully histrionic behavior and desperately strong, infantile feeling. Josephine's moments of shame consist of focusing attention on some deficiency with tormenting regret. In her (characteristically oral) words, she will "eat her heart out" with regret. Josephine's shame experience raises questions about the role of such strong, self-attentive feeling in her overall psychology.

The intensity of Josephine's feeling states constitutes one of their formal aspects and one may ask why she experiences and displays feeling in such an intense form that the feeling itself becomes a stimulus for shame or self-hate. Hereditary influences may affect the strength of felt experience, but Krystal (1975) would point to "regression in the nature of the affects themselves" (p. 216). Josephine's feelings are infantile in form. They come as powerful attacks accompanied at times by discomfort in the chest or stomach. She can have difficulty labeling her feelings with words or distinguishing one state from another:

S: Sometimes though I guess I don't recog-, I can't recognize the feeling. That's when it feels really horrible, you know.
I: Explain a little bit more.
S: Let's say for some reason the day's going badly or—no, I can't reach any of my friends or for whatever reason I don't feel right. And I don't know why, maybe there's, maybe it's a gorgeous day out, maybe I'm on vacation, maybe it's Christmas (laugh), you know, I can't figure out why I wish I was dead (laugh). And I hate that.
I: You just know that you feel lousy that day, but you—
S: Yeah, well lousy, lousy's not so bad. What about when I feel *really bad*, like I feel that there's no way anything is ever going to change and I'm going to feel this way. What way? I don't know. I'm gonna feel scared, I'm gonna feel pursued, I'm going to feel up against a wall. Sometimes I don't understand my feelings . . . And I don't know why I do stuff sometimes either.

Recognizing the form of a feeling as infantile or regressed can help us see how the feeling itself can be experienced as a profound threat to psychological integrity. The person must make dramatic efforts to shut out feeling when it occurs in potentially catastrophic form:

S: I was just getting to be sort of friends with Jay and I don't know, I started to think that he didn't want to be friends with me, or that he couldn't—he didn't want me hanging around him so much or that his roommates were saying, "Hey man, you know, she's really in motion after you" or I don't know, I just remember these couple of days—it's funny, one day I was, I was wearing black clothes. It was a grey day and Jay came over to see me and we went outside and I just was trying to explain to him these feelings that I had, how I felt bad, you know. I was low, I had the blues . . . I mean, he was very warm and friendly and, and nice to me, but I knew that [he didn't understand. I had to change], meaning I had to stop feeling this way. Because I didn't like it. So I changed very easily. *Now* I might not be as inclined to do it. I changed; I ate a couple of pills. The feeling changed and I put on white clothes, and Jay came over and he said, "Gosh, you were all in black and now you're wearing white." And I said, "Yes, Jay, I knew I had to change, that I couldn't go on wearing black clothes."

Josephine demonstrated her need to "change" many times during the interviews when she expressed some strong feeling and began to feel overwhelmed. This sequence occurred at the end of Josephine's first interview:

S: I'm starting to feel more ill-at-ease. Isn't that funny? I don't know why exactly . . . maybe it's partly because I *know*. Maybe sometimes I just wish I could stop, though, okay? 'Cause it's one thing when I con someone, to get credit in a store, or you know, to get out of work or something. I can play on peoples' feelings. I know I have this ability. Maybe that's why I also know that some people can sense this and that they don't like it. But sometimes I wish it would stop.

I: That quality in yourself, [you wish] you would stop this?

S: No, I think it's *cool*. I think it's really great I can do that.

Josephine swings between states in which she seems lost in intense feeling and sudden denial of all feeling. She also appears to be vulnerable to thought disorder characterized by conceptual contamination (to change clothes is not adequately distinguished from changing moods or identities); however, her thought disorder is difficult to evaluate because Josephine sometimes appears to be courting craziness or playing at craziness when she is capable of less regressed thinking.

Labeling Josephine's feelings as infantile or regressed highlights the traumatizing capacity of these feeling states and the motivation for Josephine to shut them out in order to maintain her sense of intactness. But this labeling fails to explain Josephine's frequent *preference* for affect in intense, chaotic, somatized attacks. Some would argue that the idea of preference has no place here: Josephine's feelings come in storms simply because she has not developed beyond this infantile form of experience. That explanation contains a degree of truth; certainly Josephine exhibits a failure to learn the usual developmental lesson that one can live more comfortably and successfully with reasonably modulated feeling states. But she does appear to prefer her chaotic states at times. Under certain circumstances, she chooses to engage them, even though they bring a feeling of artificiality or unreality. That preference invites exploration.

Evidence of Josephine's wish for a symbiotic bond with a mother-figure abounds in her protocol. She envisions herself either as undifferentiated from another or as cast out beyond reach of help. Given this limited conception of life's possibilities, when impending separation threatens, she hastens to establish a clinging tie. In these situations, intense feeling experience and dramatic displays of feeling serve her symbiotic aim in several ways. Josephine feels that dramatic demonstrations of emotion will bring the love object close. Even the internal feeling of distress, experienced without real interaction with others, brings solace through the fantasy of rapprochement. It is probably a universal assumption that a cry of distress will bring help. But in Josephine's case, the fantasy is intensified by her longstanding identification of both parents as "dramatic" in their own displays of emotion. In her family, drama brought engagement between family members. Furthermore, to behave dramatically makes Josephine feel that she has become one with her histrionic parents. She achieves reunion magically by eliminating distance between herself and them:

S: [My father] would yell at me, "Sarah Bernhardt! . . . Stop your melo-drama, stop being so overdramatic." But at the same time I'm sure I learned everything from him, 'cause he—sometimes I know when I'm acting, when I'm behaving like either or both of my parents. And that sort of weirds me out. I know when I—say when Champ doesn't wash the dishes right or he doesn't do something right and I point this out to him or I say something like, "ARE you going to take the garbage out??" And I hear my mother saying the same thing.

Josephine regards her feelings ambivalently as dramatic productions that are childish but useful for procuring attention.

Intense feeling is more than a means to attain gratification. It is itself a gratification. When Josephine feels threatened with separation, she is besieged with wishes for oral forms of gratification that will diminish her feelings of emptiness and anxiety. She craves liquor and pills. Feelings of intense disgust or shame or fear or rage themselves feel like a rich diet with which she can fill up the inner emptiness she dreads. Josephine seems similar to Frank in this respect. Her feelings are her food, her substance, and her stimulation. Although chaotic feeling frightens and hurts her, in her oral world of the empty and the full, the symbiotic and the hopelessly detached, rich feeling reassures her that things will not go dead or empty. She craves stimulation from outside and from within. The next passage illustrates a moment that brings together the conflicted wish for interpersonal fusion, the craving for oral intake, and the wish to fill herself up with exciting feeling that then becomes overwhelming. Wurmser's (1980) paper on claus-trophobic dynamics in addicts presents a number of interesting ideas that appear relevant to Josephine.

It is difficult to find a single passage that illustrates well the pursuit of intense feeling to stimulate and fill up the failing self, but the follow-ing passage gives the flavor of such cravings as they appear in combi-nation with wishes and fears regarding fusion, sex, and incest:

S: Bill and I, we both think that each other are really good looking; we like being with each other. And in this dialogue [I wrote], I just address myself to that. Bill asks me—we'd ask this, when we went canoeing—[once] he said, "Sometimes I wonder if we're not so much alike that we're really of each other, and this is what we're creating." I told him a long time ago—

I: This is what *you* said *to him?*

S: No, he said to me, that he felt that maybe I was the feminine part of him. I told him a long time—and this was true, a long time ago I was like, I don't know, I was really buzzed, I don't know, I might have even been on LSD or something, and like a character emerged for me that had a name, and it was "Bill" and I really was Bill . . . I never knew anyone named Bill either. In this dialogue I wrote, you know, Bill asks, "Are you me?" and I say, "no" and then he said, "Well, let's be twins. Adopt me." And I said, "Well, no, I mean, that would mean no you-know-what, because it would be a taboo." In the dialogue—what a cheap pun—"to boo or not taboo, that is your question." And then I was thinking about how I really wanted to get off, how if I could I really wished I had some drugs, I wished I had heroin, or some kind of narcotics. [It was a] really beautiful day. It was like the last day of school for the students and all day—it made me so tense—I heard drums, people were playing drums, Congo drums or whatever, out below my window. And people were—I could feel the excitement, this tension and I wanted to get off so bad. So I was thinking about this as I wrote, and that's sort of what happened. Bill is getting off and going into his dreams. He dreams about me all the time, apparently. And that's what I was writing about, how I was in control of his dream, and I was so happy to see him get off that way. And in my dream I switched our heads, so Bill said at the end, "You sure look cute, Bill." And Josephine says, "So do you." But our heads are exchanged.

Josephine's repeated discussions of pills focus on control over states of fullness and satiety. Pills comfort her. Unlike people, they are predictable and controllable:

S: The counselor would not do what she was supposed to do like pills do. They do what they're supposed to do.

Pills also frighten her. Although they are more controllable than people, addiction is a state of constant anxiety that she may run out of pills. Ironically, Josephine likes to make her "predictable" pills unpredictable:

S: Dangerous things are very tempting to me—taking pills that you don't know what they are or taking pills and alcohol and you don't know what's going to happen really.

Josephine explains her danger-seeking as a means of inviting catastrophe that will bring rescue. Her explanation points to the fact that pills ultimately are not satisfying; she wants solace from human sources. Josephine's dangerous ingestion also could be investigated as a possible enacting of the wish and fear to take inside herself a representation of her mother or father. Over the years, her mother has provided an unpredictable parade of comforts and cruel assaults. When in distress, Josephine struggled to assess whether Mother would soothe her or magnify her pain. As she takes pills into her body, she seems to wait and wonder what state they will bring, just as she wondered how Mother's words would leave her feeling. Father also is associated with confusing stimulation. She sees him as gentle and infantilizing at times, excessively sexual at other times.

I have emphasized the extensive data illustrating Josephine's wish for fusion because I wished to argue that rich affect gratifies that wish. Affect is food and stimulation. The excited quality of Josephine's shame states suggests that she satisfies sexual desires masochistically, through lively shame, as does Frank. For Josephine, not just shame but *all* affect and language are erotized. She wallows in words and emotion and finds oral and erotic pleasure.

Shame serves Josephine's wishes for intimacy in yet another way. Shame over her own behavior represents a denial of the faults she perceives in her mother's behavior. Josephine obviously has seen her mother as unfair, irrational, and pathetically childish, among other failings. But anger separates people and disappointment empties the world of strength and love. She fears separations will be too complete and emptiness too profound; therefore, she whitewashes her mother's personality. In consequence, Josephine takes more shame upon herself. Whenever an interaction between her and her mother fails, she is tempted to find fault with herself and to spare her mother. In the interviews, she occasionally lets slip a description of her mother displaying precisely those qualities of immaturity or hysteria that she endlessly indicts in herself. When she can tolerate the separation and anger implied in criticizing Mother, she has less need to find fault with herself:

S: [She] liked to paint—that's a very bad memory. My mother was painting, not really painting, she just used to like to paint by number. And I was excited, I was excited over something. And where our kitchen was, it was sort of longish so if you could like get a running start you could slide all across the room. So I did this and I bumped into her and I sort of wrecked up a little spot of her painting. Oh, she really got mad, she really got mad. It's funny, my parents always accuse *me* of overreacting, I think *they* overreact a whole [lot].

I: Well, what do you remember about her reaction and then how you felt in reaction to her reaction?

S: She just got, just furious. She probably called me a clod and a jerk and, can't I be careful and what am I doing and—she could really wail at me, you know, really be yelling at me, and scare the shit out of me, and make me feel bad, really make me feel like she hated me. And I'm sure, you know, she probably, that's not what she intended to do but she really came down heavily on me, mostly—I didn't want her to hate me, I figured she could fix her picture you know, I mean it wasn't that bad . . . I mean it's one thing to get mad at me but, on television it seems like the parents always go and apologize afterwards and come up in your room and go, "Well Beaver, I'm really sorry, you know, that we yelled at you" and shit, but they . . . would really get pissed off. . . .

I: Do you think that you felt ashamed when she called you a, I don't remember exactly what you said—

S: A clod, overexcited. Did I feel ashamed? No, I felt like I was, I felt like I was a victim. For a painting, a paint-by-number, you know. I mean I was pretty little but even then I think I understood the object was no big deal, that there was something else creating this tumult, that it seemed very inappropriate.

Not only was Josephine aware of her mother's poorly controlled behavior and angered by it but, as a child, she felt ashamed of such behavior:

S: When you think about like being ashamed or feeling ashamed, sometimes I used to be ashamed of my parents . . . Sometimes I was ashamed to bring my friends home because my mom used to lie on her bed and watch television a lot and smoke all the time. Sometimes I thought that our house to really stink from cigarettes and I was ashamed of that.

Although Josephine experiences powerful longings for fusion, seldom does she describe symbiotic wishes without an immediate reference to her dread that intimacy will destroy her as an independent person. The protocols are replete with descriptions of her retreat from clinging people. She abhors "addiction" to people more than addiction to drugs, and she despises psychiatrists whom she suspects to be witches engaged in efforts to dominate her will. Josephine's autonomy wishes lead to contempt for (or shame over) the intense, desperate feelings that signify the symbiotic longing. She attacks these dramatic feelings as *not herself.* They are performances that make her feel unreal. Her dismissal of intense feelings as unreal derives in part from her contempt for symbiotic states, but also from the fact that in calmer, less desperate times, she indeed does experience a more thoughtful, less histrionic self that possesses a greater feeling of agency. The feeling that she is play-acting emerges when she has refused the more thoughtful, differentiated self of which she is capable:

S: I used to run out of the house. I'd sit there on the curb on the corner and think of all the ways I wanted—all the things I would do to make Champ realize that he should be nicer to me and he should listen to me better.

I: What kind of things would you imagine in a situation like that?

S: Oh, I mean like getting hit by a car because I'm blinded by tears and having all sorts of internal injuries . . . Champ has to come to the hospital and look at my face and he would *know* that I'm there because of him (laugh) . . . Now I know that I don't want these things to happen—I hate it when I can't stop crying, when [I take] a bottle of pills [like in] a Hollywood movie and I know I'm only acting and I know that I'm just in my movie or something.

I: How do you mean?

S: Well, I don't know, do you ever do that, like maybe everything sort of feels like a movie almost, like. . . ?

I: You mean as if your feelings feel more like a part that you're playing instead of—

S: (interrupting interviewer)—instead of real.

I: —coming from inside?

S: Yeah, like the way you feel . . . when it's really beautiful outside. You feel really good or you see some scenery, you have a piece of cake and it's really delicious (laugh) and you enjoy it, or you enjoy a concert—those are *real*. And then what about, like those feelings . . . [that] someone doesn't like you at work. So instead of just going, oh wow, you know, fuck her, maybe [I'd] develop the feeling of *why*, *why* doesn't she like me, or, you know, like paranoid, what is she saying about me to the other people, you know, like that, that's *movie time*, that is not a real genuine feeling, those are just, those are from the weird side.

I: Even at the time it doesn't feel quite real, it feels more like a dramatic act?

S: Yeah, that's what's odd . . . I feel like I'm observing myself and observing things at a distance very frequently, you know? Right now I feel pretty much here, but . . . maybe this is perfect for me, because it's being recorded, and I'm being observed.

Josephine struggles to understand what she regards as a shameful addiction to the theatrics that bind her to others as a helpless, damaged child and deprive her of the feeling of being a controlled individual functioning in a simple and less dramatic world. In quieter moments, she has difficulty remembering that her fear of abrupt separation grows so intense that theatrics and loss of self-esteem can seem an acceptable price to pay for reunion.

Josephine's sense that her theatrical feelings are unreal also appears related to the difficulty of integrating a great range of feelings—of varying levels of maturity—held toward the same people. It is difficult to comprehend and distressing to accept that one can feel calm, reasonable, and realistic about someone at one moment and flooded with fury and desperate longing toward that person a moment later. The integrative, identity-establishing task is simplified, or bypassed, when one in effect says to oneself, "These chaotic feelings are not real; they are not myself because I cannot see the reason for them and cannot even imagine a reason for them." Dismissing the chaotic feelings as unreal also allows Josephine rapidly to reassociate herself with behavior and feelings that are socially acceptable and are not so frightening as rage and intense intimacy wishes can be.

In contrast with subjects like Slim and Polly, Josephine wishes not only to experience strong emotion but to give articulate verbal expression to feeling that is initially amorphous. She wants to develop a strong and individual adult self, and she experiences the accurate articulation of feeling as an aspect of the articulation of a self. When she can recognize the meaning of her emotion rather than feeling that she is a conduit through which stormy energies pass, she has a sense of pleasurable efficacy. Her turbulent, pain-filled struggles over her identity would appear to contain within them a strong desire to develop a well-defined and autonomous self.

8 Conclusions

> *The preparation of the musical effect is a process of articulating the structure of the feeling expressed, so it does much more than convey some nameable mood or emotion; it may be given different names, but best none at all, for no name such as "sorrow" or "joy" fits any actual feeling throughout its course. Feeling is a dynamic pattern of tremendous complexity.*
>
> —Suzanne Langer (1967)

In studying disgust prior to this study of shame, I turned back with interest to Sartre's (1964) novel *La Nausée* because I recalled that it was rich with subtle descriptions of emotional states. I was initially attracted to the study of feeling states by the lure to explore and describe shifting moments of experience more completely than the schematic language of science usually encourages. In *La Nausée* and elsewhere, Sartre does not disappoint with respect to vitality of observation and description. However, at times in his writings he seems to confound a broad, emotion-related category such as "disgust" or "slime" with a particular moment's experience that might fall within the category but not define it. Thus his description of slime as "a dawning triumph of the solid over the liquid" (1969, p. 774) and as a "surreptitious appropriation of the possessor by the possessed" (p. 776), or his definition of a hole as "before all sexual specification . . . an obscene expectation" (p. 781) all take liberties with the subject matter if presented as definitions of category and not as descriptions of particular moments of experience that fall within a category. Fascinating, enriching liberties they may be, but nonetheless they are liberties. In my studies of disgust and shame, I found that labeled emotion categories can be compared to the area of intersecting circles in a Venn diagram. They are the features shared by each of many moments experienced by great numbers of individuals. As such, the categories only can support rather general and limited descriptions. More specific description must be reserved for the individual moment of experience. And one finds that as one focuses on a particular, well described moment of experience, placing it in a general category such as shame comes to have limited significance. When the level of precise descriptions has been reached, category membership seems to strip a moment of meaning rather than add to our understanding of the moment.

CRUCIAL ELEMENTS OF SHAME STATES

The sole essential element of the category I have designated "shame" would appear to be displeasure about the status of the self. The displeasure occurs within a context—well-defined or inarticulate—of comparison between self and others. Such displeasure may occur in response to insults specifically directed at one's sexual attributes or at one's manner of filling a gender role. Or shame may develop in response to the feeling that, as an individual, one has no significance to someone one loves. In each case, the actual state of feeling will be somewhat different, but each state will fit within the category of states generally called shame.

The individual moment of shame represents the confluence of multiple levels of input. To begin with, gross features of the moment's situation present themselves to the person. As long as a person is attending to them, these realities establish inner representation largely independent of the individual's identity and biology. For a nonpsychotic person with normal perceptual processes either there is or there is not a chair in the person's line of vision or an argument in range of hearing. The finer points of how that chair looks to that person or how that dispute sounds result in part from his or her current state of mind and in part from a complex experiential history, which attaches highly specific meanings to specific objects and establishes important broad parameters of feeling (which become powerful motivators) such as the belief that all strong feeling is contemptible or that all people outside the immediate family are untrustworthy. Also contributing to the moment's experience will be certain basic constellations of biological response that most people appear to share. Thus situations of confrontation with foul food or with other stimuli having either a universal or a personal association with bad food evoke in most people a cluster of sensations and actions in the stomach and throat and mouth and nose, or at least they evoke vague images of such actions and sensations. These response clusters appear to represent universal human biology.

Individual biological variation also is likely to play an important role in feeling experience. Both of two infants placed in the same painful situation may show what we crudely could classify as distress. But for one, "distress" may represent a mild disturbance or an experience that is intense but quickly lost to memory; whereas for the other, distress might be a genuinely traumatizing state or a moderately disturbing state that has a sustained impact. Most people appear to have a capacity for "depression," with sleep disruption, changes in appetite, feelings that the self is worthless or harmful, and feelings that the world is empty, meaningless, or malicious. These experiences appear to represent an inherited potential experienced by almost all people under predictable circumstances. But the inheritance carried by one person may dictate that the "bad feelings about self" that form part of the depressive cluster will have extraordinary intensity, motivational power, readiness to attract ideational elaboration, and readiness to persist in memory, whereas another's inheritance promotes experience of less severity. Whether determined largely by inherited impact on the structure of feeling or primarily by environmental influences on feeling experience, individual variation in the quality of feeling life in infancy must have a profound effect on one's feeling life in later years and on the nature of one's active efforts to influence feeling experience. The child who experiences anxiety in catastrophic form—due to over-stimulation or to physical illness or to inherited intensity of response— likely will cultivate any available means of avoiding anxiety, even at staggering cost to pleasure. In contrast, the person who experiences anxiety or depression in moderate intensity may hazard these feelings if they lie along the road to some happiness that can be vividly imagined. Thus the final equation producing any moment of feeling possesses humbling complexity, comprised as it is of elements inherited and learned, newly created and long in duration, idiosyncratic and universal.

The concept of self and also the concept of boundaries are important to the study of shame and other emotions because the individual's articulation of self-boundaries is crucial in determining the specific quality of feeling experience that will result from insults, personal failures, or contacts with others who are perceived as especially powerful or degraded. For example, if an insult is accepted as truly applicable to the self, the person is likely to feel some form of shame. But if the content of the insult (e.g., an accusation of selfishness) is taken as not-self and is dismissed as the other's misconception or the other's attempt to injure or even the other's boundary failure (i.e., the insult represents a projection, as defined psychoanalytically), the person will respond not with shame but with anger or pity or some other feeling state that makes it clear that the other person is the selfish one. A person who comes into contact with something experienced as defiled or impure may feel disgust if the stimulus is experienced as not-self, or contempt if the object is experienced both as not-self and as inferior to the self, or the person may experience shame if the impurity is accepted as a self-aspect that once was cast away and now returns to its source.[1]

A person may also feel shame if he or she defines the self in a fluid manner that designates contact itself to be the criterion of what belongs to the self. Under those circumstances, merely to see or touch the defiled substance will contaminate and shame the self. In her discussion of attitudes toward impurity and sacredness across cultures, Douglas (1966) argues that numerous objects and experiences that people label as defiled originally were aspects of self, often of the body self. She implies that people in many cultures have lost awareness of the association between such objects or experiences and the self; therefore, one would expect contact with the offending objects to produce feelings such as disgust or horror or contempt, rather than shame. Awe or reverence might occur if the residual wish to contact the interesting, disowned self-aspects asserts itself in an ego-syntonic form but the person does not recognize that the powerful odor or texture or emotion once characterized the self. Lidz (1973) makes some related comments in his discussions of category formation and schizophrenia. He explains that language and culture tend to assign important experiences to distinct categories. Language and culture divert attention from experiences or forms that lie between categories, for example, that which is neither clearly male nor clearly female, neither clearly living nor definitely nonliving, neither evidently self nor evidently nonself. Lidz suggests that the schizophrenic dwells too comfortably in those "intercategorical" realms that most people deny or wrest into a clear category. Consequently, the schizophrenic occupies a more confusing world than most people inhabit. Neither Lidz nor Douglas extend their comments into the analysis of specific feeling states, but one could infer that, were Lidz correct about schizophrenic

---

[1] An equally valid argument would posit that the offense is experienced as belonging to the other, not to the self, *in order that one may avoid shame.*

fusion of typically distinct conceptual realms, one might notice a schizophrenic experiencing disgust when another person might experience shame, or shame when another might experience disgust or contempt, because the schizophrenic is not employing the self-nonself boundaries that are typical of the culture and have a determining effect on a person's feeling state. Instead of feeling disgust over vomited material, as many people do, an actively psychotic person might feel shame or guilt as if he or she were responsible for the offensive material, which is still perceived as an integral part of self. Or the person might feel some variety of interest or appetite or satisfaction in response to the material, which is seen as the inner self now positioned so that it can be seen or smelled in a manner that enhances a person's sense of being alive and physical, and of existing in the world as a strong stimulus.

Variations in voice pattern help to identify which actions or attributes belong to the self and which ones belong to others. Parents teach children the meaning of the words "shame" and "guilt" in part by tone of voice. Often "shame" is used in the context of the chastising injunction, "You should be ashamed of yourself." Perhaps even more effective is the interrogative, "Aren't you ashamed of yourself?". The solemn, disappointed, restrainedly aggressive tone of these lines, which follow some action performed by the child, suggests to the child that the fault lies within the self, and that he or she ought to identify and expunge that internal fault. The controlled aggression in the parent's voice conveys the impression that the child's actions call for punishment, but the parent will not deliver it. The child must assume the punishing role. The parent who delivers the classic shame lines in furious attack is less likely to teach the child the conventional meaning of shame, because the parent's uninhibited aggression will invite responsive aggression from the child and will locate at least some of the fault outside the self, in the assaultive parent.

This monograph does not lend itself to easy summary but one point worth highlighting involves the relationship between shame and anger. When analyzing situations in which a person complained of intense shame, I was repeatedly impressed by indications that inhibition of anger either directly motivated the shame experience, as a punishment for aggression, or it allowed shame to proliferate by rendering the person shamefully weak or by denying the person the opportunity to defend himself or herself against attacks on self-esteem. This observation should have certain implications for the notion of two separate developmental lines, one involving narcissism, the other involving instinct expression and control. It would seem that there is such constant and consequential interaction between the two lines of development that the conceptual separation is difficult to maintain. One simply cannot talk about the impact of shaming on self-esteem without exploring the management of anger, because it is the freedom to use anger self-protectively or the constraints on such expression that largely determine the narcissistic impact of the shaming. That is not to say that it matters not at all whether parents shame a child occasionally or whether they do so habitually. The world that demands constant use of anger in order to defend one's self-esteem (or constant defense against narcissistic rage) differs greatly from the world that makes no such demand. But the impact of neither environment can be assessed without scrutinizing the use of anger. I do not wish to over-state this point because I am not in the position here to consider the many vicissitudes of parental response to children, some of which may best be conceptualized, in their impact, by looking first at the child's self-esteem and identity development and secondarily at his or her management of anger. For example, consistent parental neglect (as opposed to shaming) might result in depression and diminished self-investment, and these states might be better conceptualized as primary or direct effects of the inadequate parental investment (rather than their being indirect effects of, for example, suppressed oral rage). Such a developmental picture might differ significantly from one that results from parental ridicule. The point I wish to retain though—and perhaps it is a self-evident one—is that the management of aggression interacts constantly with the maintenance of self-esteem, so that whether one begins one's attempts to understand a particular individual with ideas about aggression or with ideas about self-esteem, the interface between the two conceptual realms soon must be confronted. My tendency in this monograph to give primary importance to anger-management rather than to pervasive problems of self-esteem may suggest that shame as an indicator of narcissistic stress regularly relates to additional problems with anger. However, there are other states (of feeling and of behavior) that can reflect narcissistic stress, for example, depression, confusion, or aimlessness. Analysis of some of these states conceivably might lead to conceptualizations that give less weight to anger-management and more weight to self-development. The other point to be kept in mind is that anger can have a primarily narcissistic focus (e.g., rage following from ridicule) or an instinctual focus (e.g., rage over hunger or restriction of body plea-sure), though often anger is a response to both types of stress (e.g., oedipal rage at the same-sex parent who has what one wants, both in personal traits and interpersonal ties). Either form of rage can pro-duce moral shame if the conscience is active, however neither type of rage leads invariably to guilt or shame.

Kohut describes shame not as an immediate response to unempathic parenting, but as a part of the decompensation of self-esteem and self-organization that occurs in adults whose histories of unempathic parenting make them vulnerable to severe strain whenever self-esteem is not supported by the people and events in their lives. But such decompensations of self-esteem and self-organization can occur under a variety of circumstances other than the situation of unempathic parenting discussed by Kohut; and shame likely will attend the decompensation no matter what triggers it, because any fragmented or confused state of the self tends to be considered shameful. Such decompensation might be triggered by guilt as easily as by a basic defect of self-esteem. For example, a man who disowns his masculinity due to the guilty conviction that his masculinity caused his father to have a devastating stroke may feel acutely vulnerable, weak, self-conscious, and confused about his identity when in situations that call for manly behavior, especially if he has evolved no stable character defenses against his conflict. The ineffective state of the self then brings shame. In Kohut's formulation, too, shame may signify the self's current appraisal of its degree of coherence, but the failure of coherence is conceptualized as a decompensation due to narcissistic stress, not due to specific conflicts over aggression and sexuality such as the one just depicted.

Again I wish to state that my aim is to point to the constant interaction between shame and anger and not to criticize the psychology of the self as a point of view that adds depth to dynamic analyses already utilizing an instinct point of view. The contribution self-psychology and object relations theory makes to shame conceptualizations is that they recognize that shame is in part a response that reflects a personality comprised of relatively stable self and object representations and personal values that dictate what constitutes admirable and shameful behavior. The instinct point of view relates shame not to self-appraisal but to thwarted libidinal and aggressive energies. Both points of view are valuable to the complete analysis of a shame experience and both have been utilized in this monograph.

TALKING ABOUT FEELING, IN PSYCHOANALYTIC THEORY AND IN PSYCHOTHERAPEUTIC PRACTICE

My wish to interview people about feeling states grew out of an interest in individuals' efforts to verbalize what they experience as the inner world or the inner surface of the self. Recent literature (Schafer, 1976) has criticized psychologists' use of concepts of inner experiences.

These concepts sometimes portray the "inner world" as a concrete place furnished with "things," such as "old feelings" and "bad thoughts" and "ambiguous intentions." Critics rightfully exhort psychologists to eliminate misleading concretizations that present a distorted depiction of mental life. Schafer wishes to accomplish the dereification of language by describing all psychological functioning as actions. Although this practice would eliminate disturbing concretizations of mental process, its indictment of the concepts of felt experience and internal stream of consciousness produces a bland language that must mimic a contortionist in order to describe human activity. And after prodigious efforts to employ Schafer's language to describe feeling experience, the descriptions achieved remain paltry compared with the experience; and they misrepresent the qualitative or textural aspects of experience. Even as a language of theory, action language seems likely to discourage attention to the richness of feeling life. Concepts of feeling experience need not portray human beings as passive bystanders watching psychological "things," such as "injured feelings" and "constructive feelings" battling under their own power in some psychological inner space. Thoughtful use of concepts of feeling experience, feeling state, and stream of consciousness should reflect the person's activity in the generation and use of his or her feeling life and also the important variations in the experience of the self as active or passive in the creation of inner experience.

I prefer a concept of feeling or feeling experience that treats these terms as essentially synonymous with that aspect of consciousness describable as the felt meaning or qualitative aspect of a moment. Feeling is not a particular variety of event; it is an aspect of all conscious mental events. This conceptualization of feeling recognizes an essential similarity between complex moments of "shame" and simple moments of feeling a pleasant breeze or feeling a slight intensification of interest. And the concept recognizes subtle states of consciousness that call little attention to themselves. They simply are the quality of attention of the active self. A woman intent on algebra problems may not say to herself, "I am feeling focused and efficient." Yet there is no question that there exists a qualitative aspect to her functioning. In reviewing her morning's work for a colleague, she will feel that she gives a more adequate rendering of her experience if she says, "I was lost in my work, working easily and efficiently," than if she says, "I did algebra." A broad concept of feeling also allows for the description of self-conscious moments in which considerable attention is called to the experiencing self.

The concept of feeling offered here focuses attention on the great range of relationships between the self and its feeling experience. Of particular interest is the sense of proximity to or distance from one's own feeling. One may experience feeling as essentially not-self because emotional vulnerability brings a refusal fully to acknowledge a manifest feeling; it is seen as something evident but not real or not comprehensible or not meaningful. Feeling becomes an unexplained visitor within the experiencing self. The disowning of feeling takes many forms. A psychotherapy patient may feel the tears on her cheek while telling a sad story, yet she experiences no sadness. Or she may feel sad but quickly dismiss the feeling as having no personal meaning: "I must be getting my period." At the opposite extreme is the person who cannot dissociate any felt experience from the core sense of self. If troubled during a high fever or anxious after taking some pills known to be psychologically active, such a person cannot believe that the feeling state has been induced by an essentially external, transient influence. The chemically influenced feeling is interpreted in the same terms as any other alteration in feeling. Rather than accept that something outside his or her control is exercising an influence, the patient believes that a personality change is taking place. Distant events in the external world may also feel dependent on the person's influence. The self-experience extends too far and cannot exclude anything.

Various forms of dissociation of feeling have been conceptualized psychoanalytically by means of the concept of defense mechanisms. Repression, isolation, and reaction-formation imply varying relationships to disturbing feeling. But analytic theory and practice would be strengthened by more discriminating attention to the phenomenology and dynamics of the many types of dissociation of feeling that occur. The language of defense mechanisms has become so well established in analytic theory that practitioners too quickly dispose of complex emotional behavior as "understood" once classified as reaction-formation, splitting, and so forth. Like most terms of theory, these offer organizational advantages but they also can discourage careful, fresh scrutiny of experience and they can distract attention from intercategorical realms.

A major activity in psychotherapy is the attempt by patients to articulate feeling. The therapist encourages use of the spoken word as the primary means of communication, though patients also will exploit body language, silence, variations in promptness to sessions, grooming changes, and behavior outside the hours. While verbalizing, a person at times will think of himself as "putting my feelings into words." He makes a conceptual separation between feeling and verbalization. He does not just talk; he "looks in" at his "feelings," then he verbalizes what he experiences. He may experience himself as if he is a painter or a writer who is viewing his inner experience. He then searches for words that convey essential aspects of that experience. Some patients will be satisfied more easily than others with the descriptions achieved, as will some therapists. Some patients wish to create an exact verbal replica of the inner world and they never feel content that they have done so. These are the ones who help us glimpse their preconceptual world as they struggle to define what they feel. Others have little engagement or comfort with the world of feelings. They paint a few broad descriptive strokes, which is the best they can do without closely scrutinizing their experience. If the therapist presses for more description, they become puzzled or irritated or anxious. When not engaged in discussing a clearcut feeling or event, they say and honestly believe that they feel nothing and that they have no thoughts in mind.

At certain moments in a therapy, a patient will feel that he or she has nothing to say. The person may then simply talk, creating a succession of images and ideas either in response to his or her own inclination or in response to the therapist's suggestion. Such talk is valuable only if the one who generates it is willing to invest in it as a meaningful statement about the self. One must believe that the words either will generate significant feeling as one produces them, or that they will highlight patterns of experience one can identify and accept as meaningful indications of a potential for felt experience. If the flow of talk is not accepted as a meaningful experience, it will not be one. The person may feel that spoken words are primarily a diversion from something of genuine importance that he or she actively wishes to avoid or feels cannot be expressed because the experience has a vague form such as a deadness or a coldness or a restlessness or an irritability. Or the person may take his associations as arbitrary and thus insignificant.

The therapist's job is to recognize the meaningful feeling in the patient's verbalization regardless of whether the feeling is expressed through feeling labels, through descriptions of body feeling, through descriptions of the state of a person's house or the contour of a hillside or the rhythm of a song that has been recalled, or through intellectual ideas that point the way to emotion. The therapist also must gauge the person's relationship to the articulated feeling. Does the patient hear the same feeling in the words that the therapist senses? Does he or she hear feeling that the therapist takes to represent, in part, a flight from other, more profound potential feeling? Is the patient open to discussion of the feeling quality of the words or does the patient need to see the words as meaningless gibberish or disgusting refuse to be cast away? In certain respects, the therapist stands in relation to the patient's stream of expression as the novelist stands in relation to his or her own stream of consciousness. He or she listens actively and tries to lift from that stream what is most essential, most rich in feeling. The parallel may continue into the next set of behaviors undertaken by therapist or writer. Both may choose to find and set forth the words that most vividly restate what has been heard. In that case, the therapist simply seeks to establish himself or herself as an empathic listener who assumes that the patient will continue to work productively in such company. Or the therapist may seek to make a variety of transformations of the patient's communications, transformations that would be less likely to interest the writer. The transformation may involve restatement of feeling in new terms, for example, translation of descriptions of bodily tension into the labeled category, "anger." Or the transformation may consist of connecting the described feelings to feelings hypothetically experienced in the past or experienced in relation to a figure, often the therapist, who has not been cited in the patient's associations.

In making transformations of the patient's communications, the therapist must remain aware that he or she always violates the structure and complexity of the communication to some extent, just as the patient alters the initial reality of a dream or a fantasy when verbalizing it to the therapist. In order to subtract in this way from the patient's associations, the therapist must add to them something of value. Otherwise he or she is functioning disruptively. The therapist who equates a current figure with a parent grossly simplifies current reality. Thus the therapist must determine that the patient is in a frame of mind in which the effort to achieve an understanding of the self in terms of parental impact is a meaningful activity. Otherwise the reduction of current reality to past reality will impinge like an unwelcome assault on the meaningfulness of current experience, or it will be embraced as a basis for intellectualizing defensive activity. The therapist's imposition of feeling labels carries similar risks and potential benefits. The overwhelmed patient seeking organization for diffuse experience may welcome such labels. Because they offer some order to which one can cling, they may help to quiet the person even if they are poorly chosen and essentially inaccurate. But the patient who is much in charge of an effort to state articulately many features of a meaningful experience will not appreciate the therapist's interjection of a simplistic, "You are sad" or "You are angry." This patient knows that he has stated his feelings well. He assumes that the therapist has heard the obvious fact that he is sad or angry, and he needs no explicit acknowledgment of that communication. The label imposed by the therapist only raises the complaint, "Is that *all* you heard?" A patient who is not comfortable protesting when the therapist tears in with too dull or too large a shears for dividing up the material may dissociate himself from his feeling rather than from the therapist's categories of interpretation. He will accept and integrate a trivialization of his experience in order to remain accepting of the therapist. The middle ground of patient response would be to criticize the therapist's organization of his experience in order to maintain the integrity of his feelings; then, having strengthened the self in relation to the authority, he can accept the authority's organizing activity as contributing an additional aspect to his understanding. Generally speaking, the therapist must try to remain in contact with the feeling in the material, with the patient's attitudes of ownership and investment in relation to the material, and with the patient's need for and openness to various changes in attitude relative to the communicated experience.

In the literature of psychotherapy, and often in the practice of it, great emphasis has been placed on unraveling the patient's "dynamics," by which the writer or therapist generally means the patient's psychological conflicts. Does the man suffer in life because all other ambitious men remind him of his father toward whom he felt intense, oedipal-stage jealousy, which he never resolved? Does the woman suffer because older women bring to mind her mother who died suddenly when the child was young; thus current contacts with older women arouse unexplained tension or anger or depression? This issue-oriented variety of analytic activity always includes reference to feeling state because a person never is troubled directly by an oedipal conflict but is plagued by resulting feeling states such as envy or anxiety. However, in order to proceed with a psychotherapy, a therapist need only give grossly accurate labels to feeling states. The subtle properties of specific feeling states can remain the patient's private area of exploration. The therapist may sense the patient's feelings with depth and subtlety and this finely tuned empathy may be the guide that leads the therapist to dynamic formulations, but the therapist perhaps will never articulate, for the patient or for himself or herself, the rapid analysis of the patient's feeling state that underlies the formulation of psychodynamics. Analytic theory and practice has need to extend more attention to the qualities of feeling experience that represent the experiential end point of those conflicts that already have received so much investigation. We also must attend to the qualities of those feeling experiences that represent products not of specific, conflicting wishes, but of ongoing characteristics of the early interpersonal and physical environment. Such emphasis on description of feeling states has not been neglected entirely but, in the psychoanalytic literature, it has been of secondary importance relative to formulations of conflict. Isolated efforts have been made to describe the characteristics of particular feeling states; for example, Greenson

(1953, 1962) described the phenomenology of boredom and of enthusiasm before he turned to exploration of the psychological dynamics
leading to these states. Increasingly, writers who are interested in
early developmental deficits have labored to find their way into the
world of primitive ego states. Krystal (1974, 1975) has contributed to
the understanding of the quality of feeling response to catastrophic
experience. Because of the extensive discussion it has generated, perhaps of most significance is Kohut's promotion of the concept of self
and his attention to the impact on feeling states of the specific qualities
of attention provided by a child's parents. Kohut's work has advanced
analytic efforts to understand in detail the felt experience in the early
human environment[2] in order that the analyst may empathize with
those subtle deficiencies in quality of attention that can affect development profoundly. In theory and therapy, there remains much to
be done with the difficult task of articulating the qualitative, feelingful
aspects of the early human and nonhuman environment and with
specifying the relationship between these early environments and the
feeling world of gloom or chronic anxiety or rapidly vacillating feeling
attacks that the troubled adult creates as a major defining characteristic of self, and which he or she may impose as a living environment on
the next generation. Therapeutic empathy that extends beyond the
gross labeling of states and conflicts into the subtle aspects of early
environment and later self-experience should add to therapeutic effectiveness and to clinical theory.

METHODOLOGICAL CONCLUSIONS

Studies that aim to enhance our capacities to characterize the individual's inner world of feeling must depend on extensive subject report.
Thus an interview method, with ongoing efforts to have the subject
describe his or her experience, appears to be a preferred method of
inquiry when one seeks to picture an individual's inner world in order
to describe it for others. When the research goal expands to include
the associating of qualitative aspects of the current life with events or
ongoing conditions of childhood, the interviewing method exhibits
greater vulnerabilites. Accurate historical reconstruction is extremely
difficult to achieve and to evaluate, from a data base of four or five
interviews. One might conclude that such reconstruction should be left
to those engaged in conducting psychoanalyses or in scrutinizing

---

[2]The early environment of places, objects, and weather also creates the individual's
unique inner world, as Searles (1960) has described.

transcripts of such extended series of interviews; however, reconstructions derived from analytic hours also are subject to major sources of inferential error, especially to erroneous conclusions facilitated by the patient's willingness to incorporate, fully or partially, the therapist's preferred methods of explanation. Since major problems compromise both methods of inquiry (problems that are not solved by wresting complex questions into simplistic experimental designs), interviewing research and scrutiny of long-term therapies perhaps are best used complementarily with the expectation that false or incomplete perceptions promoted by one method will be extended or appropriately brought into question by data from the other. For example, an analyst might feel that an interviewing researcher had dismissed too quickly the possibility that a specific bodily referent would prove to be the crucial basis of a symbol system were the patient's dreams and fantasies scrutinized over an extended time period. The analyst might demonstrate, through transcripts of analytic hours, the experience of gradually evident, body-part meanings to what first appeared to be complaints related to a parent's disapproving response to all instances of spontaneous or rich feeling in a child. Then research attention must shift to the analyst's work and to the possibility that formulations he or she has presented to a patient encouraged the patient to make the penis or the breasts a symbol of the expressive self (in order to sustain the analyst's approval and interest), while the analyst believed that the increasingly well-articulated attitude toward the body-part had been the primary issue since early childhood. It is essentially an attempt at intelligent, honest dialogue about one's inference methods. But such research strategies appear to be valid if one believes that there exists no perfect external criterion of a valid inference about psychological reality. A person's own report about the meaning of his or her feeling and a listener's impression of the meaning of another's feelings always will remain highly significant criteria of valid inference; and neither source ever will establish a firm truth since psychological reality is constantly changing in response to every new construction of it generated by the experiencer or offered by those with whom he or she interacts.

As a particular category of study for interviewing research, shame has strengths and weaknesses. I had hoped that designating an emotion category as a topic of study would encourage rich descriptions affected by both primary process and secondary process meanings of the emotion category. That hope was not entirely satisfied. Highly specific, rich descriptions of states were difficult to elicit although an overall feeling for aspects of the person's inner world did gradually develop as one watched and listened over several hours. The selection of subjects who are particularly talented at feeling-state description might have enriched the research. Although I would have lost the opportunity to watch how people who deny shame experience cope with prolonged discussion of shame, more articulate subjects might have put me in a position to increase productively my efforts to elicit state descriptions and to decrease my attention to historical data that sometimes encourage excessive speculation about dynamics. Given my many shame-denying subjects, and given some subjects who lacked the inclination to verbalize feeling states, it seemed impossible to retain a steady focus on the direct experience of shame; thus I devoted much time to discussion of the person's general life story, which I hoped might provide a context for interpreting those shame descriptions that did emerge. Rich descriptions of feeling might have been discouraged inadvertently by asking subjects to focus their attention on feelings they could *label*, in this case as shame or humiliation or embarrassment. Descriptions of shame states may have been particularly difficult to elicit given the strong inclination most people feel to protect against disclosure of traits or behaviors currently experienced as shameful.

References

Alexander, F. (1938). Remarks about the relationship of inferiority feelings to guilt feelings. *International Journal of Psychoanalysis, 19*, 41–49.

Cohen, A. (1976). *A hero in his time.* New York: Random House.

Darwin, C. (1965). *Expression of the emotions in man and animal.* Chicago: University of Chicago Press. (Original work published 1872)

De Rivera, J. (1977). *A structural theory of the emotions.* New York: International Universities Press.

Douglas, M. (1966). *Purity and danger.* New York: Praeger.

Engel, G. (1962). Anxiety and depression-withdrawal: Primary affects of unpleasure. *International Journal of Psychoanalysis, 43*, 89–97.

Engel, G. (1963). Toward a classification of affects. In Knapp (Ed.), *Expression of the emotions in man.* New York: International Universities Press.

Erikson, E. H. (1963). *Childhood and society.* New York: Norton.

Faulkner, W. (1946). *The sound and the fury.* New York: Random House.

Forster, E. M. (1921). *Howards end.* New York, Vintage Books.

Freud, A. (1965). *Normality and pathology in childhood: Assessments of development.* New York: International Universities Press.

Freud, S. (1953). Jokes and their relation to the unconscious. In J. Strachey (Ed. and Trans.), *The standard edition of the complete psychological works of Sigmund Freud* (Vol. 8). London: Hogarth Press. (Original work published 1905)

Freud, S. (1953). Character and anal erotism. In J. Strachey (Ed. and Trans.), *The standard edition of the complete psychological works of Sigmund Freud* (Vol. 9). London: Hogarth Press. (Original work published 1908)

Freud, S. (1953). Five lectures on psycho-analysis. In J. Strachey (Ed. and Trans.), *The standard edition of the complete psychological works of Sigmund Freud* (Vol. 11). London: Hogarth Press. (Original work published 1909)

Freud, S. (1953). An autobiographical study. In J. Strachey (Ed. and Trans.), *The standard edition of the complete psychological works of Sigmund Freud* (Vol. 20). London: Hogarth Press. (Original work published 1925).

Freud, S. (1953). Lay analysis and other works. In J. Strachey (Ed. and Trans.), *The standard edition of the complete psychological works of Sigmund Freud* (Vol. 20). London: Hogarth Press. (Original work published 1926)

Gendlin, E. (1962) *Experiencing and the creation of meaning.* New York: The Free Press of Glencoe.

Goldstein, K. (1951). On emotions: Considerations from the organismic point of view. *Journal of Psychology, 31,* 37–49.

Greenson, R. (1953). On boredom. *Journal of the American Psychoanalytic Association, 6,* 7–21.

Greenson, R. (1962). On enthusiasm. *Journal of the American Psychoanalytic Association, 10,* 3–1.

Grinker, R., Sr. (1955). Growth inertia and shame: Therapeutic implications and dangers. *International Journal of Psychoanalysis, 36,* 242–253.

Horney, K. (1932). The dread of woman: Observations on a specific difference in the dread felt by men and by women respectively for the opposite sex. *International Journal of Psychoanalysis, 13,* 348–360.

Izard, C. (1971). *The face of emotion.* New York: Appleton-Century-Crofts.

Jacobson, E. (1964). *The self and the object world.* New York: International Universities Press.

James, W. (1890). *The principles of psychology* (Vol. 1). New York: Henry Holt.

Kernberg, O. (1974). Further contributions to the treatment of narcissistic personalities. *International Journal of Psychoanalysis, 55,* 215–240.

Kernberg, O. (1975). *Borderline conditions and pathological narcissism.* New York: Jason Aronson.

Knapp, P. (1967). Purging and curbing: An inquiry into disgust, satiety, and shame. *Journal of Nervous and Mental Diseases, 144,* 514–534.

Kohut, H. (1971). *The analysis of the self.* New York: International Journal of Psychoanalysis.

Kohut, H. (1972). Thoughts on narcissism and narcissistic rage. *Psychoanalytic Study of the Child, 27,* 360–400.

Kohut, H. (1977). *The restoration of the self.* New York: International Universities Press.

Krohn, A. (1978). *Hysteria, the elusive neurosis.* New York: International Universities Press.

Krystal, H. (1974). The genetic development of affects and affect regression. *The Annual of Psychoanalysis, 2,* 98–126.

Krystal, H. (1975). Affect tolerance. *The Annual of Psychoanalysis, 4,* 172–219.

Krystal, H. (1977). Aspects of affect theory. *Bulletin of the Menninger Clinic, 1,* 1–26.

Langer, S. K. (1967). *Mind: An essay on human feeling* (Vol. 1). Baltimore: Johns Hopkins Press.

Lazarus, R. (1984). On the primacy of cognition. *American Psychologist, 39,* 124–129.

Lewis, H. B. (1971). *Shame and guilt in neurosis.* New York: International Universities Press.

Lidz, T. (1973). *The organization and treatment of schizophrenic disorders.* New York: Basic Books.

Lorenz, K. (1963). *On aggression.* New York: Bantam Books.

Lynd, H. M. (1958). *On shame and the search for identity.* New York: Harcourt, Brace, and Company.

Mayman, M. (1974, September). The shame experience, the shame dynamic, and shame personalities in psychotherapy. Paper presented at the George Klein Memorial Address, American Psychological Association Annual Meeting. Other presentations of this paper include the Topeka Psychoanalytic Society, September, 1975; Albert Einstein School of Medicine, New York City, December, 1977.

Novey, S. (1963) [Discussion of G. Engel's Toward a classification of affects]. In Knapp (Ed.), *Expression of the emotions in man.* New York: International Universities Press.

Nunberg, H. (1955). *Principles of psychoanalysis.* (Madlyn and Sidney Kahr, Trans.). New York: International Universities Press.

Panksepp, J. (1982). Toward a general psychobiological theory of emotions. *The Behavioral and Brain Sciences, 5,* 407–468.

Piers, G. and Singer, M. B. (1953). *Shame and guilt.* Springfield: Thomas.

Rangell, L. (1952). The analysis of a doll phobia. *International Journal of Psychoanalysis, 33,* 43–53.

Sartre, J. P. (1964). *La nausée.* New York: New Directions.

Sartre, J. P. (1969). *Being and nothingness.* New York: Washington Square Press.

Schafer, R. (1976). *A new language for psychoanalysis.* New Haven: Yale University Press.

Schur, M. (1953). The ego in anxiety. In R. Loewenstein (Ed.), *Drives affects behavior* (Vol. 1). New York: International Universities Press.

Searles, H. (1960). *The nonhuman environment.* New York: International Universities Press.

Shapiro, D. (1965) *Neurotic styles.* New York: Basic Books.

Shevrin, H. (1970, April). The dreaming dreamer and the dreaming creator: A comparison of metaphor and condensation. Paper presented at the research meeting of the Chicago Psychoanalytic Institute.

Shevrin, H. (1978). Semblances of feeling: The imagery of affect in empathy, dreams, and unconscious processes—A revision of Freud's several affect theories. In S. Smith (Ed.), *The human mind revisited.* New York: International Universities Press.

Wurmser, L. (1980). Phobic core in the addictions and the paranoid process. *International Journal of Psychoanalysis, 8,* 311–355.

Author Index

Subject Index

A

adolescent issues, 10, 90, 92, 94, 113
adoption, 110-114
aggression, 32, 36-37, 44, 46, 52-53, 56, 57, 62, 65-70, 80, 90-97, 102, 107, 112-118, 120, 128-138, 140-141, 150, 170-172, *also see narcissistic rage*
  inhibition of, 53, 55, 69, 114-116, 121, 129, 131-139, 170
alcohol, use in the shame-prone person, 116-118, 149
alcoholic parent, 92, 122
anal issues, 15, 44, 57, 60, 65, 67, 69, 72-73, 79-84, 93, 102-109, 114, 119, 163
anxiety, 5, 12, 13, 79-80, 87, 120-121, 126, 127, 133, 168, *also see castration concerns*
  stranger (anxiety), 79-80, 134
audience, 32, 39, 80, 108, 143, 155

B

badness, 48-49, 142-143
biological influences on feeling, 13-14, 167, 168
blushing, 38, 40, 152, 155

C

castration concerns, 6, 11, 14, 15, 42, 100, 101-102, 103, 109, 116-117, 120-121, 132, 139-140, 152

contempt (and self-contempt), 37, 62, 72, 74, 76, 92, 137-138, 145, 169
cultural values and shame, 19, 70-71, 115, 117

D

defense
  shame as – (defense), 9, 12, 20, 33, 85, 123-147
  (defense) – against feeling, 8, 16, 20, 31, 52, 67, 80, 98, 99, 100, 118, 174, 176
dependency and shame feelings, 54, 63, 71-76, 112, 121, 122, 136, 138
depression, 12, 57, 66-70, 113-114, 123, 124, 134-136, 151, 153, 155-156, 158, 168, 171
disgust (and self disgust), 4, 10, 12, 37, 81, 83-84, 136-137, 143, 169-170

E

ecstatic delight, 126, 127
ego decompensation, 46, 97-98, 172
ego ideal, 4-5, 19, 32, 33, 109, 129
ego strain, 45, 97, 151, 172
ego strength, 45, 97
elation, 68, 89-90
embarrassment, 10, 30, 33, 35, 38-43, 46, 47, 51-52, 61, 62, 63, 64, 80, 81, 88-90, 98-99, 100, 107, 119, 124-126,